CAMEL LOT

CAMEL LOT

THE TRUE STORY OF A ZOO-ILLOGICAL FARM

MOSELLE SCHAFFER

VIKING

VIKING

Published by the Penguin Group

Viking Penguin, a division of Penguin Books USA Inc.,

40 West 23rd Street, New York, New York 10010, U.S.A.

Penguin Books Ltd, 27 Wrights Lane, London W8 5TZ, England

Penguin Books Australia Ltd, Ringwood, Victoria, Australia

Penguin Books Canada Ltd, 2801 John Street,

Markham, Ontario, Canada L3R 1B4

Penguin Books (N.Z.) Ltd, 182–190 Wairau Road,

Auckland 10, New Zealand

Penguin Books Ltd, Registered Offices:

Harmondsworth, Middlesex, England

First published in 1990 by Viking Penguin,

a division of Penguin Books USA Inc.

1 3 5 7 9 10 8 6 4 2

Photographs courtesy of the author

LIBRARY OF CONGRESS CATALOGING IN PUBLICATION DATA

Schaffer, Moselle.

Camel Lot : the true story of a zoo-illogical farm / Moselle

Schaffer.

p.   cm.

ISBN 0-670-82884-X

1. Pets—Indiana—Westfield—Anecdotes.   2. Zoo animals—Indiana—

Westfield—Anecdotes.   3. Camel Lot (Westfield, Ind.)—Anecdotes.

4. Schaffer, Moselle.   I. Title.

SF416.S32   1990

636—dc20   89-40305

Printed in the United States of America

Set in Bodoni Book

Designed by Michael Ian Kaye

To Brad Thurston,
Jack Leer, Robert Baudy,
Ruddy Edwards, and Todd Kogan,
all of whom I can count on
in a crisis, and do.
Regularly.

ACKNOWLEDGMENTS:

I'm indebted to John Burkhart
for the concept "zoo-illogical farm,"
John Macri and the late Tom Keating
for their encouragement, Hope Humphrey
for her genes, and most of all
my editor, Lori Lipsky—
a delight to work with.

CAMEL LOT

ONE

I dislike snakes. A friend who is a professional herpetologist insists it's because I know next to nothing about them, which is true. The only thing that interests me is how to put the greatest possible distance, in the shortest possible time, between them and me. But even though I wish God had quit after the first serpent and hadn't bothered with the rest of the creepy, crawly things, I never harm them. On the contrary, I am unfailingly courteous and accommodating. Whenever one slithers into my path, I stop dead in my tracks and graciously give him the right of way.

The same learned herpetologist insists there aren't many poisonous snakes here in Indiana and that it's easy to identify those few. The good guys usually have rounded jaws, he says, their opposite number, diamond shaped. But I'm not around long enough to scrutinize their features. Even if they wore labels clearly spelling out their intentions, I wouldn't have time to read them.

I now know boa constrictors are of the nonpoisonous variety. I also know they are indigenous to central and South America. But had I not met one right here in my own backyard I might never have found that out.

One day when I had to be away for several hours, a nineteen-year-old buddy of mine, Buster, came over to give a baby camel her bottle and keep an eye on things in general. Besides being ever affable, Buster is also conscientious, so I had no qualms about leaving him in charge. And everything was calm when I left—or as calm as it gets around here. Three hours later as I drove up to the house, I saw two of my dogs, a Doberman pinscher and a German shepherd, racing round and round the base of a fifteen-foot-tall prickly pear tree at the edge of the driveway. Barking hysterically, they interrupted their frenzied circuit only long enough to catch their breath so they could bark some more.

I assumed they had treed a cat or a squirrel, one of their favorite pastimes, and I sauntered down to satisfy my curiosity. Curiosity killed the cat, so it's said, and I can vouch for what it can do to a Homo sapiens. My heart missed more than a couple of beats when I made eye contact with the largest, most ferocious-looking reptile I have ever seen outside the confines of a zoological exhibit. Yards and yards of his vast body were coiled around a branch at the top of the tree and what I could see of his midsection was about six inches in diameter. He was mostly dark gray in color with splotches of a lighter hue that probably matched my sudden pasty gray pallor. As I stood mute and motionless gaping at the monster, Buster rounded the corner of the house on the double.

"Oh, there you are," he said cheerfully, obviously addressing the snake. "I've been looking all over for you."

Then he turned to me. "You've never met Perry, have you, Moselle?"

Nor had I expected to. I had known about Buster's pet boa constrictor but assumed he was always at home—where he belonged, in my opinion.

"Buster, why did you bring Perry over here?" I asked, hoping my voice didn't reveal the fright and annoyance I felt.

"Because usually he gets outside some by now, but this spring it's been too cold for him. This is the first warm day and Perry wanted a sunbath."

How one knows when a boa constrictor wants a sunbath still eludes me, but I don't much care. And pursuing the subject then could only delay the snake's departure and work to nobody's benefit except possibly Perry's. I wanted him elsewhere. Anywhere elsewhere. Even the term "boa constrictor" made my skin crawl. Boa—which is also the name of a fashion accessory worn wrapped around the neck—combined with a variation of constrict, conjured up a grisly image of someone, namely me, being choked to death by the enormous serpent.

"If you'll put the dogs in the house, I'll get a ladder," Buster said. "I've gotta get going, so I guess we'd better get him down."

I, as the other half of the "we" in this rerun of *Bring 'Em Back Alive*, got to brace the ladder while Buster attempted the rescue, and I was unhappy with even so minor a role. Then, what I feared most came to pass when Buster climbed on to the top rung and extended his arm toward the boa. Perry was still a three-foot reach away from captivity.

My eyes darted back and forth between roly-poly Buster and the tree's spindly branches. By any standards, Buster was chubby, close to six feet and two hundred pounds. Only someone half his weight could climb out on a limb and unwind Perry, I figured. Certain that Buster would also reach that disturbing conclusion, I shouted my refusal before he had a chance to make the suggestion: "No! I will *not* climb up there and I will *not* touch Perry!"

"He's not poisonous, he won't hurt you."

"I'll take your word for it—I'm not going to find out for myself. You'll have to go borrow a longer ladder somewhere or stand here until Perry decides to come down on his own."

I had barely finished that emphatic declaration when Clark, a meter reader for the power company and a frequent visitor, walked up. How long he had been observing this little melodrama, I didn't know, but long enough to recognize the problem and offer a possible solution.

"Our linemen are working just a mile or two down the road and they've got a cherry picker. Do you want me to see if they'll come down here?" he asked, as if he were in doubt of my answer.

About twenty minutes later, Buster crawled into the bucket of that versatile contraption, was hoisted up next to the branch Perry had staked out for his own, and offered the snake his arm for a substitute. But Perry refused to cooperate. So Buster grabbed him by the tail and middle, at which point the cherry picker lowered boy and pet to the ground, with the twelve-foot-long Perry writhing in protest. In a matter of minutes, the mission was a fait accompli.

Buster and Perry departed immediately, at my suggestion. Clark left too, but the cherry-picker team of Hank and George wanted to meet the other animals, the permanent residents at

Camel Lot. So we started with the Siberian tigers who were the closest. Their large, sturdy pens are only fifty feet from the back patio, just around the corner from where we were standing.

As always, I tried to prepare the uninitiated twosome for this unique experience and, as usual, they ignored my warnings. Ivan, the most majestic animal I've ever known, is large—even for a Siberian tiger, the largest of all the big cats. And this particular cat has more idiosyncrasies than any animal I've ever known, be he two legged or four. Ivan is a ladies' man. He loves them all and is delighted with their company. Getting as close as possible, he rubs against the cage and chats nonstop, puh-puh-puh, puh-puh-puh. Women are enchanted with the lovable seven-hundred-pound tiger with the demeanor of a pussycat.

Ivan hates all men, without exception, but with varying degrees of intensity. The bigger they are, the more rabid his behavior becomes. He also despises head gear of any sort and any man wearing a hat is subjected to an unabridged, nerve-shattering display of his wrath. Since Hank and George were both masculine, large, and wearing Chicago Cubs baseball caps, I suggested that they remove the one irritant they could control. They didn't bother.

As we approached, Ivan began to rev up his act, crouching down in the classic position of any cat about to attack, neck extended and eyes bright with excitement. As opposed to any ordinary tabby, however, there was a lot more cat involved in Ivan's threatening posture. The twitching of his tail was also significant. It indicated he was making plans, and the plans weren't good for anybody but Ivan.

At my insistence, we stopped about six feet short of the enclosure just before the tiger put his plan into action. Ivan shot across the width of the pen like a rocket, his face contorted with rage, and hit the fence full force with his two front feet. Simultaneously, a deafening roar erupted from the huge mouth, opened wide to display an array of teeth that had a language all their own. They could rip up these measly, two-hundred-pound targets faster and more efficiently than a can opener and that message was eloquently conveyed to Hank and George.

The two new believers' reactions were typical. They jumped as if they had been zapped by a cattle prod and then, in a state of shock and unable to move under their own power, they remained rooted to the spot. The entire scene was enacted in less than thirty seconds, but it was a minute or so before the two men could beat a hasty retreat to the patio to avoid the impending encore. There they removed their caps, after it was too late to do any good, and mopped the perspiration splashing down their faces.

"Good God!" was all George could manage by way of comment.

Hank was still unable to speak.

Both of Ivan's newest victims were relieved to learn there were no more full-fledged carnivores on the premises and meeting the other animals—the camels, zebras, llamas, ostrich, kangaroo, and goats—proved uneventful. At least by comparison. One small incident took place when we went into the primates' quarters in the barn where the marmosets, plus Biddy and Joe Jo, who are woolly monkeys, and Buddy, a capuchin, all live in relative harmony.

Before I could warn Hank, Buddy—a little wisp of a fellow, not more than seven or eight pounds—played his favorite trick on his visitor. He dropped down from his hiding place in the rafters and landed on Hank's shoulder, where he quickly wrapped his long, itchy tail tight around Hank's neck and grabbed onto both his ears. It was one of the harmless pranks Buddy enjoys, but to Hank, whose nervous system had already undergone severe trauma, it was somewhat less than amusing. When I plucked Buddy off, Hank recovered quickly, but I think what helped most was my saying, "That's it. Now you've met all the animals."

On the quarter-mile walk back down the driveway, there were the usual questions that follow a visitor's first tour of Camel Lot.

"You live alone and take care of the animals by yourself?"

My affirmative reply to George's question meant we were edging up on the inevitable, the question virtually certain to arise.

"Don't you have any help at all?"

We were no more than one or two questions away now, for sure.

"Oh, yes, I have marvelous help, friends I can count on any time I need them, and a high-school boy who comes over one afternoon a week. He's great with things like taking a fifty-pound frozen chunk of meat for the tigers and breaking it up, or anything else I need help with. Maybe a zebra has kicked a fence board loose and it has to be replaced—all sorts of unpredictable things happen."

And the predictable one was about to happen. Hank was poised for it.

"Tell me," he asked. "What's your normal day like, anyhow?"

TWO

A normal, ordinary day? There were some—before Camel Lot. Twenty years ago, my then-husband, Ed, and I lived in a suburb of Indianapolis in a conventional community where the neighbors were friendly and close enough to drop in for a cup of coffee. Our house was equally conventional, a white shingled bungalow with green shutters, a conventional mortgage, and a conventional, inedible lawn. It was small but comfortable for a household of three, which included the two of us and our dog, Dirty Sam.

Dirty Sam was an unclipped standard French poodle, white when he was born and white for fifteen or twenty minutes after one of his frequent baths. But he was inordinately fond of wallowing in mud and rooting around in the ground and any other activity that ended with the same satisfying result. A lot

8

of my "normal" days were spent trying to turn the rascal back into a reasonable facsimile of a French poodle.

I also did a good bit of volunteer work, dunning friends and neighbors for contributions to worthy causes more times than they or I would care to recall. There were other types of fund drives, too, the ones that call for salesmanship, of which I have none. Every year after the Medical Society Auxiliary's spring geranium sale, our flower beds were ablaze with the merchandise I discovered was a whole lot easier to buy than to sell.

For recreation, my husband and I played golf and bridge and took the normal two-week vacations each year. But because he chose not to be away from his busy medical practice for more than one week at a time, we split up our holiday into two segments. That was fine with me. It meant I could engineer short jaunts by automobile as opposed to longer distances that would make flying mandatory. My unreasonable fear of airplanes had degenerated into such a phobia that I broke out in a rash, literally, when confronted with just the possibility of having to fly. Ed was fairly tolerant of my problem, at first, but in the fifth year of our marriage it precipitated a crisis.

"I've blocked out the first week in December," he said, settling back comfortably in his Barcalounger.

"Great. Does Sea Island appeal to you? Or Pinehurst?" I named two of our favorite spots that were strategically located one day's drive from home.

"I was thinking of someplace different this time, somewhere neither of us has been. Mexico."

Mexico! Ed launched that bombshell as casually as if he'd suggested a trip to the hardware store. Mexico! Even taxing my imagination I could think of no way to cram a five-thousand-mile road trip into seven twenty-four-hour days. In rapid succession I came up with one alternative after another to keep me on the ground. I'd start ahead and drive. I'd take the train. I'd go by bus. I'd stay home. Ed vetoed them all and unleashed a tidal wave of guilt that brought about the calculated result.

"If you won't fly, I can't go."

I did wangle one concession. Ed agreed to drive to New Orleans where the flight originated, and back. Benevolence, however, was not the only motivating factor. That was the only convenient nonstop flight he could find, and experience had taught him well. He'd already learned the folly of luring me aboard any airplane that pulls up to a gate and stops—whether or not it has reached its final destination.

Our flight's scheduled departure at 11:00 A.M. meant getting up early to prepare for the horrendous ordeal ahead. By the time the wheels left the ground, I had swilled two Bloody Marys, two old-fashioneds, and two whiskey sours, and was still cold sober. Fortunately, it was a champagne flight, and I hastily guzzled each glass so I could present an empty one each time the flight attendant came by. I consumed enough "sedation" to drop a bull elephant and was still stiff from fright the whole wretched trip.

But that state of affairs changed abruptly. When the airplane landed in Mexico City, I crashed. The altitude, combined with the prolonged tension and enormous amount of alcohol, hit me immediately and I could keep my eyes open only long enough to crawl into bed at the hotel. Four hours later, when I woke up, it was time to start agonizing over the return flight. The only enjoyable part of that miserable vacation was the drive home from New Orleans. There wasn't an airport in sight.

Ed frequently flew to medical meetings and was mildly annoyed when I declined his invitations to go along. I, in turn, became more than mildly annoyed as he stepped up his barrage of propaganda: The only dangerous thing about flying is the drive to the airport; thousands upon thousands of flights each day arrive safely at their destinations . . . on and on and on. Had Ed not been six feet and 180 pounds, I would have grabbed chunks of his dark wavy hair and shaken him until he was either mute or bald.

To make matters worse, our good friend Dean Wildman began flying lessons and became a fellow crusader. Dean and his wife, Jo, were among our favorite bridge partners, and we got together once a week for a relaxed, enjoyable evening. We weren't experts, but we played rather seriously, and in between hands the conversation revolved around the game, rehashing and discussing the score. Only when someone got up to replenish the popcorn did we veer off onto other subjects. When Dean took up flying, bridge took a back seat to aviation while Ed and Dean pursued their common cause, brainwashing me. Dean's instructor, Ted Lisec, also unknowingly took part in absentia.

"Ted says only two-tenths of one percent of all small airplane accidents are the fault of the airplane." Dean.

"Interesting. Did you realize that, Mosie?" Ed.

"Yes, yes, I seem to recall that from last week's dissertation. Are you going to bid, partner?" Me.

"One heart. And, Ted says when it's pilot error, most often it's due to weather, running into heavy weather, which doesn't happen with proper preplanning." Dean.

When Dean got his private pilot's rating, the obsessed duo became insufferable. They never had to steer the conversation back to flying because they never left the subject, and I had not only ceased to enjoy these weekly get-togethers, but I also dreaded them. I was sick and tired and generally fed up with this variation of group therapy with me as the only patient. Although I didn't realize it, I'd reached the breaking point. Nothing else could explain my rash decision.

"I'll tell you what I'll do," Ed said during one such laborious occasion. "If you'll take five hours of lessons and still feel the way you do, I'll never mention flying again."

The offer caught me totally by surprise and my first inclination was to dismiss the idea as absurd, out of the question. But I hesitated, weighing the potential benefits against the exorbitant price.

"You mean I'd never have to get on another airplane again?"

"Right."

"No more badgering, no more harassment, not even subtle references to flying?"

"Right."

"Does that include you, too?" I directed that question to Dean.

"Absolutely," he replied.

Five hours of self-inflicted torture. But oh, the rewards! I continued to mull over the proposition, unintentionally dramatizing the moment.

"Okay," I said. "You're on."

Since no performance timetable was stipulated, my commitment doubtless would have remained tucked away in the recesses of my mind until some new threat arose. But Dean had anticipated that probability. Three nights later, Ed and I were attending a party where the Wildmans were also guests. It was a gregarious, festive group, undoubtedly made more so by large bowls of Christmas cheer, and I was chatting with a group of people when Dean walked up. With him was a tall blond man in his middle to late twenties.

"Mosie," Dean said. "This is Ted Lisec."

"How do you do," I acknowledged the introduction, wondering why the name sounded familiar.

"Ted's my flight instructor. And," he added with a devilish grin, "yours too, now."

I stared at the stranger I knew so well by reputation as he smiled and extended his hand.

"Your first lesson is scheduled for Monday morning," he said, his deep voice about one octave below impossible. "I'll see you at Sky Harbor at nine-fifteen."

"Ne-ne-next Monday?" I stammered.

"Day after tomorrow."

The party was over.

On Sunday, a fierce winter storm that felled trees and power lines hit Indianapolis and temporarily crippled the city. Unfortunately, it spent all its fury that day and there was nothing left over for Monday, nothing to postpone this exercise in depravity I'd agreed to. Monday dawned bright and clear and cold. Sunday's violent winds had turned calm, and all I had going for me was the perilous driving conditions. With any kind of luck at all I'll skid into a ditch, I consoled myself as I crept along the ice-glazed roads to the airport. But the only reprieve I won was negligible. Arriving five minutes late wasn't much help.

Ted was waiting for me. Wearing a dark gray business suit, tie, and white shirt, he shattered my notion of a professional pilot. With the exception of airline crews, I thought they at all times slouched around in old leather jackets, baggy pants, and a helmet with goggles. A silk scarf, necessarily orange, had to be wrapped around the neck with the ends streaming backward as if the wearer were bucking a thirty-knot headwind. That phenomenon persisted whether he was on the flight line being blasted by prop wash or inside Operations becalmed behind his desk.

Ted's conservative dress made a statement. Loud and clear it said he expected to return to the ground unscathed an hour or so hence. I, on the other hand, was geared up for survival. My snowmobile suit, zipped up to the chin, was topped off with a wool knit stocking cap pulled down over my forehead, and I was firmly anchored to the ground by heavy waterproof boots.

Ted, not one to dwell on small talk, confined the amenities to a succinct "good morning," pulled on a trench coat, and ushered me out into the bitterly cold 5-degree morning. But it wasn't the weather that caused me to shiver. While I tagged alongside like a zombie, he led the way to a shiny red-and-white airplane, a single-engine Cessna 172, and indicated I should follow him around as he conducted his preflight inspection. He kept up a running commentary on what he was doing and why, most of which bounced off my impenetrable cloak of terror. Only when I was ensconced in the left seat of the cockpit, seat belt fastened securely, did Ted's direct order get through to me.

"Put your hands on the controls and follow me through," he said calmly.

"I can't."

"What do you mean you can't?"

"I don't want to touch anything."

"Moselle." His voice became gruff as he repeated his instructions slowly, pausing between each word for emphasis, "PUT YOUR HANDS ON THE YOKE AND KEEP THEM THERE."

That command I obeyed, and soon we streaked down the runway and up into that menacing wild blue yonder. For the next forty-five minutes we flew around the area, my eyes fixed straight ahead as if I were in a trance.

When we finally landed, I staggered into Operations to officially finalize my first flying lesson. Like a visit to the dentist, it is one of the ironies of fate to undergo a solid hour of unremitting torture and then have to pay for the ordeal. At Ted's insistence, I even had to invest in a log book to record this memorable occasion, as if I were ever likely to forget it. Also at his insistence, I joined him for a cup of coffee.

"It wasn't so bad, now, was it?" he asked, lapsing back into the charm that automatically disappears when he's instructing.

"Yes," I answered.

"Then let me try to relieve some of your fears. Even if we had lost the engine, with a glide ratio of nine to one, we could have glided nine miles. And in Indiana, flat as it is, we'd have a choice of dozens of places to land in that distance. Small airplanes are safe."

"I know that."

"If you know that, why are you so frightened?"

"Because there's a big difference in knowing something, accepting it as factual, and actually believing it, feeling it."

"You will in time."

"When?"

"It isn't something that happens abruptly, like turning on a light or opening a window. It will be so gradual you won't even realize it's happening."

Ted was right. After the fourth lesson, I didn't have to make a beeline for home, the aspirin bottle, and a long hot bath. I could also actually grasp the controls and keep the airplane from dropping out of the sky—although my straight and level flight and the gyrations of a roller coaster had an awful lot in common. I was still far from being at ease in the cockpit, but considering how I had started, the improvement was dramatic. I began to believe Ted's assurances that in time, if I stuck with the program, this obsessive phobia of mine would be permanently laid to rest. He'd been right so far. So had Ed and Dean, and for once I welcomed "I told you so." I'd gotten a lot more than I'd bargained for.

But I continued to brush aside Ted's oblique references to "after you solo." Me tooling around in the sky alone was about as likely as a frog sprouting wings. Or so I thought . . . until it happened.

An apt student will solo after four hours of dual instruction, an average student requires about eight hours. I'd logged eighteen hours when Ted decided to sever the umbilical cord. Even then his drastically revised procedure reflected my shaky standing in the world of aviation.

Usually an instructor tells his student to make three takeoffs and landings, then he gets out of the airplane at the end of the runway, thrusts his hands deep into his pants pockets, and saunters casually into Operations with never a backward glance—at least while the student can see him. The whole scenario is designed to impart confidence to the fledgling, and possibly to the instructor. Among other things, Ted's revised version eliminated two out of the three acts.

"Pull over there and shut off the engine," he said, indicating a turnaround in the middle of the runway.

Then he went through a dress-rehearsal pep talk and climbed out of the airplane before issuing his final instructions: "Take off, go around the traffic pattern once, *just once*, land, and pick me up here."

As I taxied out onto the runway, I caught a glimpse of my instructor, hands behind his back, jaws locked tightly together and feet spread wide apart in a defiant stance. He was an almost perfect picture of a man about to be carted off to the gallows, lacking only the blindfold.

It was not an image to instill confidence in a novice singularly lacking that attribute, but it prompted the same end result. Determined to get the airplane back on the ground in the same configuration in which it left, I concentrated so intently there was no time to be scared.

Ed was ecstatic over my soloing. He regarded it as a milestone, a positive sign that my aggravating hang-up would eventually become a thing of the past. But to make sure, he acted quickly to prevent any backsliding. He decided we should buy 1348 Yankee, the trainer in which I'd logged most of my flying time.

Ted was pleased, too, and/or relieved by the near-miracle of my getting off the ground and back down again without incident. Immediately, he set a new goal of a private pilot's rating—as much for him as for me. There was very little difference between my instructor and *Pygmalion*'s Henry Higgins. George Bernard Shaw's fictional character had a waif from the streets of London to mold into "my fair lady"; Ted had the oaf of the airways to transform into a pilot.

Messrs. Higgins and Lisec both had formidable challenges. And both were persistent. I was feeling proud, extremely proud of accomplishing the impossible when I did pass the FAA private pilot flight test. In fact, I was downright smug. I would have enjoyed an afternoon off to revel in my smugness, but the Henry Higginses of the world are tough taskmasters. After a quick sandwich, I was back at work, this time on my commercial license.

When that was accomplished, there was a hiatus—through no fault of Ted's—before the quest for an instrument rating began. The 172 I had become devoted to was not instrument equipped, so we traded it for a Cessna 175 with more sophisticated navigational aids. The one-week delay was caused by the installation of an additional radio, but that time did not go to waste. No siree. Ed, enthralled with the convenience of having a live-in pilot to ferry him around, decided bigger and faster was better, and we acquired part interest in a Piper Twin Comanche. That move gave me the opportunity to get to work on a multi-engine as well as an instrument rating.

It was easily understandable why my instructor was Sky Harbor's leading salesman, and I was astounded by a question from another one of his students, Chuck Galbraith. Chuck was head of Merrill Lynch's Indianapolis office and was interested in recruiting Ted as an account executive.

"Do you think Ted has any sales ability?" he asked one day when we were chatting in the airport restaurant, the equivalent of a pilot's lounge.

"Ted? Are you kidding? In two years' time he sold me on a private, commercial, instrument, and multi-engine rating, plus two different airplanes and a one-seventh interest in another one. And I didn't even want to fly!"

But once addicted, I was flying, flying, flying. Professional pilots are fond of saying their job is "hours and hours of boredom punctuated by moments of stark terror," but I didn't find that to be the case. It was mostly hours and hours of pleasure in those days I look back on as normal. Before I got out of bed in the morning, I knew what I'd be doing that day, although the passengers and destinations would vary.

Usually I was home in time to begin dinner preparations and fill the ice bucket before Ed arrived. Cocktail hour was a daily ritual in our house, a chance to relax and talk over the events of the day while we theoretically safeguarded our health.

Ed contends dilating one's arteries with a bit of libation provides long-range benefits to the body.

Friends often dropped in, so there was nothing unusual about Hiram Rogers's visit. Not until he stated his purpose. Hiram is the realtor who sold us our house, or rather allowed us to buy it. I was in favor of several we had seen until he pointed out some major drawback, a proposed waste disposal plant across the road in one instance. We had the utmost confidence in Hiram's judgment and integrity.

"I'm here on business and pleasure," he said, loosening his tie as he sipped a Scotch and soda. "I've found a place you've got to look at."

"Why? We're perfectly happy here," Ed said, voicing both our sentiments.

"Because it's an excellent buy and . . ." He paused to build suspense. "It's a small twenty-six-acre farm with an eighteen-hundred-foot sod runway and an airplane hangar."

That bit of news got our undivided attention. Hiram knew his clients well. Besides my having flown him on several business trips, he was also aware of Ed's longtime ambition: A bona fide New Yorker born and raised in the city, Ed had always wanted a farm.

So had the man who was selling the property—until his two teen-age boys found out that girls are a lot better company than tractors and lawn mowers. Hiram filled us in on the rest of the particulars, insisting we must see the place for the first time from the air. Accordingly, the three of us met at Sky Harbor at the appointed time and, with Hiram functioning as navigator, easily spotted the property from an altitude of 3,500 feet.

An elongated rectangle with a number of white, red-roofed buildings, it stood out as an oasis in contrast to the newly plowed fields surrounding it. I descended to 1,000 feet to check out the runway, and one look at the hostile approaches prompted me to drop down to 500 feet and circle a second time. Obstructing the east end was a row of thirty-foot evergreens, and at the opposite end was a swamp with a bunch of trees and bushes and jagged stumps rising up from mud and pools of stagnant water. Both approaches called for the shortest short-field landing I'd ever attempted, but there was no need to try to pick the less ominous of the two. An orange wind sock fluttering on top of the barn dictated a landing to the west, over the evergreens.

Surely those trees doubled in height while we were on the downwind leg, and the opposite phenomenon occurred as the 1,800-by-400-foot runway shrank. It looked like a diving board, the same size and shape, complete with water at the opposite end. I slowed the airplane down until it wallowed in the sky just short of stalling speed, skimmed the treetops, and dropped in with a thud. Surprisingly, the heavy grass—coupled with my standing on the brakes—slowed the 175 so quickly at least half of the runway still stretched out ahead of us unused as we rolled to a complete stop. John Kirk, the owner of the property, drove up on a tractor and motioned for us to turn around and taxi along behind him to the large asphalt parking pad on the other side of a fence.

"Nice landing," he said as we climbed out of the airplane. "You'll like it here."

I already did, and at that point all I'd seen was the runway, all I needed to see. For Ed, the pièce de résistance was the eight-stall barn. Its whitewashed walls rose up from the dirt floor to the high rafters, above which was a hay loft that still sheltered links with an era long since past. Old horse collars, buggy whips, and churns and pitchforks were stashed there among the hay and straw and bags of grain. It also housed a livelier collection. Colonies of field mice grew fat on the haute cuisine, sometimes dining out on leftovers at the adjacent facility, a low, flat-roofed chickenless chicken house.

We walked the entire length of the runway and wandered around the pastures crisscrossed with white board fences, taking in the beauty of the gently rolling terrain. Here and there a giant oak or maple provided patches of shade, or a spring burst of golden forsythia lit up the landscape. It was a toss-up as to who was the more enthralled, Ed or I.

Hiram wound up his guided tour with the semicircle of buildings clustered around the parking pad. At one end was the T-hangar, housing a single-engine Mooney. Next to it was a new three-car garage, also of concrete block, with a two-bedroom apartment above it. The garage/apartment was jammed so close to a swimming pool it would be logistically feasible, assuming a reasonable degree of proficiency, to dive from the second-story kitchen smack into the middle of the pool. And only four or five steps on the other side was the spacious four-bedroom house.

Ugly might be too harsh a description of the sixty-year-old frame structure. Stark, or plain, is a bit kinder—also less accurate. But for the porch of drab-red brick jutting out in front, it was a square clunk of a thing devoid of any esthetically redeeming qualities. Neither Ed nor I cared. We'd never devoted a lot of time to gazing at the exterior of our present home.

John, who had discreetly remained behind mowing, chugged up on his mechanical steed when we came out of the house.

"Do you have any questions?" he asked.

Hiram had a couple, but Ed and I were still a bit overwhelmed by the vastness of the place. Although twenty-six acres with five buildings is minute for an Indiana farm, compared to our bungalow on an average-size city lot, it was the King Ranch.

"By the way, I'm leaving this for you to mow with." John indicated the tractor.

He behaved as if the sale had already been made. Which in fact it had.

THREE

By the time the mortgage and swing loan were approved, the title search completed, and all the loose ends tied up, there were five of us to make the big move to the country. Besides Ed and me and Dirty Sam, we had Bismarck, the pedigreed German shepherd we deliberately acquired, and Fat Charles—the full-fledged mongrel who deliberately acquired us.

Fat Charles didn't start out fat. He ate his way into his nickname. The first time I saw the dog he was stretched out fast asleep on the asphalt ramp under the wing of my airplane as if he were too exhausted to look for a more comfortable place to rest. A scrawny little fellow, probably eight or nine pounds, his smooth fur was black except for a light brown spot about half the size of a dime over each eye, floppy hound-dog ears in matching brown, and a long white tipped tail.

Afraid he'd be mangled by the propeller if I started the engine, I first tried calling to him and then shooing him away. When neither of those approaches worked, I resorted to bribery. While my lone male passenger waited patiently, I hoped, I ran to the restaurant, bought a hamburger, and lured the dog over to Operations.

In one gulp the quarter-pounder disappeared. Obviously the animal was ravenous and I debated what to do about him. Too much food at once would surely make him sick, so I decided to forgo seconds and started back toward the airplane; my new friend trotted right along beside me.

We were back to square one. Nothing had changed—other than Fido being one hamburger to the good and my having at least learned a little something. The next time around, I awarded custody of the hamburger to the lineman and asked him to parcel it out bite by bite until I could at least make it out to the taxiway.

It was dusk when I returned, peak time at Sky Harbor, and the ramp was a maze of airplanes, engines idling, as pilots waited in line to refuel. I was glad to see the same lineman on duty so I could inquire about the dog.

"No, I haven't seen him since"—Tony stopped mid-sentence and pointed to the far side of the ramp—"up until now."

Defying all odds of survival, the dog zigzagged his way toward us through the congestion, scooting under and around the whirring propellers with the agility of a broken field runner.

"Good God!" Tony gasped as the daredevil presented himself unscathed at our feet.

The dog's tail was a study in perpetual motion, signaling his pleasure more effectively than a semaphore, and he was panting so hard he appeared to be sporting a wide grin. He just might have been. To him, Tony and I probably looked like two king-size hamburgers standing side by side.

"This guy's been hanging around here for a week. He's got a charmed life," Tony said as he reached down and picked up the dog. "But he's sure pushing his luck. At this rate, he won't make it through the night."

"I'm afraid you're right," I agreed. "Can you think of anything we can do with him?"

"Yeah. You can take him home with you."

Tony handed the little guy to me and, as if he'd been coached, the dog licked my hand and then for the clincher fixed his beautiful brown eyes on mine.

Patting him on the head, Tony laughed and said, "Now you've got it made, On Top Charlie."

Indeed he did. "On Top Charlie" is pilot-ese for one who has everything under control, and from the first moment we met, Charles had called the shots. It was a singularly appropriate name, but it was short lived. At first it was a concentrated effort on my part to put some weight on the dog's gaunt frame, not much of a chore since Charles was cooperative to a fault. He swooped up his food so fast he couldn't have known he enjoyed it, and in between meals he snacked. If there was nothing tastier around, Charles licked the glue off sandpaper.

In less than one month, the dog went from emaciated to plump to chubby. And that was in the city. It was pretty slim pickings there with access only to the house, garage, and the fenced-in backyard. But the country presented Charles with a five-square-mile smorgasbord generously, if unwittingly, provided by our neighbors. Singled out for regular visits was a dairy farm down the road where sweet feed heavily laced with molasses was stockpiled by the ton, and twice each day at milking time puddles of fresh milk were temporarily on the menu. Charles adjusted his timetable accordingly. He loved the country life.

We all did. By choice, our days began early. The sun was just peeping over the horizon when the three dogs and I started down to the road for the morning paper on a pathway rife with temptation. Soon my companions deserted me. They darted off in pursuit of some furry creature who unfortunately had let down his guard, and although I rooted for the potential loser, my team seldom won. Dirty Sam, the gentlest and most affectionate of dogs where people were concerned, was fleet of foot and adhered to a policy of take-no-prisoners. Any unwary rabbit who dawdled over his breakfast was likely to *become* breakfast. Bismarck always followed Dirty Sam's lead in the chase, and Charles, waddling-fat, ran a poor third.

My only companions on the return trip were those more inclined toward an arboreal way of life. Squirrels scampered close to the trees and songbirds flitted about on the branches, tuning up for their casually orchestrated a capella choir. Ed always had the coffee ready and, after a quick cup and a glance at the sports pages, he was off to the hospital. But my routine had undergone a change. No longer did I peruse the paper from front to back as the first order of business. My newly acquired lifeguard duties took top priority.

Although a four-foot fence around the swimming pool kept the dogs out—except when they really wanted to get in—it was an ineffective deterrent to a lot of wildlife that regarded the pool as their watering hole. In our first two weeks at the farm, I rescued two squirrels, one opossum, and so many birds I lost count. For sheer clumsiness, I'd match our local feathered flock against all comers. They would glide in gracefully and execute a flawless landing, these perfect aerodynamic specimens, but it was after that that everything went haywire. The klutzes stubbed a toe or leaned over too far for a drink and all of a sudden they'd be in the water, thrashing around frantically, unable to escape.

Usually I could effect a rescue by slipping a broom under them, sort of a makeshift raft, and towing them to safety, but occasionally more heroic measures were in order. After twice plunging in fully clothed, I made a few changes in the M.O. The pool patrol was moved up into an earlier time slot before I got dressed for the day's activities—at least the ones that had been planned.

The rescue missions were so numerous, Ed's evening greeting was frequently, "What was the bird count this morning?" It was a benign conversation opener that carried no particular significance, as opposed to the loaded, "Guess what I did today?" That question usually preceded a bombshell. Naturally it was the forerunner for his all-time blockbuster. It came a mere week after Ed's newly adopted role of gentleman farmer.

"I bought eight Black Angus steers today."

"Huh? You did what?"

"They're young ones. We'll fatten them up to sell and keep one for us to eat."

Eat! *Us to eat!* The idea was appalling. Although I enjoy a good steak as long as it's an anonymous one selected in a butcher shop, putting a knife and fork to somebody you've met personally is one step removed from cannibalism. Just the thought of it brought back recollections of a traumatic experience still vivid even though many, many years have passed.

My older sister, Carolyn, and I were avid animal lovers, probably from the day we were born. As we frolicked our way through childhood, our parents were indulgent and tolerant up to a point, so we were allowed such conventional pets as cats and dogs—and the goldfish and guppies that were our parents' idea. The unconventional pets, those we secreted in our bedrooms, weren't actually forbidden, but only because we had taken the precaution of not asking permission beforehand.

Phil, a six-inch-long alligator, was our first triumph. We smuggled him home from a Florida vacation. That in itself we considered something of a feat. But keeping his presence unknown to the powers that be, we looked upon as the stuff of genius. It did require considerable maneuvering on our part and remarkable flexibility on Phil's.

A constant threat to his health and well-being always hovered over us—the unexpected appearance of Mother or Daddy. Room inspections were no problem. Since the whole purpose was to bring about some semblance of order in the chaotic habitats of two young hooligans aged five and nine, inspections were announced well in advance. Phil sat out those occasions in Willie's bathroom.

Willie, our beloved second mother, had lived with us as long as we could remember. She had snow-white hair by then, a lovely contrast with her chocolate-colored skin, and an ample lap that was always available to either of her "chillun." Cooking and caring for all of us—including the various pets—she was not just a member of the household, she was part of the family. Carolyn and I could trust her implicitly, but there were always drawbacks to Willie's involuntary assistance. Whenever we called upon her to act as an accessory, she protested vehemently and vowed never again. But more significant in this situation were the logistics. Our confederate's quarters were on the first floor, not far removed from Mother and Daddy. Trips to and from Willie's place had to be swift and stealthy.

Once we'd gotten Phil there, all was well. But it was our parents' impromptu social visits that kept our reflexes sharp. Not only were Mother and Daddy in the habit of dropping in, there were always visitors to contend with—out-of-town clients of our attorney father, relatives, friends of the family. Any adult was automatically deemed dangerous, and the usual security was in effect. If Phil was on the loose, a sweater was always handy to throw over him, or a drawer open to toss him into. When we were away, our contraband, mistakenly thought secure in his cardboard pen, was tucked under a bed until one of us returned.

Even after a couple of months, the alligator caper was still so successful we grew bold. We branched out. When a playmate, Ralph, offered us his two white mice, we readily accepted. Mice met the criteria of our covert operation; they were small, quiet, and the little bit of food they required was easy to pilfer.

Ralph had bought the animals without permission, and in a classic example of poor judgment, proudly showed off his new purchase to his parents. They lacked their son's enthusiasm for rodents and they were vocal about it. "Get rid of them right now!" was how they expressed their sentiments.

We were sorry for Ralph's loss, but not very. The mice were a bonanza we'd never anticipated and, because of the haste in transferring ownership, the wire-mesh cage came along with them. Pleased and excited, we whisked our new pets home with us where Carolyn, four years wiser as well as four years older than I, decided some precautionary measures were in order. "Maybe we'd better leave them in their cage for a while until Phil makes friends with them," was her four-years-wiser suggestion.

But one look at the glint in Phil's narrowed eyes told us they wouldn't be here that long. It told the mice the same thing. They went into such a frenzy, orbiting their metal cage and ricocheting off its sides, the resultant racket sounded like a dozen tambourines in action. We had to snatch up their cage and hustle them off to Carolyn's room to rethink our strategy. It was suddenly in need of a drastic overhaul.

"They're quiet now," I observed as the mice settled down. "Why don't we just keep them in here with you, and Phil can stay with me?"

"Yeah, knucklehead, but what about room inspections? Willie's afraid of mice. We're going to have to think of something else."

Time was not on our side. Two days after we acquired our new friends, Carolyn padded quietly into my room early one morning and whispered, "Quick! Come quick! I have a surprise."

Since the expression on her face indicated that whatever prompted this urgent invitation was pleasant, I hurried along behind her to her room. It was a surprise, all right. It was also a shock. There in the cage with Mickey and Minnie Mouse were seven shiny-pink, furless little mites that looked like small wads of slightly chewed bubble gum. We were ecstatic.

Willie was not. Before we'd had a chance to convince her that two caged mice were harmless, we had a deal four times more difficult to push. Three weeks later when another litter of five arrived, Willie was visibly shaken by the news, and even our enthusiasm was somewhat tempered by anxiety. Our clandestine operation had burgeoned into a mob of fourteen, and at this rate things could get out of hand. All we knew about the birds-and-bees principle was that it took one mama and one papa to produce babies, and we had no idea how to curtail production. We began to worry.

But that concern was soon replaced by a more pressing one. Mother and Phil met, due to an unfortunate circumstance. They both happened to be in the same place at the same time, walking along the upstairs hallway. The news of that catastrophe reached us almost immediately even though we were playing outside at the time.

"Carolyn! Moselle! Come here this instant!"

The tone of Mother's voice told us more than we wanted to know.

The timing could hardly have been worse. Ten days hence, Easter Sunday, was the targeted date for our big coup, one we'd worked toward for almost a year. And now our punishment put me in a severe financial bind that jeopardized the entire project. Since barnyard bedrooms hadn't been outlawed up until then, we hadn't broken any rules nor had we disobeyed. But we were convicted on our parents' flimsy "you-knew-better" charges, a catchall covering everything from high crimes to misdemeanors. Our allowances of twenty-five cents each were suspended for that week, except for the nickel earmarked for the Sunday school collection.

For years, Carolyn and I had been longing for a duck of our very own. It had become our hearts' desire ever since we'd seen the fuzzy little ducklings in a pet-shop window several Easters ago. Mother and Daddy, however, had taken a non-negotiable stand against buying one for us. Some of their objections were probably even legitimate; but the one about the harsh winters? In Birmingham, Alabama? Obviously we'd have to employ a more indirect approach, since reasoning or begging was futile. Once Mother and Daddy said "no"—or "yes"—they never wavered.

Carolyn masterminded the scheme, one that called for substantial sacrifice on our part. A duck cost fifty cents, a princely sum for youngsters with a disposable income of twenty cents, particularly ones who got paid one day and were broke the next. But my sister, systematically squirreling away a penny at a time, was prepared to ante up her half when the time grew near. I was a nickel short, and my situation was desperate.

The options were limited. Mother and Daddy sometimes granted an advance, but a full disclosure of its purpose was a prerequisite. Out of the question. Then there was the Sunday school nickel, cold, available cash—also out of the question. Even though the concept "misappropriation of funds" was over my head, the difference between right and wrong was not. Willie was a last resort.

"I've told you and I've told you, I am not going to get in the middle of something I know your mama and papa would disapprove of," she railed . . . before she handed over the nickel.

Willie also advised against the project on the grounds of bad timing. We were still in disfavor from the alligator-mice disclosure, as she pointed out. Accurately. And futilely. She might as well have suggested we voluntarily forgo Easter, Christmas, and both our birthdays.

The first step of the plan went smoothly, since window shopping was almost an Easter tradition, thanks to my sister and me. As we pressed our noses against the window of the pet shop and looked longingly at the Easter ducks, Carolyn opened the well-rehearsed dialogue.

"Oh, how I wish we could have a baby duck," she opined. "Are you sure you won't get us one?"

Mother's response was almost letter perfect. "Now don't start that again, Carolyn, you already know the answer."

That was my cue to move in for the kill.

"But if we had fifty cents of our own we could buy one, couldn't we?"

Secure in the belief their daughters were paupers, Mother and Daddy nodded absentmindedly.

"Of course. That would be a different matter altogether," Mother said, and the trap was sprung.

Carolyn, poised for action, immediately whipped out our fistful of nickels, dimes, and pennies and Quack Quack went home with us.

Unlike most pet-shop Easter attractions, Quack Quack thrived. Every day he grew plumper, louder, and more popular—at least with the children in the neighborhood. He was a delightful pet, so extraordinarily tolerant he put up with outrageous indignities, allowing us to suit him up like Disney's Donald Duck, wheel him around in baby carriages, and join him in his tail feather–deep wading pool. We needed no explanation for our companion's behavior, he was a good sport who enjoyed the games. Adults explained the phenomenon with a different theory: The term "bird brain" was solidly grounded in fact.

But even adults were enchanted with the people-oriented, personality bird—with two notable exceptions. Daddy was particularly displeased each time he strolled through the yard and skidded on some incontrovertible evidence of the clean-up crew's negligence. He was also bent out of shape when our feathered friend's loud honking disrupted his Sunday afternoon nap. Carolyn and I thought up a sure cure for that disruption, a mate for Quack Quack, but our idea was not well received.

On the contrary, in their quest to rid themselves of their own personal albatross, Mother and Daddy came up with some pretty creative solutions. One was a twenty-dollar cash offer to purchase Quack Quack, which would have amounted to about one dollar per pound—impressive capital gains for someone looking to make a profit. We weren't and we didn't.

Eventually, in desperation, our parents overwhelmed us with a hard sell loaded with such key words as *honor* and *obligation* and *responsibility*. If we really loved Quack Quack we'd want to give him the life of freedom he deserved and yearned for, a life amongst his own kind where he could have the mate we *knew* he wanted and baby ducklings of his own. It was a humdinger of a pitch, and we succumbed.

Mother and Daddy let no grass grow under Quack Quack's feet. Daddy left the office early the following day and all five of us climbed into his car for the twenty-mile drive to Lake in the Woods. Friends had a cottage there, and it was an unofficial wildlife sanctuary where a lot of animals made their home and a variety of birds, in search of balmier climes, stopped off on their annual migrations.

Daddy lugged Quack Quack, by now thirty pounds, down to the lake's edge, where Carolyn and I hugged and kissed our precious pet and splashed him with our heartfelt tears as we dragged out our good-byes as long as possible. We knew what would happen the minute we released him. As advertised by the powers that be, Quack Quack would be so elated when he spotted the kinsmen he'd been deprived of, he'd dash into the deep water and paddle furiously across it to claim the bride he'd been waiting for.

But Quack Quack wasn't in favor of changing his life-style. Instead of making a break for it, he stationed himself between Carolyn and me, never dampening a toe, and stared at the unfamiliar creatures bobbing around on the other side of the lake.

"Take off your shoes and socks and wade into the water so he'll follow you," Daddy instructed us, thus indicating the degree of his consternation.

It was a sweater-cold day when ordinarily we would have
been admonished to stay out of the water, but we were glad to
oblige. When we advanced, so did the duck. We stopped, he
stopped. By the time we reached ankle depth and Quack Quack
hadn't sailed off into the sunset, our father had another idea.
He gathered up Quack Quack in his arms and, with the two
of them leading the procession, the rest of us trooped along
behind them to the end of the pier.

"How deep is the water?" Carolyn asked.

"Oh, five or six feet," was Daddy's answer.

"What if Quack Quack can't swim?" she continued.

"Of course he can swim. All ducks can swim," our father
assured us.

In all fairness to Daddy, he didn't deliberately dump Quack
Quack into the water. It's tough hanging on to a chunky thirty-
pound bird who's protesting vocally and vigorously, his feet
churning the air as if he were pedaling a bicycle. It was an
unceremonious launching. Quack Quack sank. Straight to the
bottom he went as a trail of bubbles gurgling upward marked
his downward path. Carolyn and I shrieked at top capacity
until Daddy, pausing only to hand his wristwatch to Mother,
dove in and, with Quack Quack in tow, made it safely back
to dry land.

Quack Quack was never threatened with eviction after that—
but not because of any sudden surge in popularity. Another
melodrama quickly followed on the heels of the last one.

Uncle Bob and Aunt Ella, relatives by mutual adoption,
were neighbors as well as close family friends. A gourmet cook,
Aunt Ella frequently concocted mysterious delicacies neither
Carolyn nor I recognized, and she never objected to our asking
about them.

"What's this?" I inquired, looking at the unidentified slices of meat on my dinner plate.

"Peking duck," Aunt Ella answered.

"He came all the way from Peking?" asked Carolyn, whose geography class was currently studying China.

"No, this duck walked in from a block away," Uncle Bob joked.

The rest of the meal was a fiasco. Although I realized that Uncle Bob, the kindest and gentlest of men, was only teasing, the implications of his remark were devastating to a six-year-old, and I was excused from the table in tears.

The aftermath was worse. For many months my screams, brought on by the recurrent nightmares, had Mother and Daddy racing to my room in the middle of the night to comfort me. Countless hours they spent at my bedside, reassuring me that Quack Quack was alive and well and living, regrettably, right outside their bedroom window.

Although the childhood nightmares were long since a thing of the past, nothing else had changed. My dinner plate as the final resting place for somebody I knew was still a distressing prospect, and I took measures to lessen the emotional wallop. Selecting savory names for the steers was the start of my do-it-yourself brainwashing attempt. But since Porterhouse soon became Porter, and Béarnaise, Bernie—and the rest of the animals' names went through the same refinement—it wasn't much help.

At first they all looked alike, with the exception of BurgerKing. King, for some unknown reason, was a redhead, a real standout against seven black Black Angus. But when I got to know the others, I realized each one had some distinctive feature, such as Porter's wavy bangs or the warts on Bernie's chin. One characteristic all eight shared was equally blank, expressionless faces. They were as dull a looking bunch as ever assembled in a barnyard. But they were sweet, docile animals with never a malicious thought between them. In fact, scratch "malicious" and the statement is still accurate. Their number, eight, was quite likely the sum total of their collective I.Q.'s.

Having such a retarded group of playmates was another aspect of country life that held great appeal for Dirty Sam, Fat Charles, and Bismarck, and they devised a new game with the steers as the focal point. The barnyard bounced with beef as the poor dumb animals raced round and round in endless circles to escape the trio of dogs nipping at their heels.

In our introductory phase, I gave the steers credit for opening gates and deliberately engineering exits where there had been none, but it was a compliment they didn't deserve. Even at their relatively diminutive two-hundred-pound weights, it took just one of them stumbling against a loose fence board to create a handy new doorway to the big wide world beyond. They were also athletically inclined and any one of them could clear a fence with the agility of an Olympic pole vaulter, soon followed by the seven other members of their close-knit group.

My days took on new dimensions when "we" began raising beef cattle. As my husband blithely motored off to the city, my half of the "we" got to ride herd on the herd. When they strayed only as far as the runway, I let them linger there undisturbed as long as feasible. Keeping the grass down to a satisfactory height for takeoffs and landings was a time-consuming effort, and their assistance was welcome. The other function they performed there was not. Cow pies splattering

on the airplane as I rolled down the runway were a bit
disconcerting.

Usually their junkets took them farther afield. Rare was the
day they didn't amble down the road several miles to taste-
test another pasture, and I, the inept, unwilling, horseless
cowgirl, had to lure the boys home on foot with a pail of grain
for incentive. After one of those cold, rainy treks into the land
of plenty, I could have shish-kebabbed the culprits with never
a palpitation; but such was not the case as the day of infamy
drew closer.

After fourteen months, the steers were becoming perilously
fat, and each passing day saw my charges getting closer and
closer to their execution. Days they spent munching the sweet
clover and alfalfa in the pastures, and evenings I escorted them
to their individual stalls and plied them with more lethal nourishment in the form of grain—the hot fudge sundae of the cattle
crowd. They thrived, blissfully oblivious to their temporary
tenure on Death Row.

"I can't do it. They can't go," I moaned to Ed as the time
of their demise approached.

"Mosie, for God's sake! Eventually their bones would crum-
ble under the excess weight if they kept on getting bigger.
They're bred for this purpose," was his less-than-persuasive
rebuttal.

"I'm sorry. I just can't do it. They're my friends and they
trust me."

Nevertheless, the day of doom arrived, and I had to be on
hand to sign the death warrants that would take my friends on
their journey to the slaughterhouse. Sobbing convulsively, I
fled into the house to escape the commotion that meant the
animals were fast on their way to becoming has-beens. But the
noise of the struggle penetrated the closed windows. The shouts

of the cattlemen as they rounded up their quarry, the protests of the poor, dumb beasts being poked and prodded through the chute, and finally the rumble of the engine as the bulging truck lumbered away toward its sinister destination—it was a grim funeral dirge. I felt like a Judas. And for good reason. It's exactly what I was.

FOUR

Robert Baudy's visit was a particularly welcome one. Our good friend, always a delightful houseguest, arrived a few days after my despicable deed.

We had met the fascinating Frenchman five or six years earlier when Robert and his seven Siberian tigers were the major attraction in the Shrine Circus held each spring in Indianapolis. As guests of the PR man for the event, we had excellent seats with an unobstructed view of Robert's act, and our eyes were fixed on him as he strode into the arena, whip in hand.

His costume, what there was of it, was flamboyantly show biz. From the waist up he was bare except for an extraordinary amount of jewelry, more than likely his entire inventory, hanging all over him. Heavy gold bracelets were stacked up on his left forearm and a bear-claw necklace plus some silver and gold chains were draped around his neck. He wore tight-fitting kelly green trousers tucked into ornate leather boots, and a nail-studded belt with a jeweled dagger completed his outfit. The whip was not part of Robert's ensemble. As far as the tigers were concerned, it was flesh and blood, an extension of their trainer-keeper's right arm.

As the PA system blared: "And NOW, Robert Baudy and his seven Siberian tigers," the big cats were admitted one by one into the arena, where the star of the show was waiting. He had already established dominance as the "chief tiger" by having them enter *his* territory, and he continued to prove his superiority, of necessity. These were not docile cats. Any one of them could put their boss out of business and themselves out of a job, and some of them have tried to do just that.

"Deutchka, *en place*! Alexandra, *en place*!" Robert barked commands in French, and each tiger loped over to his or her assigned pedestal, leaped up, and sat down on all fours. When six tigers were *en place*, a crack of the whip cued the big cats to sit upright and remain so while Robert swirled the whip over his head, ending with a dramatic flourish that cued the animals to revert to their seated positions before they went on to other things.

I wondered fleetingly about the discrepancy between the seven tigers in the billing with only six performing, but it was of no significance—at that time. It was a spellbinding performance, a smooth-flowing symphony in grace and motion.

When the act was over, our host for the evening appeared in the aisle close to our seats, signaling for us to follow him. On the way to the animals' quarters outside the building, he explained why.

"I can't get hold of a vet, Ed, and Baudy needs someone to give a sick tiger a shot."

"You mean me?" asked an incredulous orthopedic surgeon about to turn veterinarian—reluctantly. "Lew, I don't know a thing about tigers."

"Oh, Baudy will show you how," Lew announced laughing.

Introductions and amenities were kept to a minimum, after which Robert explained where and how to insert the needle in the tiger's tail as soon as he—Robert—managed to pull it between the bars of the cage.

"I can't hold on to it long, so you'll have to be quick, very, very quick," he said.

Robert's emphasis on haste was quite unnecessary. Calm, cool surgeon's hands had developed a noticeable tremor, and Ed's normally ruddy face was ashen. With one swift jab the needle was in and out of the indignant cat's tail. Whether Ed was actually faster than the speed of light—as he claims—is debatable. That he was very, very quick, is not.

Robert came out for dinner the following evening, and we saw a good deal of him during his Indianapolis engagement. From that chance meeting, the Baudy-Schaffer friendship grew, with many visits exchanged between Indiana and Robert's home base in Florida, where he pursued numerous other animal-related interests.

I was especially glad to see Robert when he popped in unexpectedly right after the steer debacle. Having a sympathetic ear to bend was a comfort, and I regaled him with my woes:

"No sooner had the Black Angus departed for the happy hunting ground than Ed announced he had arranged for eight replacements. I mutinied. With a firm, defiant, irrevocable 'no,' I mutinied.

"And do you know what he's talking about now? Milk cows. *Milk cows!* That have to be milked twice a day! 'We'll get someone to do the milking,' he says. Sure we will. Me. I can just see it now, 'Sorry Mr. Umpsty Umps, I hated to leave you stranded at O'Hare but I had to get home to milk Elsie, eight Elsies.'

"I have discovered an interesting facet of Ed's personality. He abhors an empty stall as badly as nature abhors a vacuum, and they both react the same way. They've *got* to fill them up. Did you notice the chickens? Twenty-five of them. The chicken coop was empty," I raved on and on.

"You know what you ought to raise, Moselle? Camels and zebras," Robert said thoughtfully.

"Camels? In this climate?" Sun-drenched deserts and sweating Arabs came to mind.

"Oh, sure. Camels are such hardy animals they can withstand a hundred-degree temperature variation in twenty-four hours. As a matter of fact, the largest camel-breeding farm in this hemisphere is in Canada. It would be a good business for you. You could start with a pair of each and sell the offspring."

"I'd probably be scared to death of them, they're so big."

"The babies are only about seventy-five pounds at birth. You'd want to start off with young ones."

Ed thought it was a good idea, too. Although I much prefer waving good-bye to corn or soybeans, to which I develop no emotional attachment, those sorts of crops are much too bland for a gentleman farmer and Robert's plan sounded like an equitable compromise. It sure beat raising perishables.

Even though I should have anticipated problems parting with any camel or zebra babies, there weren't any at that point, and giving up somebody not yet born isn't too difficult.

———

Camel salesmen move quickly. Ten days after Robert's visit, a large horse van pulled up and the driver, wearing a filthy cap, clothes to match, and a three-day growth of beard, knocked on the door. "Where you want these here camels?" he asked, as casually as if he were dropping off a crate of oranges.

Ed and I hurried out to open the gates, and the driver backed up to the barn doors—his last physical contribution to the cause. Climbing out of the cab, the camel chauffeur sauntered over and propped himself up against the barn, a position he never deserted until—some two hours later—the camels were ensconced in their new quarters.

"Take hol' of the chute there," he said to Ed. "Jus' slide it out then hook it on them side rails. They slip into them li'l grooves."

Ed grabbed on to the heavy wooden contraption and pulled it to the ground, then together we struggled with the awkward side rails until we got the director of operations' approval.

"Okay. Now open the back doors. Go ahead," he added as Ed hesitated. "They got restrainin' straps."

Ed slowly opened the doors, behind which was the largest, shabbiest, most intimidating "baby" I'd ever encountered. In none of my telephone conversations with Robert was there any reference to the size of the fellows en route, and I assumed they'd be a relatively petite seventy-five pounds, which they had been when they were born eleven months before. Now the guy had to be six feet tall and five hundred pounds. Shedding profusely, the remains of the camel's coat dangled in long streamers, the only fur intact being the mop of reddish-brown curls on the top of his head. He was homely.

I had second thoughts—and third and fourth ones—about

this venture, and they were all the same. "What have we gotten into?" didn't just race through my mind, it moved in and stayed put.

"Here, miss," the driver handed me an eighteen-inch whip. "Go open up one stall door and stand on the other side of it. Then keep flickin' this li'l whip so when the camel comes out he don't go past the stall."

"Do *what*?"

"Like I said . . ." and he repeated his instructions.

"I don't much think I want to do that," I protested.

"Go on. He ain't gonna hurt you."

I walked slowly to my position and flicked the whip. Effortlessly. Activated by a panic they'd never known, my muscles were jumping around of their own accord as I stared, wild-eyed, in the direction from which the impending disaster would come. I felt like an ancient Christian in the Colosseum waiting for the onslaught.

Fumbling with the buckle, it took Ed a good five minutes to get the restraining strap unhooked and, as the outraged beast roared, he jumped nimbly over a side rail out of the way. All that was left between me and the one-humped behemoth was a few strands of loosely plaited leather and twenty feet of space. That distance was reduced to twelve inches as down the ramp he thundered, stopping abruptly just before he smeared me into the floor.

I didn't have time to move, even if I could have, before the camel reared back on his two hind legs then executed a ninety-degree left turn and stormed into the empty stall. At that point, I dived at its sliding door before he could turn around, and half of this exercise in madness was over. I no longer felt like an ancient Christian, I *was* an ancient Christian.

"That wasn't too difficult," was Ed's comment, and from his vantage point it hadn't been. "Let's get the other one out. She's probably more docile."

In a matter of seconds, the pundit's optimistic prediction bit the dust. The instant the female's restraining strap was off, she went berserk. Without advancing one step forward, she bucked and kicked and bellowed and foamed at the mouth, behaving in general like the hysterical female she was. The soothing words, the coaxing, served only to increase her agitation.

As the awesome sounds reverberated over the countryside, half a dozen neighbors from as far away as a mile arrived to investigate. Word of mouth, camel mouth, travels fast.

One farmer, used to handling contrary animals, recommended roping the animal and pulling her down the ramp by sheer force; his offer to do the lasso bit was readily accepted. On his eighth attempt, the rope dropped over the camel's head, down onto her neck, and full-scale warfare ensued. But four men tugging on the rope couldn't budge their determined adversary.

Improvising a makeshift shield was a prerequisite for the next plan, one that called for a combination push-pull strategy. While the scraps of plywood and two-by-fours were being nailed together, I attempted a graceful escape from the melee.

"You don't really want me here anymore, do you?" I called out over the din.

"Don't worry," came the answer from our director, still propping up the building. "She's more a'scared of you than you are of her."

"No, she isn't," I replied with conviction.

My notion of a camel's disposition was totally shattered—

along with my nervous system. According to the artwork on a
box of Dromedary dates, from which I'd gleaned my expertise,
camels are a placid lot. The imaginative artist depicts one lone
Arab, his docile herd of dromedaries padding along behind
him, out for an afternoon stroll around the pyramids. A tranquil
scene, that, but a far cry from the brouhaha in progress. The
company has since changed their packaging—and probably
canned the artist—but too late to prepare me for reality.

Camels are by no means docile, malleable animals. They
are stubborn, firmly opposed to change of any sort, and have
the resources to back up their opposition. While their kicks
and bites may inflict serious injury, two other nonlethal weapons in their arsenal can usually stave off the enemy. Spitting,
for which they're notorious, is not always the judicious use of
saliva the term implies. The ruminants are able to summon
the contents of their stomachs at will and drench their oppo-
nents in a vile, poison-green puree—most effective on a frontal
attack; diarrhea protects the rear.

The three stalwarts on the rope crew and the other dispirited
trio behind the camel were subjected to those unforgettable
experiences before they could claim their feeble victory. But
judging from the appearances of all six, it looked like the
winning team had actually lost the war.

Once the commotion subsided and the mob dispersed, the
animals calmed down and Ed and I were able to get our first
good look at the camels. What neither of us had noticed before
became obvious then, a swelling in the male's left cheek about
the size of a baseball, in the center of which was a cut in the
form of an X. It appeared to be an incision with some stray
bits of black thread, probably sutures, dangling from it.

"What do you think that means?" I asked.

"I think he's had an abscessed tooth that's been lanced, but only because I can't think of anything else it could be."

"Do you know what to do for him?"

"Yeah, call Harry Kerr."

I got the oral surgeon on the telephone and gave him a brief rundown on his new, unsolicited patient. A long silence followed.

"Moselle," he said, and another silence ensued. "I have treated a poodle and I have even treated a crocodile. But I have never treated a camel, particularly a camel I've never seen. And certainly one I've never seen on such a flimsy diagnosis. Well, let's see. Start him on five hundred milligrams of penicillin every six hours and see how he does."

Not for an instant did I consider prying open those enormous jaws and thrusting my arm halfway down a hostile gullet to deposit a pill. Sugar, I thought, might be a good vehicle. Horses like sugar. Subsequent research has proven that some camels do indeed like sugar, but this one didn't. He put his nose into the bucket I hung onto his door and blew the offensive grains out of the way, leaving the medicine untouched.

I tried apples next, the tablets subtly wedged into the fruit. Nothing doing. But with Pepperidge Farm whole-wheat bread, I hit pay dirt. Rolling up the sort of doughy little marbles a six-year-old concocts at the dinner table, I stuffed the medication into some of the wads and left the others as decoys, and he gobbled them with enthusiasm. But no other brand would do. It was Pepperidge Farm or nothing for this discriminating quadruped, and I was happy to cater to his whims. The possibility of our becoming friends didn't cross my mind at that point, but survival did.

The next morning I set an unofficial record for the forty-yard dash trying to get the newcomers out into the pasture. Leaving both ends of the barn open for escape routes, I eased up to the male's stall, quickly slid open the door, and streaked out the closest exit faster than a comet. Not until I'd hurtled the barnyard fence did I break stride—or look back. The camel never budged.

Half an hour later, I repeated the process in reverse, first closing him back in and then opening the female's door. The results were identical. We seesawed back and forth the entire morning, until I reluctantly concluded they weren't ever going anywhere unless they went together. Recalling the camel driver's observation that they were more "a'scared" of me than I of them, I told myself he was right and opened both their doors at the same time before my hasty retreat.

They did eventually step out into the runway of the barn, and I did eventually lure them out into the pasture, but only by walking along with them outside the pasture fences. Even so, the minute I, their security blanket, was out of sight, they hotfooted it right back into the barn. To get them used to the wide, open spaces, I set up camp with a canvas folding chair and a table for the long stints of baby-sitting that lay ahead.

As we got to know each other better, a mutual affection began to develop between us. At least I hoped it was mutual. I was still afraid of the big dudes, but the more I learned about them—up to a point—the more relaxed I became. I learned more than I ever wanted to know about their dental prowess, but then I hadn't reckoned on becoming a tourist attraction.

Friends, casual acquaintances, and total strangers flocked out to ogle the camels, who had become "Reverend" and "Roxie," and there were always various comments about the animals. The seven callous pads they're born with—one on the middle of the chest and six others on their limbs where they bear weight in their "folded-up" resting position—was usually a topic for discussion, as was the toothless midsection of the camels' upper gums. But one woman, a *grown woman*, became belligerent on the subject and chose to demonstrate her half-baked theory that camels have no teeth at all. For this exercise, she shoved her elbow into Roxie's considerable mouth and Rox, displeased with the demonstration, immediately clamped her powerful jaws together and planted the teeth she supposedly didn't have deep in the demonstrator's flesh. Roxie's performance convinced everyone present that the toothless theory, as well as the nincompoop's arm, had a lot of holes in it.

As a matter of record, the camel has a single outer incisor, a canine, and an advanced premolar on each side of the upper jaw, and three normal incisors, a canine, and an advanced premolar on each side of the lower jaw—sixteen teeth in all. I came by this bit of information the easy way, reading up on camels, rather than by any perilous excursion through Reverend's or Roxie's mouth.

The same reference book provided a factual account of the first *Camelus dromedarius* in North America, coincidentally offering a glimpse of bureaucratic shenanigans as long ago as the mid-1800s. Not much has changed.

Way back in 1855, some politician in Washington boned up on the attributes of the camel and was enthralled by what he learned. Although the animals drink from five to seven gallons of water per day, depending upon the amount of work they do, they can go for as long as thirty-four days without liquids and are able to transport four hundred pounds over long distances with ease, much heftier loads for shorter treks. Traveling 100 miles per day, with water breaks, is routine; in fact, one lone supercamel covered 115 miles across the torrid Sahara in a mere eleven hours.

Then there was the notable caravan consisting of forty-five camels and one ignoramus, the herdsman, that covered 530 miles *sans* water. That is, two of them did. The rest conked out one by one and the two pathetic animals who managed the entire trip reaped their heavenly rewards shortly afterward.

Drawing on that information, our man of vision in D.C. concluded camels would be extremely useful in the arid Southwest, where there was some skirmishing between our side and a few disgruntled Indian tribes who had gotten there first. Exactly what the camels were supposed to do is anybody's guess. Most likely they were to be used as pack animals, an auxiliary of sorts to the budding railroads. Whatever the long-range plan, our bureaucrat wandered over to Congress and presented his idea and, after deliberating a moment or two, that august body appropriated $30,000 for the experiment, plus expenses.

Just as quickly, the idea man stuffed the money in a satchel, dusted off his passport, and junketed off to Smyrna. There he lolled around for a couple of weeks, finding the climate pleasant and the natives friendly. They found him gullible and acted accordingly. The local camel hucksters rounded up thirty-three specimens, easy to do since dromedaries were overrunning the place, and collected the thirty large bills. That's $30,000 in 1855 dollars, approximately $450,000 in today's buying power.

On February 15, 1856, our agent and his thirty-three companions boarded the ship *Supply* for their long, rocky voyage across the waters. The seas were stormy at that time of year, so the 33-plus-1 were actively ill during most of the journey. It being the camels' first voyage, they were the sickest.

Once back on dry land, the animals still didn't take kindly

to their new surroundings. One or two at a time they disappeared, and even those who hung around were eventually turned loose to roam the countryside. Soon they became a menace to both crops and horses: They ate the crops and terrified the horses.

Understandably, the ranchers grew more and more irate and legislation had to be passed outlawing camels at large. Any found running wild were to be shot on sight. None of these developments fazed Washington, however, so Uncle Sam continued to underwrite camel shopping sprees to exotic faraway lands.

Private industry also ventured into the camel market, purchasing two-humped Bactrians as well as dromedaries. One company, Comstock Mines, tried to use the animals for hauling ore, but things didn't work out too well. The last Comstock camel died in Yuma, Arizona, in 1899, was roasted, carved, and served as the main course at a swanky Indian powwow. It was a bit of a switch from the original intent. Whether the occasion was noted on the society pages or the obituaries isn't clear, but a newspaper commented at the time: "The venerable beast was one of the herd of camels brought from Asia Minor years ago to carry ore from Comstock Mines. So ends the greatest attempt of acclimating foreign animals ever made in the United States."

That isn't quite the conclusion of the Western Saga, though. Even today camels supposedly appear there from time to time. They saunter into the backyard of some unwary little homemaker who's hanging out the wet laundry, tiptoe up behind her, and startle her clear out of her canvas tennis shoes.

Eyewitness accounts of same are understandably scarce.

FIVE

Our camels stayed home. Unlike the steers, they weren't afflicted with wanderlust, which in one sense was a pity. They were no help at all with runway maintenance. Time *and* grass wait for no one, I discovered. They're too busy maintaining the balance of nature, making sure that when you have too little time you have too much grass. That way things equal out and Mother Nature is happy.

My little Cessna 175 could operate safely when the grass was fairly long, but that was not so for some of the other airplanes that used the sod strip, notably the Twin Comanche. Our Twin Comanche group, known as Merrill Lynch, Pierce, Fenner, and Schaffer, was composed of six pilots from the Indianapolis Merrill Lynch office and me, and although we hangared the airplane at Metropolitan Airport, several of our members were fond of swooping in and out of eighteen-hundred-foot Camel Lot International. I was not among that elite few. Flying twin-engine aircraft, I preferred a hard-surface runway and a lot more of it than home base had to offer. If it's possible to be overly cautious, I admit to being just that and wish I could say the same for two air force pilots who dropped in, literally, for a surprise visit. It was a surprise, all right, and a whole bunch of people were flabbergasted.

I was in the barn when I heard an airplane and looked out to see it approaching much too fast to land at Camel Lot. Assuming, wrongly, that he'd pull up and go around, I watched in horror as the pilot got lower and lower and nearer and nearer to the end of the runway. With about two hundred feet remaining, the wheels struck the ground with a thud and the airplane bounced back up in the air, veering crazily out of control. The nose pointed up, then down, and there was a horrendous sound like a loud clap of thunder as the aircraft crashed into the swamp.

Dropping the feed bucket in my hand, I raced down the runway thinking that any minute an explosion only Divine Providence could prevent would turn the swamp into a fireball. As I got closer to the crash scene, I saw two young men, apparently unscathed, climb out of the mass of mangled metal and shattered glass that no longer bore any resemblance to an airplane.

"Are you all right?" I screamed when I was within shouting distance.

"I think so," the pilot answered, shaking his head as he wandered aimlessly around in the wreckage.

"Then get out of there. Quick! It could blow any second!" I shrieked.

"Oh, we have to be flying back to Grissom, can you pull us out of here?" he asked, as casually as if he'd just stepped out of a whole airplane.

Not realizing both men were in a state of shock, the question left me speechless. What was left of their airplane was face down in the swamp with the main landing gear completely severed and the right wing impaled on a tree stump. The fuselage was crumpled like an accordion, and gasoline gushing out of the ruptured fuel tanks meant fire was a strong possibility.

When we regrouped one hundred yards or so back from the wreckage, the insane discussion continued. The dazed men couldn't grasp the idea that the airplane they had so recently flown would probably never fly again, a fact I pointed out repeatedly with more and more annoyance.

"Why don't you think it will fly?" the puzzled pilot asked.

"If for no other reason, it's out of gas," I answered, hoping that line of reasoning would get through to him. It didn't.

"We can get some gas, can't we?" was his solution.

"And pour it in that hole in the tank?" Sarcasm didn't work either. "Look, fellow, I think I'd better take you two to the hospital. You've just survived a serious crash, apparently unharmed, but you do seem to have a problem understanding the airplane is wrecked. *You* can't fly it. *Nobody* can fly it."

"We'll have to get a mechanic over here," he persisted.

At that point I gave up. "Come with me," I said, leading the way toward the house. "What happened, anyhow?"

"I shouldn't have landed here," he said, obviously considering that statement an explanation.

"Uh—I don't believe what you accomplished is generally considered a landing," I commented.

"I just got checked out yesterday," he continued.

"I have no reason to doubt that."

"I think I should have gone around."

"Yes, but why did you try to land here at all?"

"I saw the wind sock," was his astonishing answer.

The mere concept of United States Air Force pilots landing every time they spy a wind sock was too frightening to even contemplate. I tried to switch the subject to something unrelated, such as their imminent departure, but Pilot continued to pursue his chosen topic of conversation. While his buddy remained virtually mute, we argued all the way to my car and all the way to the bus station in downtown Indianapolis. There I lured them on board a four-wheeled vehicle for their return trip to Grissom Air Force Base as Pilot proclaimed, in the proud tradition of the military, that he would return.

And he did. The following day, Pilot, his commanding officer, his flight instructor, and an assortment of mechanics and technicians all arrived together, via surface transportation. With much shaking of their heads, the grim-looking party proceeded to slosh around in the swamp to get a closer look at the wreckage. It took them quite a while to locate the main landing gear as it had, meanwhile, sunk.

After a comprehensive study, which included diagrams and measurements, the thoroughly vexed C.O. began asking all sorts of questions that obviously made Pilot uncomfortable: "Why, for God's sake, did you try to land here in the first place?"

I was relieved when Pilot, instead of coming up with the wind-sock explanation, remained silent except for a deep breath and continued to concentrate on the state of his shoelaces. His buddy was not on hand to field any of the questions, since he had wisely elected to remain at the base. At least I guess it had been his own decision, since Pilot was still running around loose.

Considerable discussion ensued as to what to do and how, after which the somber group departed. A few hours later, an enormous four-engine job buzzed in so low over the runway it rattled the windows in the house, and I rushed out in time to recognize an air force bomber. The thought did cross my mind that if this kept up, the swamp was likely to become a bit congested. It turned out, though, they were only taking pictures of the place, one of which they presented to me.

Late that same afternoon, a tow truck arrived and dragged the wreckage out of the muck so the mechanics could separate the one remaining wing and the propeller to get them ready for traveling. They left the dismembered components, as well as all the other loose parts, strewn about the fuselage, explaining that another truck would be down soon to pick up the remains. Exactly when it would appear, they neglected to mention, and for the next month the lawn was a real attention-grabber—so much so that I was called upon by an official of the Federal Aviation Administration. He happened to be flying over, duly noted the airplane fragments all over the grass, and stopped in to inquire as to why the FAA had not been notified. It appeared to him to have been a great deal more serious than any taxiing mishap he could imagine, he explained, making an accident report mandatory.

When I gave the gentleman as accurate an account as possible of the events that prompted his visit, carefully avoiding any editorial comment, he was aghast. But since he was standing square in the middle of the evidence, he had no choice but to accept my version.

Eventually, a series of trucks did arrive to haul away the debris, but before the clean-up job was completed, Pilot was transferred to Okinawa. Whether that move was calculated strategy on the part of the air force or sheer coincidence is anybody's guess. Personally, I like to think they deliberately dispatched the fellow to a diminutive little island, as far away as possible, so he could practice up on his shabby short-field landings.

The airplane wreckage littering the lawn didn't interfere with the use of the runway other than psychologically. Most people are aware airplanes have mishaps occasionally and sometimes even crash, but having those facts spread out in front of them is less than reassuring to a passenger. It doesn't do a whole lot for the pilot either.

During that period, no charter flights originated from home base. Up until then, I sometimes gave clients a choice. They could take off from the sod strip or they could choose a more conventional airport, one with hard-surface runways and a control tower and all sorts of sophisticated amenities. That option was only open to those who scored high in their evaluation: Before accepting any charter flight, I indulged in a bit of amateur psychiatry. If the client's voice sounded shaky over the telephone or if I detected any tendency toward nail biting or hand wringing when the arrangements were made face to face, they were automatically relegated to Category II (the conventional airport). I figured they were going to be nervous in any event, and there was no sense in aggravating their condition, so I selected an airport convenient for them and picked them up there. I also prayed for a strong tail wind to shorten time en route, not altogether an altruistic act on my part.

Those who qualified for a Category I classification, most often people I knew personally, could select Camel Lot International as the point of departure, if that was their pleasure. Since they had usually been to the farm or heard about it, I assumed they knew what to expect, an assumption that was not always justified. I almost lost a huge macho of a man, an FBI agent who was the picture of complacency until he climbed into the right front seat.

I got the first clue he was somewhat apprehensive when he secured his seat belt with such vigor he had difficulty breathing. When I started the takeoff roll, beads of perspiration broke out on his forehead. I must admit, however, my variation on the standard short-field takeoff procedure provided an unintentional thrill. Instead of lining up at the end of the runway, standing on the brakes, and applying full power before releasing them, I used a technique that shortened the takeoff roll. Barreling down the parallel taxiway as fast as possible, I made a sharp ninety-degree turn onto the runway, then another one to line up the airplane, and we were officially on the takeoff roll with considerably more speed than the textbook method could provide.

After we were airborne and heading for the trees at the end of the runway, I pulled on the flaps to give us a few feet extra clearance over the obstructions, and we hiccuped over the evergreens. That did it as far as my passenger was concerned. He grabbed a sick sack and squeaked, "Let's go back. I think I'll drive to South Bend." I was more than willing to oblige.

The poor man never flew with me again, his choice, but several of his fellow agents did. One, in fact, was such a regular customer, he qualified for my frequent-flier bonus. That award was purely honorary. It consisted of the privilege of helping to preflight the airplane.

Out in the country there is more to that ritual than kicking the tires and draining the sumps. There are birds to contend with, mostly sparrows and pigeons. They love to build their nests in the airplane's engine where it's snug and warm. If they're not removed before the engine heats up, it's likely to get a whole lot warmer for everybody. Sometimes they select a spot in plain view, but more often the nests are wedged into some obscure crevice with only bits of straw and grass and a few feathers as clues to their presence.

The feathered menaces also perform another disservice, the one for which pigeons the world over are renowned. They drop their cargo on everything in their flight path—trees, roofs, automobiles. Nothing is immune and my airplane was no exception. I don't contend our birds were more adept at hitting their target than any others, but the effect of their bombing runs was unquestionably more repulsive. Gorging themselves on an ever-present supply of berries, the end result was a purple commodity that polka-dotted everything on which they trained their sights. The airplane's windows had to be cleaned in order to see out of the cockpit.

In search of a solution to the problem, I poked around in a hardware store and found a product guaranteed to repel the airborne nuisances without harming them physically. It was a sticky substance to be spread on surfaces the birds frequented, and it worked on a premise that sounded simple and logical: The gooey concoction provided an unpleasant sensation to the birds' toes and they took off immediately never to return to that spot.

"Does this really work?" I asked the clerk.

"I've never tried it, but it's been around for a long time," he answered.

It didn't occur to me to ask for an interpretation of his remarks. Had it been in use for a long time or sat there on a shelf for a long time? Well, I followed the directions and so did the birds. They did land and they did find the gummy stuff unpleasant and they did try to take off. But they couldn't.

Mired in up to their ankles, they were permanently grounded until I came to the rescue and gouged them out with a spatula. They were not idle, however, during their period of captivity. They stepped up production and their deposits doubled and tripled in quantity.

That was the end of the bird eradication effort, a success at least from some points of view. The birds lived happily ever after.

SIX

Gertrude fell into the same classification as the messy birds. She was uninvited, unpopular, unwelcome, and unforgettable.

I got a call from the Indianapolis Humane Society where several years before I had attempted to help out on a regular basis. My first assignment was a fiasco, in the receiving station where people brought in animals they were parting with for one reason or another. If it was a sad farewell and they cried, I cried; if it was a cold, businesslike transaction because the pet was being casually discarded, I was enraged. The job was an emotional roller coaster and a three-hour stint left me drained.

My second assignment, working with the animals, was worse. Cleaning the cages of a dog or cat who had just been adopted was a pleasure, but looking into the eyes of one who was fast approaching the limit of his stay was devastating. My time at the Humane Society was short, but the memory of one staff member was long.

"She's already over her time limit and if you don't take her we'll have to put her to sleep," Ernie said of the monkey he was pushing. "That would be such a shame. She's tame and leash trained, a real beauty. And she's no problem. She's only eight pounds and used to running around the house loose."

When I picked up Gertrude at the animal shelter, she was already installed in a small, plastic-domed traveling case. Harnessed and leashed, she was ready to roll, and for good reason. There was cunning behind that seemingly efficient move. Confined along with Gertrude was the nose-punishing stench that was part of the stump-tailed macaque's heritage, unbeknownst to me.

Hints of this undisclosed characteristic began drifting up to my nostrils as we drove home in the car side by side. After I opened up Gertrude's traveling gear to release her, that regrettable trait was no longer a mere suspicion, it was hardcore news. Gertrude was the vilest-smelling creature ever to single-handedly pollute this hemisphere.

Selecting the basement for the monkey's liberation had been a matter of luck. I'd accepted Ernie's highly embellished profile of Gertrude word for word and intended to install her as a permanent member of our household after she had met the dogs. That was now out of the question.

Pondering my next move, I closed the basement door behind me and left Gertrude alone to become familiar with her new surroundings, and she did. The "well-behaved" monkey was busy, busy, busy. An hour later when I returned to check on her, the place was a shambles. All of the tools light enough to handle—hammers, sanders, drills—had been examined and discarded; boxes of nails and staples had been torn open and their contents strewn around at random. Gertrude herself was perched high atop a cabinet, crossed legs dangling over the front as she munched on a tulip bulb, taking one bite before she tossed it to the floor and reached into the handy plastic bag at her side for another.

"Gertrude!" I shrieked. "Come down here, Gertrude."

The monkey ignored my summons, as she could well afford to do from her secure position aloft, so I switched tactics. Lowering my voice to what I hoped was a persuasive tone, I tried again. "Come down, Gertrude," I cooed irresistibly. Gertrude resisted.

Ernie had mentioned Gertrude's weakness for ice cream, so I resorted to bribery, hastily dishing up a scoop of vanilla. Before I offered it to her, I rummaged around in the garage for a bulky but lightweight cage big enough to accommodate a full-grown German shepherd and dragged it down to the basement to serve as Gertrude's temporary quarters.

The ruse worked. Gertrude scrambled down from the cabinet and began delicately licking the booby trap while I stood by feigning innocence. When I figured she was sufficiently engrossed, I grabbed her from behind and stuffed the scoundrel into the cage as she screamed in protest.

With Gertrude's activities curtailed, my next concern was how to break the news of her presence to Ed. It was a needless worry. Gertrude introduced herself before they ever met.

"What is that horrible smell?" Ed asked the minute he opened the door.

"Gertrude," I answered without elaborating.

"Who is Gertrude? Where is Gertrude? And when is she leaving?" followed rapidly.

I explained the Humane Society's predicament, which had become our predicament, but Ed was not terribly sympathetic to Gertrude's cause. "Surely you don't intend to keep her?" was not really a question.

"I don't know what to do about her. I can't take her back, they'd have to put her to sleep."

"Maybe Robert would like to have her," Ed suggested, his whole demeanor suddenly brightening. "Call him."

Wildlife at the Rare Feline Breeding Compound is not limited to cats or even to carnivores. Since a group of macaques were already in residence there, Robert Baudy was agreeable to the prospect of another female joining them and I had only to get her down there. Before I could relay the glad tidings to Ed, the sound of a crash, then another, then a third, came up from the basement. Bounding down the steps two at a time as I followed slowly and reluctantly, Ed met the cause of his distress face to face. Gertrude's dexterous little fingers had managed to release the latch on the cage and the monkey was free as a bird. She'd found a stack of clay flowerpots and was happily tossing them into the air, watching in fascination as they shattered on the concrete floor.

"Don't worry about a thing," I said. "I know how to catch her."

Having been duped once, however, Gertrude was suspicious of the second bowl of ice cream, so it took a lot longer for her to succumb to the temptation. When I was finally able to make my move, I just might have put more pressure on her rib cage than was absolutely necessary and the monkey went into another tantrum on her way back to captivity. Ed chained the door, padlocked it, and handed me the key.

"What did Robert say?" was the first sentence he uttered.

"He'll take her."

"Good. How's the weather tomorrow?"

"I don't know, but it doesn't matter. I took 'zero six tango' over for its one-hundred-hour inspection, and the Twin Comanche is in Canada."

"For how long?"

"A week or so. Don't worry. I'll drive Gertrude down tomorrow," I said, realizing Ed, who was seldom even ruffled, was pretty agitated.

In need of help for the nine-hundred-mile journey with Gertrude, I called a buddy, sixteen-year-old Jack Owen, who was our "farm hand" during his summer vacation. Jack was more than willing to trade a pitchfork for a trip to Florida, not having met Gertrude, and a classmate of his also wanted to go along. Pat would join us if we delayed our departure until noon, a small concession to make for another delightful companion and another driver to expedite the monkey's relocation.

After Gertrude had her cooked-to-order breakfast of one scrambled egg, a sliced orange, and half a cup of hot chocolate, Ed gladly helped me move her to a smaller cage. The door was chained and locked in deference to the ingenious one's track record, and she and I were all set to go when the boys arrived.

As soon as they got a whiff of her, a spirited discussion ensued as to where exactly our passenger would ride, front or back seat. But Jack, having already offered to take the first shift behind the wheel, had in so doing unwittingly decided the issue. Pat's motion that Gertrude ride shotgun beside the driver was quickly seconded by me, and the proposal was railroaded through by a decisive majority that soon had the one-third minority gasping for breath.

Riding in the car posed no problem at all for the monkey, though the same could not be said for her fellow primates. She settled down and made herself comfortable by turning over her feed dish, which she used as a stool, then proceeded to splash the contents of her water dish all over the disgruntled driver. When that got old, she amused herself rolling up spitballs from scraps of paper torn from the bottom of her cage. Then she spied the ashtray on the dashboard. Before we could stop her, she reached between the bars of her cage, grabbed a handful of cigarette butts, and ate them, carefully spitting out the filters before she swallowed the tobacco right along with the paper.

I was afraid she'd be sick, but she wasn't. Not much bothered Gertrude. Initially, she flinched each time we passed a truck, but before long she became blasé and didn't seem to even notice them. Tunnels disturbed her, though. Covering her eyes with both hands, she spread her fingers and peeked nervously between them until we emerged on the other side. She never did get used to tunnels.

And we never did get used to Gertrude. She provided powerful motivation to exceed the speed limit. Because both young men, even under normal circumstances, tended to press heavily on the accelerator, I felt a moral obligation to caution them to obey the law. I felt no compulsion, however, to check the speedometer, not even when we slowed down perceptibly each time a state trooper loomed up on the horizon. We sped onward.

Every fifty miles or so we stopped to catch a breath of breathable air and change drivers. It was essential for the survival of the one at the wheel. Gertrude's close proximity guaranteed the chauffeur of the moment would stay alert, but it was high-priced stimulation. As soon as the car rolled to a stop, the three of us leaped out in unison while Gertrude protested vehemently. In a frenzy, she screamed and shook the bars of her cage until we were all back inside, seating rearranged, and once again in motion.

Originally, we'd intended to drive straight through, stopping only for food and fuel, but after ten hours cooped up with Gertrude our resolve crumbled. When I suggested we stop for the night at a motel, the boys were grateful, but by taking on Gertrude as my roommate, I won their eternal gratitude. Or put more accurately, I earned and deserved their eternal gratitude.

"I thought we'd get stuck with her," Jack sighed. "But don't change your mind on that account."

"Okay, guys. If you'll park her in my room, I'll feed her and meet you in the restaurant."

We had a leisurely dinner, so I was probably out of the room an hour, maybe an hour and a half. It was ample time for Gertrude to plan and execute a disaster. When I opened the door and eyed the devastation, I shrieked, "She's loose!" and the boys came running from their room halfway down the hall. The three of us slipped inside and slammed the door behind us as Gertrude, covered with face powder, scampered to the bathroom, and shinnied up to the top of the door where she perched and began nonchalantly brushing the powder from her fur.

The lock and chain still in place on the door to her cage hadn't been any handicap to her at all. Obviously she'd shaken the bars so vigorously she'd gotten the top section moving and had managed to drive off and leave the sliding tray that served as the bottom. After that it was a simple matter to lift one side and depart. The escape hadn't taken her too long, because she'd gotten quite a bit done. She'd had time to open my cosmetic case and dump the box of face powder on herself and the carpet, pour all of the perfume out of a small bottle, and hurl the remaining items around the room—toothbrush, nail file, and such. Streamers of toilet paper were draped around the furniture, mounds of Kleenex were heaped in the bathroom sink where she'd turned on the water, and the waste basket was wedged in the toilet. The place was in shambles.

While I stood mute surveying the carnage, the boys were more practical. Pat's six-foot-two height served us well. He sneaked up on the prisoner at large, shouting, "I got her," as he plucked Gertrude off the door. For the next go round, Jack put the front of the cage against the wall and weighted the top down with an overstuffed chair. Even enterprising Gertrude couldn't make her way out of that improvised Alcatraz.

After cleaning up the mess as best I could, I crawled into bed hoping for a good night's sleep before the final leg of our strenuous journey. But no sandman could cut through the noxious atmosphere thick with overpowering odors. Consequently, we got an earlier start the next morning than we had planned.

At exactly 3:47 P.M. EST, Gertrude took up residence at the Rare Feline Breeding Compound, moving in next door to a male stump tail who was obviously delighted with the new arrangements. So were we.

SEVEN

It was a long time before I succumbed to any more sad monkey tales or tails of any sort. Other than the arrival of the zebras, the increase in Camel Lot's census over the next two years was due almost exclusively to an influx of people. Norma Mings and Monica Myer, two young nurses, rented the garage apartment, and a flying buddy joined us, bringing his own living quarters along with him. Fred Storer telephoned first, explaining that his marital status had changed abruptly that morning; that afternoon he appeared, house trailer in tow, and settled in next to the hangar.

Then Jack Dellon decided to keep his Cessna 150 tied down at Camel Lot International along with the skeleton of a Piper Tripacer he and its two other owners were perpetually recovering. The job was, is, and probably forever will be a work-in-progress largely because of Jack's affinity for smoking big, long cigars and his penchant for paying close attention to his work. Oftentimes, he forgot to remove the stogie before leaning over for a better look, after which another easily explained hole appeared in the fabric.

It was a delightfully gregarious group, and with all the comings and goings the farm was lively. The "comings" were of special significance because there was usually someone around to pinch-hit for me with the animals when I was delayed or weathered in somewhere. Ed could usually do the honors before he left in the morning, but emergencies make an orthopedic surgeon's schedule so erratic it was anybody's guess when he'd get back home.

The camels and zebras were fed twice a day and were free to graze in the interim, with access to the barn at all times. It was the dogs who were a major concern. Lest one of them tangle with the propeller, they were always confined before I took off, but when they were on the loose, the only thing that could be expected with any degree of certainty was the unexpected. Fat Charles, ever fatter, had refined his scavenging techniques, and although they worked well for the most part, sometimes they caused him problems.

During the winter when neighbors put milk outside for their cats in metal or plastic bowls and the cats were slow to lap it up, that fit right in with his plans. He picked up the whole thing, transported it home in his mouth, and as soon as he had access to the house, brought it inside where he stood guard impatiently until his ill-gotten gains thawed. The problem arose when the container was glass that shattered en route and left him with a cut and bleeding mouth full of shards, though still holding onto his loot.

Despite Charles's gluttony, his injuries were usually minor, merely an inconvenience to him, which temporarily curtailed his activities. Once, however, he almost put himself permanently out of business. In his zeal to ream out a discarded can of pork and beans, Fats got the bent back lid irretrievably wedged into his mouth and staggered home with the can still attached. I managed to cut the container part off with a pair of tin snips, but the jagged edges of the lid were imbedded deep in his flesh, impossible to dislodge without inflicting further injury. With Charles bleeding profusely and moaning in pain, we made a frantic trip to the veterinarian, who had to anesthetize his patient to remove the obstruction and suture him back together.

Presumably, Charles did learn from the ordeal. At least he never came home in the same predicament again. Dirty Sam, on the other hand, was a sportsman. It was the thrill of the chase not the quest for calories that kept him charging around the countryside systematically depleting the local wildlife. I was unaware he had branched out into the private sector until I got a call from an immediate neighbor.

"I know you don't realize it, Mrs. Schaffer, but if you'll look out your front window right now you'll see your dog running across the cornfield with another one of my chickens." The lady was almost apologetic.

I did look out and I did see the object of her distress, but I already knew who it was. Dirty Sam was happily trotting home with a Rhode Island red clamped firmly between his jaws.

"Oh, Mrs. Fisher, I'm so sorry. I'll replace the chicken right away," I assured her.

"No, I won't hear of it. I really didn't want to complain, but it's the sixth time I've had to chase him away," she said.

Mrs. Fisher was so emphatic I didn't want to risk an insult by going against her wishes, so, by way of reparation, I bought her a trunk load of chicken feed. It was an unfortunate choice. The nice neighbor had failed to mention there were six chickens to begin with, none after Sam's last visit.

The third member of the canine corps presented another serious problem. Bismarck was to most people what Dirty Sam was to the wildlife in the area, a menace. When we acquired him from a German shepherd breeding kennel shortly before we moved to the country, he appeared to be a normal, clumsy six-week-old pup. At about six months of age we began to detect congenital deficiencies that became increasingly more pronounced. By that time it was too late to accept the kennel's offer of a healthy replacement; Bismarck was already an important part of our lives. The big, lovable oaf was friendly and affectionate with Ed and me and the few people he knew and trusted, but the poor dog was mentally retarded and couldn't remember anyone he didn't see on a regular basis. Almost any person he hadn't seen in the last five minutes was a stranger, and he was death to strangers. Bismarck's circle of friends was extremely limited.

In addition to a single-digit I.Q., the shepherd was deceptively crippled in the hind quarters, so unstable he wobbled when he walked. He was well coordinated when he ran, and there was nothing, absolutely nothing, wrong with his mouth. Aggressively compensating for his handicaps, Bismarck was always ready to attack and frequently did. He marked his fourth birthday in the mailman's backside. He hadn't seen him since the day before.

Convincing Norma and Monica and Fred that "to know him was to love him" took three months and called for the hard sell. We rarely tried to win other converts. It was easier to confine the dog when any of us expected visitors, because meeting Bismarck was an experience most people chose to forgo. For the few who ignored the "attack dog" signs posted around the property, meeting Bismarck was a terrifying experience, best forgotten.

One morning, I was in more than my usual hurry when I went into the chicken house. Even though fresh eggs were a treat and collecting them plus taking care of the laying hens was no big deal, it was not a favorite pastime. Eggs delivered by messy chickens, gathered from messy nests in a messy henhouse are not the same spic-and-span items one removes from a grocery-store carton of same. With feathers stuck to the shells in globs of chicken uglies that are often still damp, they're unpleasant to handle, and I always rushed through the chore, anxious to leave the smelly place.

In my inordinate haste that day, my feet slipped out from under me and I fell. Flat on my back I skidded the length of the twenty-foot building, cutting a wide swath through the vile inch-deep carpet of manure. Half of me was smeared with it, and all of me reeked. I could hardly keep from gagging.

Still clutching the brown paper bag with its meager harvest of two eggs, I struggled to my feet and cautiously made my way out of the building before making a run for the house. Once inside the back door, I stripped off my shirt and jeans and underwear and kicked off my loafers. The two fresh eggs were still intact but, intent on ridding myself of the last vestiges of the disgusting episode, I took them over to the kitchen sink and dumped them into the disposal.

Ours was no ordinary disposal. When in use, the metal blades grated against each other and created a racket that could be heard as far away as the barn. Besides that, it had another idiosyncrasy. It would start in the usual fashion by rotating the lid which pressed a button, but to stop the action required minor surgery. I had to remove the lid and disengage the button by gouging it back out with a long, sharp butcher knife kept handy for that purpose.

I completed the series of steps and, knife still in hand, turned around, idly curious, wondering if I had really heard what I thought I had, someone clearing their throat. I had. In the doorway stood a man I'd never seen before. He didn't appear to be a burglar or someone with malevolent intentions; he looked like a businessman. In one hand was a briefcase, and he was wearing a dark suit and tie and a thoroughly bewildered expression. Apparently he had not anticipated meeting the lady of the house under quite these circumstances.

"Get out!" I screamed, still clutching the cutlery.

The confused citizen was probably eager to do just that. He turned around immediately and exited rapidly through the back door, where yet another surprise awaited him. Bismarck.

Bis, who had not been around for the stranger's arrival, was on hand to liven up his departure. Hiding behind the curtains, I peeped out to see the dog lunge at the man's back and miss, try again, and manage to sink his teeth into the fellow's calf. The man swung his briefcase at Bismarck, and I yelled at the dog through the window, but the tenacious animal held on. Fortunately for the intruder, his car was parked close enough that he could hobble over to it, with Bismarck still attached, get the door open, and finally shake the dog loose. In his eagerness to depart, the stranger didn't even spare the time to turn his automobile around. He sped down the driveway backward with Bismarck, an unwelcome escort, racing along beside him.

Blood was spattered all over the concrete walkway between

the house and the parking pad. Starting with small drops by the back door, it spread into an ever-widening trail that continued to the edge of the asphalt.

"What the hell happened?" Ed asked that night.

I described the sequence of events, and we tried to figure out who the stranger was and the purpose of his visit. With no clues to go on, we could only guess.

"We'll probably find out. Most likely we'll hear from the man, or his lawyer," Ed concluded.

But we never did. To this day the case of the silent stranger remains an unsolved mystery.

EIGHT

I fall a lot. Being innately clumsy is only one of the reasons; having a railroad conductor mentality is the major contributing factor. Granted: On any given day there are things that must be done, but with the exception of commitments that involve specified times, most of my obligations can fit comfortably into my schedule. The chickens, never down to their last kernel of corn, didn't care if their supplies were replenished at 7:45 in the morning rather than 7:15. I did. In my head I'd already programmed the day, so if 7:15 sneaked up on me and I hadn't been to the chicken house, my timetable was off and I compulsively began hurrying to catch up. Hurrying was what preceded the other events that led to the stranger-versus-Bismarck bloodbath in the driveway.

My mishaps aren't *always* followed by melodramas. It was

sheer coincidence that the next one was. Catching a heel in the carpet at the top of the back stairway, I tripped and fell down the entire flight, smacking each step on the rough journey to the bottom, and ended up in the hospital with a broken back. Even so, I was lucky. After a week of complete bed rest, I was fitted with a brace that kept my back rigid and allowed to go home. All my activities were restricted until the fractured sacrum mended, and I was grounded for six months, but the brace made it possible to get around.

Ed bought me a mynah bird we named Jack, and I spent a lot of "down" time trying to teach the bird to talk. As the manual directed, I said the same phrases over and over, but I was a dud as a teacher and most of Jack's repertoire he picked up on his own. Every time the telephone rang, he joined in with an imitation of my "hello," and he developed a raucous cackle of a laugh I hoped didn't sound like mine. If I were out of the room, the bird's shouting "Moselle!" duped me every time. Since the back door was never locked, friends in the habit of wandering in announced their presence by calling my name, and Jack could mimic each call to perfection. He never failed to elicit a "Be right there!" from me.

The dogs were fascinated by this psychedelic collection of feathers that moved in with us. Jack's head and torso were basic black tinged with iridescent green; a clump of yellow whiskers bloomed on each cheek and his face came to a point in an orange beak. The skin on the knock-kneed bird's legs was so shriveled he might have been too long detained in his bath, and the yellow legs merged into the ugliest pair of feet so far designed. Unfortunately, most of him was feet. They were yellow, four toes on each—three of which pointed forward and one the opposite direction. Each toe was composed of a series of gnarled lumps where they bend, and at the end of them protruded a black Dracula claw. He was as homely a creature as was ever put together by our Creator.

Everyone who knew the bird greeted him by name with "Hello, Jack," so he adopted that phrase and used it indiscriminately. If it were a Margaret or a Henry or a Steve, it made no difference. But a lot of Jacks were in and out of the house, and occasionally the bird stumbled onto the right name. The comic aspects of a solemn exchange of greetings, a "Hello, Jack," from a bird acknowledged with a "Hello, Jack," from a human always brought on laughs from any bystanders, and that in turn triggered the feathered one's guffaws. Then everyone present got caught up in the ongoing hilarity until the bird's entire audience, tears streaming down their faces, rocked with laughter.

The comedy routine was a daily event during my convalescence. Jack Owen rearranged his own schedule so he could handle both the morning and evening animal chores, and I always accompanied him—except to the chicken house—and hung around outside the fences to watch. I didn't dare run the risk of the animals getting frisky.

The camels, by then four years old and more than twice their original five hundred pounds, played a game that usually ended with my clearing a fence in something like two-tenths of a second, maybe less. If they were at the far end of the pasture and spotted me, they'd aim for me, revving up to full speed on the way, and stop on the proverbial dime just before they smeared me into the clover. The first time it happened, I stood my ground, thinking any minute they'd turn aside, and when I finally realized that was not in the game plan, it was too late to get out of their way. Terror was a good teacher. From then on I was off and running, heading for a fence before Rev and Rox could shift into second gear.

Most zebras are not so playful. They are extremely high-strung with an instantaneous flight reaction. The run-first-investigate-later policy is prevalent amongst animals that are a popular entrée on a predator's menu. Being the "fast food" of the carnivore crowd makes them edgy. Even so insignificant an event as the unexpected fluttering of a leaf can startle the animals into a frantic dash with tragic consequences. The nervous beasts will sometimes bolt and run headlong into an obstruction in their path, a barn or tree or some other immovable object, and break their necks. "Death due to behavior" is the zoological term for one of the primary causes of death in the species. But zebras, I was surprised to learn, are highly intelligent. It had been my opinion after seeing films of a pair crashing headlong into a wall, that they were somewhat lacking in the cerebellum.

The wagging of the tail is another misunderstood characteristic. It does not indicate the zebra is receptive to a friendly pat on the head, as in the case of a dog. It merely signals the animal is excited. But in contrast to the canine, who is probably excited in the anticipation of pleasure, the zebra is in a state of nervous excitement, prepared to take whatever remedial action is deemed appropriate. The faster the tail moves, the more agitated the animal is.

All three species of zebras still in existence vary somewhat in appearance. Mountain zebras are the smallest and are identifiable by the fold of loose skin, a dewlap, that hangs from their throats. The Grévy, named for François Paul Jules Grévy, the president of France in 1882, has exceptionally large ears, which may or may not have been the case with Monsieur Grévy. The Grévy also has narrower, more sharply defined stripes than the more common Grant, and a white belly. Both the Grévy and mountain zebras are on the endangered species list.

Our guys were Grants, a subspecies of the *Equus burchelli* members of the Equidae family. Less formally they were known as Mac and Alice. Mac should have been named for Emmett Kelly because somewhere amongst his ancestors there must have been a clown. When I'm in the barn putting hay in the racks and drop a small wedge, Mac appears out of nowhere, falls to his knees on top of it, and looks up at me impishly as if to dare me to take it away. I don't try, instead I tease him by deliberately scattering one hay wedge after another to keep him zigzagging from pile to pile guarding his prizes.

On winter days when the temperature bottoms out at zero, I'm bundled up in an ugly shambles of a coat that could best be described as an atrocity. It's made of a coarse canvas fabric, drabber in color than just plain olive, and lined with some sort of gray fuzzy synthetic. The thing begins flaring out right under the sleeves, and by the time it ends up just short of my ankles it looks like a badly constructed tepee. Mac was fascinated with the hood that at one time was attached to the collar. He loved to slip up behind me, grab the material in his teeth, and give it a quick yank, each time ripping it farther from its moorings until eventually it and the coat were two separate units. I still wore it with the drawstring tied under my chin and he continued to attack it from the rear. Having fun was his only purpose, although every time he got a firm grip, I got a minor whiplash.

It was springtime when I hurt my back, and even though Mac had never shown any interest in my sun hats, I didn't want to take a chance on aggravating the injury in case he'd gotten new ideas. I stayed out of range and enticed the animals over with treats. The same delicacies that appealed to the camels also made a hit with the zebras. Persnickety Reverend held out for Pepperidge Farm bread but the other three were not so discriminating and any sort would do. They all liked other things, too—carrots and apples—and it was carrots I had relied on when I was cultivating the zebras' friendship.

That was a much less traumatic project than getting to know the camels. For one thing, the camels provided my introduction to the world of unfamiliar animals; for another, the zebras *were* more "a'scared" of me than I of them, which they readily demonstrated. Until the zebras became accustomed to me and their new surroundings, they darted for the nearest exit at the mere sound of my footsteps. Hours at a time I stood at the fence trying to lure them over, but it was several months before they would venture close enough even to check out the bribes I was offering, carrots. Bread couldn't be trusted. It was likely to sag in the middle and shorten the distance between my hand and those big square formidable teeth. I chose crisp carrots, the longest ones I could find, as the best bet for keeping my fingers intact.

When Mac finally gave in after several months of diligent coaxing, Alice soon capitulated. In six months' time they were hooked and reversed their routine, running toward me when they heard me approach—but only if I were alone or with someone they knew. Strangers, however, posed no problem for the nosy camels, particularly if there was a possibility of a handout. They became increasingly more friendly, thoroughly enjoying attention, and I loved to run my hands down their long, satiny smooth noses.

Most evenings when the weather was pleasant, the barnyard at Camel Lot was like the clubhouse in an apartment complex. Everyone who happend to be at home gathered there. Often friends and acquaintances dropped by and sometimes total strangers who'd heard about the animals. Camels and zebras are like magnets, attracting animal lovers as well as the interested and idly curious. We had all become used to living in a tourist attraction and none of us minded—at least not for the first three or four years. After that things gradually began to get out of hand.

Two years after we acquired the farm, developers bought up all the surrounding land, and cornfields became cul-de-sacs and the crops, houses. We hoped for the best and feared for the worst, and our fears were justified. Civilization began creeping up on us and we could do nothing about it but grumble—and sometimes laugh.

One evening about twilight, as our group of regulars stood around chatting, several carpenters were still at work on a house close by. We paid no attention to the buzzing of saws and the rap, rap, rap of hammers in the background until the activity stopped. The sudden quiet attracted our attention and we all looked over to see one man on top of the roof, hammer still poised in midair, and four openmouthed workmen on the ground gazing in our direction. The total silence was shattered just as suddenly as it had come about when the lookout aloft yelled for all the world to hear: "Dammit, you bastids, I told you them was ------- camels."

There was no humor involved when children began running through the pastures with sticks and stones and other weapons. Nor was it amusing when I got back to flying and youngsters scooted across the runway, necessitating aborted takeoffs and landings dangerous to everyone involved. Even the caliber of our uninvited visitors deteriorated to the point where they had to be policed rather than enjoyed.

People are infinitely more unpredictable than animals, and one fourteen-year-old boy proved that point more effectively than I would have cared to see it demonstrated. The young hooligan was gnawing on a Popsicle, which in due course he finished and, to dispose of the stick, he jabbed it into Reverend's left nostril—which was empty up until that time. Acutely unhappy over the chunk of lumber imbedded in his nose, the camel decided to share his unhappiness with the one who brought it about and did so with his teeth. There are still scars on the obnoxious brat's thumb and forefinger that aptly illustrate the depth of Rev's unhappiness—and the unpredictability of humankind.

The very next day, Ed announced with no fanfare, "We're moving."

"We are?" I was jolted by the suddenness of the proclamation.

"There are too many people around here now to mix with animals and airplanes, and it's going to get worse."

"But . . . where exactly are we moving?"

"I don't know, but start looking," he answered, sliding the real estate section of the Sunday *Star* across the breakfast table. "I've already circled one farm that sounds like it might have possibilities. See what you can find, I'm off to make rounds."

That afternoon we drove out to see the property that had attracted Ed's attention. Located twelve miles northwest of Indianapolis and near the Interstate, it was close enough to make his office and the hospital accessible but remote enough to remain relatively undeveloped. Once again, there was the refreshing sight and earthy fragrance of plowed fields ready for the spring planting.

A handsome white barn with black trim stood back about forty feet from the gravel frontage road, and close by were several outbuildings of various sizes. None of them, I was happy to note, appeared to have had any truck with chickens. Most of the fifty rolling acres were devoted to pastures and hayfields bisected by a narrow lane that led to a heavily wooded area at the north end of the farm. The owner, who happened to be on the premises, Dan Hollibaugh, showed us around.

"I raise and train racehorses," he explained, taking us inside the barn. "Since they run mostly at Lexington, I decided to move my operation there."

The twelve stalls, six on each side of the asphalt driveway, were constructed of stained and varnished oak up to a height of four feet, with black wrought-iron bars from there to the ceiling. Doors to each stall were in two sections, so the top or bottom could be opened independently of the other, and every unit had its own window on the outside wall. Impeccably clean and orderly, it was the personification of elegance.

Much less glamorous but strategically located among a cluster of foaling stalls, was a small apartment for the caretaker. Windows along two of its sides permitted a clear view of any new equine arrival as well as constant surveillance of the mare prior to and after foaling.

After our tour, we met a delightful Dutchman and his wife, Herman and Janie de Boer, who lived across the road on a farm they operated in the usual scrubbed, efficient manner of their Dutch heritage. Other than their place, there were no houses and no people in sight. Not one single armed kidnick prowled the pastures.

Ed asked the usual pertinent questions about utilities and septic systems and taxes and then turned to me.

"What do you think?" he asked.

"Well . . ." That was as far as I got before Ed resumed his conversation with the owner.

"Assuming Hiram, our realtor, thinks it's a good idea and we can get suitable financing, we'll take it," he said without further ado. "Moselle can take care of those things tomorrow."

Sure. Assuming she had recovered by then. Moselle was dazed from the speed of the day's developments. We got up from a leisurely Sunday morning breakfast on one farm and before the coffeepot cooled off we almost didn't live there anymore. Now I was supposed to call Hiram Rogers almost five years to the day since he had propelled us into the country life, to say we were moving.

"How long do you think it will be before we move?" I asked Ed on the way home.

"As soon as the deal is closed?"

"Are you joking? Of course, we weren't there very long, but you did notice there's no house, didn't you? Do you plan to live in the barn?" I thought I was being facetious.

"Right. Until we can get a house built. You don't mind, do you?"

"No, not in the least. But you're going to have severe claustrophobia in a year's time, Ed."

"We're not talking more than three or four months to build this time of year. Then Norma and Monica can have the barn apartment if they want it, and there's plenty of room for Fred's trailer. It's a great place, don't you think?"

"Mmmmmm," was my noncommittal answer, in case that was a question, because I'd had virtually no time to think about it.

There was no runway but no chicken house either, not exactly an even trade but considerable compensation nonetheless. But twelve stalls? I knew what that meant.

NINE

Since the barn apartment we'd be moving into would accommodate only a meager amount of furniture, the basic necessities, almost everything would remain at the old place until the new house was built and ready for occupancy. My only immediate concern was how to move the animals, a monumental problem. I called Robert and, as usual, he provided a solution.

"If you can wait until next month, I'll fly up there and move them," he said.

"Bless you! We'll wait until next month or next year for that, if need be."

"Line up a horse van and don't feed the zebras for two days before I get there, I want them good and hungry. Give them

87

plenty of water. You still have the crates they were shipped in, don't you?"

"Yes."

"Good, we'll move them in those."

"What about the camels? Don't feed them either?" I asked.

"No, you can feed them, they won't be any trouble. They lead, don't they?"

"No," I had to admit.

"Oh, well, I'm not worried about them."

That statement will surely haunt Robert to eternity.

On the day of the big move from Camel Lot I to Camel Lot II, the heavens split wide open and the incessant rain that persisted throughout most of the long, strenuous day made our already difficult tasks almost impossible. Ed, with splendid foresight, had surgery scheduled—which left Robert, young Jack and four of his buddies, and me. Jack's recruits, all of whom were selected on the basis of their muscles, were given only the slightest hint of what was in store for them. They were in for a few surprises. So was I. Figuring my little dab of strength wouldn't add appreciably to the overall effort, I thought of my role as more of an observer and errand-runner for those on active duty.

"Moselle, which of the zebras is the least nervous?" Robert asked, as we assembled in the barn.

"Mac, the one in the first stall," I told him.

"We'll move him first then. The doors open out, I see. Okay, Moselle, open the door and stand in it so the zebra won't come out while you fellows help me get this crate into position. We'll need to put one end right up in front of the doorway."

"Robert," I interrupted. "I don't have a whip."

"You don't need one. He's not going to want to come past you."

Not past me, I thought, just through me. But I knew from experience the futility of protesting. I planted myself in the doorway and stared at the agitated animal, who moved in jittery spurts, three or four jerky steps at a time, while Robert and team shoved the cumbersome crate in place and boxed me in.

"Just a minute and I'll let you out," Robert said as he climbed up on the top and lifted the guillotine door so I could crawl through the crate and emerge from the other end. "Now put a bucket of feed at the very back of the crate, Moselle, and let that door back down. I'll stay up here on top so when the zebra goes in for the grain, I can let the door down."

But Mac, hungry though he was after his two-day fast, chose to go nowhere at all.

"I'll tell you what we'd better do," Robert said after half an hour of squatting on top of the crate. "I think we'd better leave, except you, Moselle. He knows you and we may be scaring him. You take my place up here and drop the door the minute he goes in. But don't drop it prematurely, you could break the animal's back. We'll go outside where he can't see us."

Robert came down and hoisted me up as his replacement. Then he and the boys moved outside and six heads peered around the corners to watch the action, of which there was very little. Mac may have been hungry but not hungry enough to fall into our trap. We waited and waited, my muscles twitching from the strain of the crouched position, but the zebra made no move toward the food. I've never weighed the doors to the zebra crates, in hopes I will never have another occasion to find that bit of information useful, but I'd guess one to be about twenty pounds. Holding it up was tough duty, and I feared I'd drop the door and ruin any chance of success. After another twenty minutes, Robert apparently reached the same conclusion.

"Okay, we'll do it another way. Take his water away and then we'll give him time to get used to the crate and wait until this afternoon to try again. Might as well load the camels first. I want to make a chute to lead up to the ramp. Is there any lumber around?"

"In the basement," I answered.

Jack and an assistant sloshed back a few minutes later with two four-by-eight-foot sheets of plywood.

"Is that all you could find?" Robert wanted to know.

"It's all there was," Jack answered.

"That won't be enough."

"I think there are some old fence posts around. Would they do?" Jack asked.

"Anything will help. Moselle, what about some rope?" was Robert's next request. "Never mind, I've just stumbled onto a gold mine of baling wire."

When the Rube Goldberg of a chute was in place, I got to determine which camel would be the least difficult to maneuver and I selected Rev. I was right.

"Here's what we'll do. You fellows stand outside the chute and brace it—you understand it's a little fragile." Robert laughed. "Moselle, you get in the van. I'll slap the camel on his rump, and he'll run up the ramp. As soon as he gets inside the van, fasten the restraining strap."

I was not crazy about that assignment either. The only thing that made the situation tolerable was the rapidity with which Reverend made each round trip. He'd zoom up the ramp, turn around, and race back down into the barn before I could get the restraint in place. Six tries we gave it. So far we had moved no zebras and no camels and we'd been going at it for over two hours.

"We'll do it differently," Robert decided, redesigning the

CAMEL LOT · 91

monstrosity of a chute to substitute fence posts for one section of plywood. "We'll use this plywood instead of the strap. This time when he comes up, Moselle, slip the plywood across in front of him. That will be easy."

"Slip" and "easy" were not the terms I would have chosen. But the new strategy did work. Robert swatted Rev once more, and up the ramp he stormed; I gave a mighty heave and shoved the barrier into place. At that point I was cooped up with one extremely perturbed animal and I would have liked to have been someplace else.

"Can you get the strap across now?" Robert called.

"I'm trying." I finally got the catch in place after much fumbling. "Okay, it's done."

Robert moved the plywood aside and I took a deep, relieved breath. I'm hard pressed to decide which pastime I'd forgo first, loading or unloading wild animals who don't want to be messed with—but I was never granted that option.

"We'll do the same thing with the female," Robert announced.

But we didn't. Roxie became hysterical. Up and down the runway she raged, bellowing fiercely as she flung her legs in all directions at once. Only with difficulty could the boys keep the chute from collapsing when a hefty foot crashed into it with the force of a battering ram. One superblow split the plywood as she surged to the other end of the barn and ran into the closed door. Shattered glass and splinters of lumber were everywhere as the poor animal, in her frenzy, created havoc.

"There, there girl, you're all right," Robert tried to soothe her, leaping aside each time she roared by.

Roxie would not be soothed. She continued her rampage to the point of exhaustion. For over an hour she raged, until she crumpled up, folded her legs under her body, and could not be budged. The pathetic beast's face was bleeding, she foamed at the mouth and, of course, there was the inevitable manifestation of nervousness, rampant diarrhea.

"Get some rope, Jack," Robert said.

Resourceful Jack cut off the rope dangling from the hay loft and Robert fashioned a loose collar that he dropped over Roxie's head.

"Jack, you go around back and pull on her tail, the rest of you get on the rope with me and we'll see if we can pull her up."

Jack grimaced with profound displeasure as he grasped the disgustingly slippery tail and strained to enlist the rebellious camel's cooperation. Meanwhile, the forward team tugged mightily. But Roxie was adamant in her determination not to travel. They tugged and tugged some more, all to no avail. I was still on board the van watching the struggle and waiting, more and more reluctantly, for my part in the drama. All of us were grateful when Robert suggested we take a break, but we hadn't gotten out of the barn before he had another idea.

"Wait a minute. This may get her up. If it does, you men get the rope around her shoulders, right behind her front legs, and Jack, back Moselle's car up to the other side of the van. Then run the rope through the van and secure it to the bumper. When I give you the signal, move the car forward very, very slowly. We have to be extremely careful not to injure the animal."

Working his arm under the camel's middle, Robert twisted a nipple, and the results were instantaneous, an explosion of fury as Rox lunged to her feet. Immediately Jack began inching the car forward, and Roxie, foaming and gurgling her wrath, was slowly towed on board. Ten minutes later, both camels were placidly nibbling a bucket of grain as if nothing in the least bit noteworthy had occurred this hot, rainy, summer day. The rest of us were bushed.

Late that afternoon we had another go at the zebras, who were by then thirsty enough to fall for the water ruse. First Mac succumbed to entrapment, then Alice.

After all the turmoil subsided, Ed arrived, cool and unrumpled as he stepped out of his air-conditioned car. Boos and hisses greeted his heroic announcement that he would drive the van to the new farm, although we secretly welcomed that prospect. We were weary. Heads did turn as we made our way slowly along 116th Street with both camels poking their sizable necks out the windows. Drivers and pedestrians alike stopped to gawk at our unusual passengers.

Our hegira completed, all of the brawn assembled and lifted the zebra crates off the van, positioning them so each animal could be released directly into its individual stall. I didn't receive an assignment for that phase of the operation and didn't request one. There were distinct advantages to the role of observer. But my turn came with the camels. Robert removed the restraining straps and invited them out, but Rev and Rox didn't care to leave. They looked calmly around, surveying the new scenery, and showed no inclination to move.

"Moselle, come up here and see if they'll follow you down the ramp," Robert said.

For once the camels cooperated. They sauntered down the incline behind me and ambled together into one of the stalls.

That was the end of a long, strenuous day and, exhausted from the effort, nobody had much to say. Except Robert. He requested in the strongest possible terms that we do one of two things: stay put once and for all or forget we ever knew him.

Getting the rest of the household to the new Camel Lot the next day was anticlimactic. It wasn't much of a feat for Robert and me to transport three dogs, a bird, and the smattering of essentials that could be crammed into four hundred square feet, albeit three rooms.

The kitchen consisted of an enormous stainless-steel sink, a yellow Formica counter attached to the wall, and a two-hundred-gallon water heater that hissed a constant jet of steam onto the brown linoleum floor. Space being critical, we acquired a small refrigerator that fit under the counter, and on top went the hot plate, toaster, and electric coffeepot. Except for a box in the corner that contained a few dishes and cooking utensils, that was the kitchen. That and a copious supply of spiders, several battalions of militant ants, and a dozen or so field mice that commuted from other parts of the barn.

The "parlor" furnishings were limited to six canvas folding chairs, a small drop-leaf table, two floor lamps, and a cot for overnight guests. In the four corners of the cozy ten-by-ten-foot salon were stacks of books, magazines, and stationery; a television set; a radio; letters, bills, and checkbooks; and an iron—things one tucks away in cabinets or desks, if there are any. In addition to twin beds and a nightstand, we wedged three trunks into the bedroom, one for linens and one each for our clothes. There were no closets. The shower-curtain rod in the bathroom was the only place to hang garments; consequently, there was no such thing as a quick shower. They were all productions.

Robert spent three sleepless nights with us getting folded up in his bed with great regularity. Whenever he dropped off to sleep and changed positions, the springs snapped and he suddenly found himself folded in two, head and feet elevated and his middle weighting down the center of the mattress. That unique feature of our "guest room" did not contribute to a sound sleep, but it did make for early rising, not all bad from Ed's and my point of view. We awakened to the aroma of freshly brewed coffee instead of the irritating summons of an alarm clock.

Ed assumed the coffee-making duty after Robert left, but only for a short while. Cabin fever was quick to set in, and just as quickly Ed discovered the advantage of making early-morning hospital rounds. Patients soon began to expect their doctor, the insomniac, to appear at their bedsides at four or five o'clock in the morning.

Life in such crowded quarters never did get better, only worse. Heavy trucks roared up and down the gravel lane to the construction site back by the woods, kicking up dust when the weather was dry that sifted into the apartment and coated every surface with a fine, white powder. When prolonged wet weather set in, we were invaded by hordes of worms—fat, red, wiggly things six inches long that had to vacate their underground premises. By the hundreds they drowned in the puddles of standing water, but dozens of them crawled into the apartment to join the throngs of creepy-crawlies already settled in there.

Because the dogs weren't used to contending with vehicle traffic, I kept them inside during the day, and they were bored and restless, with the exception of Fat Charles. He stayed busy with his never-ending quest for calories.

"What happened to my bed?" Ed growled one evening shortly after climbing under the covers.

Charles had snitched a coffee cake from the kitchen counter, dug a hole in the foam-rubber mattress—through the sheets— and buried the half he couldn't finish inside Ed's bed.

Though it was delicately suggested that I leave nothing edible lying around, occasionally I forgot. Four times Fat Charles pulled the same stunt—new holes, new treasure. Ed failed to show any appreciation for the dog's ingenuity. The master of the manor was becoming a little testy as more and more symptoms of claustrophobia surfaced. The bird annoyed him, too. The close proximity of the dogs disturbed Jack and kept him flapping around in his cage, adding to the general uproar.

"Good God!" Ed complained one evening when Jack was being unusually obstreperous. "Let's put him in the bedroom. Maybe that will quiet him down."

Ed had had a rough day and was further irritated when he asked for the morning paper to peruse. Unfortunately, it was being useful in the bottom of Jack's cage and it is difficult to pick up much news from the bottom of a birdcage. That soothed nobody's ruffled feathers. Ed wasn't even amused when I related the day's humorous antics with the camels and the utility crew that was trying to lay the power lines.

Because the site for the house was a quarter mile back from the barn, it was important to get power there to facilitate construction. The lines were to be installed along one edge of our property just inside the pasture fences, which meant men and machinery had to invade the animals' home turf.

When the teams of technicians arrived with their gigantic, ear-shattering equipment, the agitated zebras took off at a rapid clip and remained as far away from the commotion as possible. Not so Reverend and Roxie. If anything interesting is going on, they want to be in on the action, so they loped over to check things out, which created somewhat of a problem for the men. None of them had ever worked around camels before, and they were reluctant to start then.

"They're quite gentle, really," I told them. "They won't bother you."

"Lady, I've heard how mean camels are. They spit and they bite and they kick."

"But not under these circumstances, only when they're upset."

"Uh huh. And might they take offense if I reach into my tool kit?"

"Here, let me show you." I climbed the fence to demonstrate my point by stroking the camels' noses. "You see, they won't hurt you."

"No, I don't," replied the unconvinced spokesman.

"I just showed you!"

"No, you didn't. You showed me they won't hurt *you!*"

It took a great deal more persuasion before the skeptical group would enter the pasture and, hoping to ease their anxiety, I escorted them across the open terrain. With the five men looking back over their shoulders apprehensively, we crossed the pasture without incident, Rev and Rox strolling amiably along behind us.

Only when the men set about their business did the camels become playful. Every time someone put down a hammer or a drill, one of the clowns grabbed it in his or her mouth and lumbered off in the opposite direction. Since the men hesitated to take their newly acquired toys away from the big guys, I spent the day retrieving the pilfered articles. Conducting business on a camel lot does present a few problems.

TEN

It was a toss-up as to which was the more intolerable to Ed, the lack of space in the apartment or the unoccupied space in the barn. He had discussed llamas with Robert before, so when Robert called to say he was on his way up from Florida with a trio of them, it was no surprise. It was surprising when he opened the doors of the truck and out tumbled a mob of pygmy goats before Robert could release the llamas.

"Aren't they nice?" Robert indicated the goats. "They'll never get taller than eighteen inches. I thought I'd surprise you with them."

"And you did," I said.

"Snow White, the female with the red collar on, is the alpha animal, the rest will follow her lead. But there's no need to pen them up—they won't go anywhere."

He should have said there's no need to try to pen them up, because you can't. Goats can go under, over, or around anything they please. And if those tactics don't work, they rear back and butt their way through whatever object stands in the way of progress. Sure-footed animals, they love to climb and will make use of anything handy, including a camel or two if nothing else beckons. When Reverend and Roxie stretched out in the pasture for a siesta, either or both of them had a pygmy capering up and over their massive frames. The camels, genial hosts, showed no displeasure when one of the little guys decided to do a dance routine on their rib cages or simply leap on and off their huge bodies, a king-of-the-hill game with a camel as the hill.

The llamas fit in well with the rest of the pasture crowd and were quick to learn the zebras' and camels' strategy for securing a handout. Whenever I was in the kitchen, one face after another appeared at the window, and there it stayed until a goodie was forthcoming. They had their own pecking order, which in this instance was according to size. First it was the camels, then the zebras, and the llamas at the end of the breadline. The goats knew they were missing out on something, but they weren't big enough to get up to the window. They made up for the exclusion by ambushing me as soon as I stepped out the door.

Living so close to the animals was such a delight it made up for many of the apartment's disadvantages. Nevertheless, I wasn't dismayed when the house was completed and it was time to forsake our cluttered quarters in the barn. We made the move in early November, when the leaves had changed to their splendid reds and golds and the woods behind our new home blazed with color.

The three-bedroom house was conventional in most respects, a sprawling, one-story, gray stone similar to those scattered around the English countryside. But, designed for the way we lived, it had a few not-so-standard features. Ed and I were both addicted to fires, so there was a two-way fireplace between the family room and the master bedroom that allowed us to doze off to sleep with the flickering of the flames for a lullabye. And our red-and-white bathroom was admittedly unusual. After our first few weeks of no tub at all in the barn, we chose the largest one available. The rest of the features in the house were fairly standard—other than a garden in one corner of the den that consists of earth with no foundation beneath.

Wayne Sturtevant, a young law student, and his wife, Jeannie, who was a professional photographer, replaced us in the barn apartment and were a delightful addition to the new Camel Lot. They were also excellent help with the animals when I was delayed or stranded somewhere, so I was able to get back to flying. It was not much more time-consuming to drive ten miles to the airport, where my plane was now hangared, than it had been to reclaim the airplane from the birds, or clear the runway of snow, or tend to any one of the many preflight requirements of Camel Lot International. However, I flew a lot less, by choice.

Although the grazing group was fairly self-sufficient, I enjoyed their care and their company and there was also the myriad of details to be reckoned with in the sale of the old house and getting settled in the new one. Only one new furry friend, unsolicited, joined us during that period.

It was blizzard weather when the stray dog, a short-haired

black mutt, began hanging around the house. Hoping he had a home to return to, I resisted him for several days, but when I caught him scrounging the bread crumbs I scattered on the snow for the birds, that was the end of the resistance. I took him into the garage and fed him, wishfully thinking he'd move on after a few good meals, and knowing better.

Kozby was a sleek forty pounds of brains and brawn that had served him well. He was a tough hombre and an excellent businessman, having made his living for years dealing in the succulent creatures hereabout that lack—or lacked—his foresight. Some, when Koz invited them for lunch, objected to his choice of an entrée and became disagreeable, as evidenced by the wedge missing from his left ear and his vast collection of old scars. Obviously not all of his transactions were painless.

To no one's surprise, certainly not Kozby's, he rarely missed a meal once he retired at Camel Lot. In return for board and room, he performed numerous services, one of which was announcing all arrivals. His hearing, whether from heredity or necessity, was far superior to the other dogs, so he was the one who alerted the rest of the group, barking boisterously at anything or anybody that approached. He also provided an automobile escort service. Whether I was going up or coming down the driveway, he preceded my car at precisely 7 mph, tail straight up in the air and ears flopping as he bounced along glancing from side to side. Occasionally he came to an abrupt halt when something attracted his attention, in which case I had to stomp on the brakes and wait until Koz was ready to get back to work. I would gladly have given up that special courtesy, but Koz was as persevering as the postal service and not even the sleet and snow of an Indiana winter deterred him from his self-appointed task.

As spring approached, Ed set aside a week for R&R and we planned to fly down to Robert's place, one of our favorite spots to visit. But winter had saved back one last snowstorm and spent it the day of our scheduled departure. So, instead of winging down to the sunshine, we mushed out of the snow and ice in a four-wheeled vehicle.

ELEVEN

The Rare Feline Breed-
ing Compound, tucked away in a remote area of central Florida,
is the next best thing to the Promised Land for animal lovers.
There in the shade of the huge live oaks are cats of every
description, from the small margay to the largest of all the big
cats, the Siberian tiger. Numerous other species are at home
there, too. Lemurs, the lowest form of primate, live next to the
maned wolves, and close by them are the chimps and orang-
utans. Hoof stock ramble around the forty acres and white
rhinos are confined, when it suits them, to a paddock with
their own personal freshwater pond.

It's a large operation with emphasis on the preservation of
endangered species, a cause dear to my heart. Endangered is
but a brief reprieve from extinction. If we fail to save these

magnificent animals God intended to share our world, we'll face the grim irreversible consequences of losing them forever. Too little *or* too late and there is no second chance. Ever.

Being allowed to help care for the animals was for me one of the special attractions of the Compound. Although mine was but a meager contribution to their battle for survival, it was a gratifying one.

"I have two new tiger babies," Robert greeted us as we stepped out of the car.

"Marvelous! May I see them?" I asked.

"Of course. You may even feed them," Robert answered, leading the way to his living quarters attached to the barn. "I had to pull them from their mother, Tara; for some unknown reason she's never taken care of any of her cubs."

Snoozing soundly in their cardboard boxes until we disturbed them, the babies looked like little wads of frizzled light brown cotton with disorganized stripes that resembled the tracings of an electrocardiogram. At ten days of age each had only one eye open—a hazy, blue button—below which was a nose that seemed to have been smeared on as an afterthought. Serving as a mouth was a gently curved slash with patches of whiskers on each side, delicate white wisps emerging from small black polka dots the size of pinheads. Their ears were limp, black, half-circle flaps decorated by a splash of pure white in the center.

"They look like little pirates," I whispered, already smitten. "Little one-eyed pirates."

"They're both males," Robert said. "The small one weighed two and a quarter pounds at birth, the larger one, three and a quarter pounds. The little guy has a feeding problem. I have to hold his mouth closed for him, he doesn't seem to know how.

"I'll get their bottles and show you how to feed them."

Robert returned with two four-ounce plastic baby bottles containing the warm Esbilac formula, and picked up the larger tiger by the scruff of the neck. Immediately the baby's four legs jutted forward stiffly at thirty-degree angles to his body.

"The mother holds them this way and the cub goes into a catatonic state," he explained, as he sat down by the "bassinet."

Arranging the tiger so its hind legs were on the floor while his front claws dug into Robert's thigh, Robert cupped the head with one hand and touched the nipple to the baby's mouth. Almost simultaneously the mouth sprang open and snapped shut to capture the nipple, and away he went. As the little fellow drank enthusiastically, a stream of bubbles gurgled backward like the wake of a motor boat.

"This fellow's no problem," Robert commented, when the bottle was drained in forty-five seconds. "But the other one! He's something else."

Robert exchanged the full tiger for the empty one and proceeded in the same manner, except he made a circle with thumb and forefinger and clamped the cub's mouth shut around the nipple. The little runt downed a couple of swallows, at which point he choked, and Robert reacted instantly. Jerking the nipple from the baby's mouth, he snatched him up by the loose folds of skin on his neck and shook him upside down until the excess liquid sputtered out of the tiger's nose and mouth. Then they had at the bottle routine again, the eager baby climbing Robert's jacket to get back to his lunch.

"Now," he said when the traumatic feeding was over. "You see how to do it. You can give them their next feeding. And be sure to record their intake on this chart, and the time of the feeding, and the amount of medicine for Number Two tiger.

"The records are extremely important, they give you an accurate picture of their progress. See"—he indicated the account of the preceding day—"Number Two has been running a low-grade fever, a hundred and two degrees, which isn't much for a tiger. Normal is ninety-nine degrees. By looking at his chart I can tell how long I've had him on penicillin and the dosage. Relying on memory can be dangerous. I've found that out the hard way."

I found out the hard way that tiger babies' fingernails are honed to the sharpness of hypodermic needles. Before they first took the bottle they sank their claws into my arm, but that location never suited them. So they dragged the nails to a more satisfactory site and replanted them, leaving bright crimson trails to mark the path to a final, acceptable spot. Armor was a must.

Feeding that pair was not only physically painful, it was terrifying. I panicked when the little fellow choked, and I never overcame the fear he might not regain his breath. After a few supervised feedings, I soloed. Then Robert eased me into mixing their formula, a simple matter of stirring up sixteen tablespoons of Esbilac with thirty-two ounces of warm water.

"Don't forget the medicine for Number Two," Robert cautioned. "And I'd better show you how to take his temperature. You'll want to keep him on penicillin for twenty-four hours after his fever is gone."

I will? The comment puzzled me—at the time.

A demonstration followed. Grease the tip of the thermometer with Vaseline, hold the tiger firmly in whatever position he is the least unmanageable, and gently insert the glass cylinder into the slot under his tail that nature provides for temperature readings.

"Be very, very careful," Robert warned for the third time. "If you should slip, you could injure him internally."

That warning, imperative though it was, did nothing to boost my already low level of confidence.

There was more to come for that end of the tiger. Tiger babies cannot have normal bowel movements without assistance. If their mother is a bona fide tiger, she licks the appropriate territory and causes nature to function, but these babies had to be "pittled." That is accomplished by standing him up, lifting his rear end off the floor by his tail, and stroking his derriere with a wet paper towel until he cooperates. If he refuses to perform, it calls for a suppository. Pittling is a sport I don't think will ever catch on big.

One function tiger babies can perform on their own is making little tiger puddles. They do it with more frequency than I, personally, think necessary. It isn't a big deal; it only involves lifting them out of their boxes and exchanging the damp newspaper and paper towels for dry ones. It sort of takes up the slack time between mixing formula, dispensing medicine, taking temperatures, feeding, weighing, washing bottles, keeping records, pittling, and keeping tabs on the box temperature. And, of course, there's lots and lots of cuddling to be administered.

It was news to me, not to Robert, that caring for tiger babies is such a time-consuming, often nerve-wracking job. The fact that Robert viewed my arrival at the Compound as opportunity knocking at his gate was also news. It became apparent when our week-long visit came to an end and he let me in on his plans, the ones he'd made for me.

"You're doing such a good job with the tigers I've decided to let you take them home with you for a while," he said matter-of-factly. "With the little runt's feeding problem and the big one running the fever, they're much more susceptible to disease here with all the cat germs around than they would be at your place."

"But Robert—" I didn't get to finish. I didn't get to *begin* my series of objections, first and foremost of which was my lack of experience caring for these priceless animals.

Although I welcomed the opportunity to participate more actively in the endangered-species program, the impending responsibility was awesome. Being den mother while Robert was within shouting distance was one thing, quite another if I were on my own. Robert didn't help much with his next volley.

"They're going to be extinct if the situation doesn't change. These two tigers represent three percent of all the Siberians in the free world."

"What if something should happen to them?" I protested.

"I have complete confidence in you," he said, handing me a pen and tablet. "Now, there are a few things I should mention."

There were quite a few. He mentioned fifteen pages worth while I scribbled rapidly, hoping I could decipher them. I was not just apprehensive about the undertaking, I was downright scared.

"They'll need normal feline serum every ten days, one cc per pound. It should be injected subcutaneously in either the neck or shoulder blade. And they should have some vitamin-B complex, and after three weeks, more vaccine. When they're—"

"Robert," I interrupted, visions of his enormous "working cats," the performers, messing up my mind. "How long do you want me to keep them?"

"Oh, until sometime after they're weaned. I'd suggest you

apply to the United States Department of Agriculture for a license. Now, when the cubs are two and a half to three months old they'll also need a shot of Leucogen and you'd better keep some Neumovex on hand for feline pneumonitis, an upper-respiratory virus." He caught his breath. "In two more weeks, add half of the yolk of a raw egg to thirty-two ounces of formula. In another week, add another half if there's no change in their bowel movements. The tigers' teeth will turn yellow after you start adding the egg, but don't worry, they're just the milk teeth and they'll all fall out eventually. When their permanent teeth come in, they'll be as pretty and white as you ever saw."

The brightness of the tigers' smiles very likely would have been the last concern to cross my mind. But I didn't even attempt to insert that subjective consideration into Robert's nonstop monologue.

"Vitamins. Put a drop in each bottle and gradually add more drops until you finally get to twenty-four drops per day. That's twenty-four a day, not each bottle. Any children's vitamin will do. If they should get diarrhea, give them streptomycin, and if they should have any constipation problem, lower the proportion of the dry formula to the hot water.

"And you can gradually lower the heat so that in a few weeks they should be comfortable at seventy-two degrees. Watch them, if they pant you'll know they're too hot. Oh, they can be off a few degrees for a few minutes at a time, but on the whole they must be maintained at a steady temperature."

"Er, Robert, when do they get weaned?" I asked hesitantly, hoping for a clue as to the duration of my tiger-mama status.

"Oh, that's a long way off, when they're eleven or twelve weeks old. Tiger cubs are extremely immature. They only have a hundred-and-five-to-hundred-and-nine-day gestation period. Before you wean them, you take a little chicken, about one tablespoon for thirty-two ounces of formula, chop it up very, very fine and put it in the blender until it's pureed, then add it to their bottles. After a while of that, rub a little chicken on their mouths so they get used to the taste. Eventually they get red meat, but not at first. With chicken you don't get the diarrhea problem that you risk with beef. When you start giving them chicken, bones and all, you take chicken backs and crack them up with a meat cleaver into extremely small pieces. Then you give it to them with the bones in it. Tigers love it."

Robert left the room with the explanation he wanted to get something from the barn and returned dragging a fifty-pound moth-eaten old lion skin from an animal who had died of old age.

"They'll love to snuggle in the fur, it feels like their mother. There are a few other things I want to send with you, too."

The few things took up all of the trunk and most of the back seat. Thermos bottles, heat lamp, clip board, baby bottles, a metal scale contraption with "Purina Feed Saver and Cow Culler" woven around the clocklike face, stacks of newspapers, rolls of paper towels, Vaseline, two thermometers, and a case of Esbilac. Tiger babies are big on luggage.

I climbed into the right front seat next to the cardboard box the cubs would ride in, Ed started the engine, and Robert delivered the two babies. They were mute during that short trip from the house to the car, suspended by the napes of their necks, one fuzzy, striped kitten with stiffened appendages and large unseeing eyes dangling from each of Robert's hands. Immediately upon being placed in their box, they became vehemently vocal. Having done no touring other than from their mother's womb to their corrugated homes, the vibration of the car disturbed them and they shrieked like banshees.

"Don't worry, they'll settle down once they get used to the car," Robert assured us, as Ed, the two bawling cats, and I started slowly out the drive with Robert waving good-bye.

"Good luck," Robert called, as well he might have.

And so began our portable safari to the heartland of America.

Robert was dead wrong. The cats never did settle down. They squalled in unison with only brief intermissions of my contrivance. Whenever I reached in their box and rubbed the tigers' tummies, they were placated for the moment, until that became old hat and they proceeded to insert their claws into my arms, climb up to my neck, and dig in in earnest. It's difficult to dislodge a tiger burrowed into one's neck, twice as difficult when there are two of them to remove. Tiger babies are tenacious.

Even when the cubs were quiet there was only a fifty-fifty chance all was well. Satisfying the natural tendency to nurse prompts them to latch on to almost anything to serve as a substitute for Mama, and that can be dangerous. If one of them settles for his brother's tail or ear there is no harm done, other than esthetically, but usually he chooses the distinctly male portion of the anatomy and that has to be stopped immediately before he draws blood.

Offering them their bottles was a successful diversion, but that necessitated at least a half-hour stop each time, with all the ensuing commotion. While I gathered up the gear, hauled it into a ladies' room to fill and warm the bottles, Ed decided on a suitable place for our picnic. Whether we had stopped at a restaurant, or gas station, or a rest stop, we always attracted a crowd. Everyone who spied the cubs had to have a closer look and pose the routine questions: Are they really tigers?

How old are they? Where are you going? The oglers were always polite, with one exception, two clods who made unnecessary remarks about the appearance of my precious little runt.

"That little 'un, he don't look like no tiger. You can't hardly make out his stripes. He looks like an imitation tiger," one bumpkin said to his buddy.

"No, he don't. He looks like some kid's stuffed toy that's done been through the washing machine a hunnert times," the other yahoo responded.

It was steamy hot, and even with my constant fiddling with the air conditioner the temperature bounced back and forth from 80 degrees to 70 degrees. Then, after no more than one hundred miles from Robert's place, Murphy's Law went into high gear. The heavy traffic came to a complete stop when an accident blocked the interstate, already clogged with homeward-bound vacationers. Nothing moved but the soaring mercury. The engine overheated and the air conditioner had to be switched off altogether.

At 85 degrees, the cubs were panting, and Ed pulled the car off onto the berm, turned off the engine, and raised the hood as I grabbed up the babies and headed for a sparse patch of shade under a scraggly palm. In a matter of minutes, a Florida state trooper stopped, got out of his car, and approached us.

"Are those tigers?" he asked, running true to form.

After providing the standard information, I added an explanation as to why we were sidelined. The officer asked if he could pick up the cubs, and when he did he was hooked and our problem was well on the way to a solution.

"This bottleneck only lasts twenty or thirty miles," he said. "Follow me and I'll get you around it."

In high style with the red lights flashing, we zoomed up the highway on the wrong side of the road, weaving in and out of traffic, until we were five or six miles ahead of the glut. At that point, the trooper motioned us around him and I waved a thank you as we motored onward *sans* fanfare on the right-hand side of the road.

Even with the police escort we had only covered two hundred miles in six hours on the road. When nightfall came, we were all exhausted and Ed pulled into the first motel that had easy on-and-off access, hoping they had no objection to pets. The sign PLEASE USE OUR KENNELS led us to believe tigers would be unwelcome guests, and we chose not to risk finding out for certain. While Ed stayed with the cubs, I went in and registered, and then looked around for the usual outside entrance to the room. There was none. The front desk was situated squarely in the middle of the lobby like a command post, and nobody came or went unobserved.

Spiriting the little cats up to the room called for something creative, but short of knotting up a couple of bed sheets and hoisting them up through our second-story window, we could come up with only one alternative. I tucked both tigers under my sweater, folded my arms under them for support, and, striding briskly through the lobby behind Ed, headed for the stairway.

The babies were snug and warm and quiet, which we had counted on. What I hadn't anticipated was the pain little tiger nails can inflict on a midriff that's led a sheltered life. I hoped the grimace on my face passed for a permanent smile as we hustled through hostile territory up to the designated tiger den. Our exit the following morning was brazen by contrast. While Ed packed the car, I sauntered through the lobby with the tigers in my arms, two little striped heads bobbing up and down in full view. So what if they threw us out when we were already on our way. We'd had a good night's sleep and I was Mercurochrome-d and Band-Aid-ed and braced for a whole new crop of holes in my epidermis. We still had a long way to go.

Covering the nine hundred miles between the Compound and home chewed up most of two days, and most of me.

The tiger babies adapted well to their new life at Camel Lot. The "mud room," a small utility room at one end of the house, made a perfect den for the little cats. Adjacent to the garage, we used it for an entrance during inclement weather so its linoleum floor was used to muddy boots and wet coats, ideal indoctrination for little tiger puddles. Lots of built-in cabinets and a closet were handy for stowing the babies' gear, and there was also a sink plus a washer and dryer. An old Naugahyde lounge chair and side table were there, too, but only because we had no use for them elsewhere.

In addition to two windows, it had doors that led to the side porch, the back hallway by the kitchen, and the garage. It was a bright room with light beige walls and woodwork painted with an easy-to-clean semigloss, fortunately. Even though the cubs couldn't yet see, whichever one was not being fed at the moment was very much aware his twin was noisily slurping up a bottle and took measures to remedy the inequity. If he didn't succeed in slapping the bottle all the way out of my hand, he'd manage to get the nipple directed to some place other than the intended target, and the inevitable result was Esbilac splattered over the wall, the floor, and the three of us.

Before long I had to modify the procedure and feed each one by himself in the kitchen. It wasn't a strenuous undertaking, the eight or ten steps to the kitchen, but it did mean having to corral all the dogs, since they had not yet been formally introduced to the newcomers. All of them were very much aware of some major development five seconds after the tigers were ensconced in the house, and they stationed themselves at the mud-room doors, sniffing and pawing and barking at the mysterious creatures who had moved in. I had kept the dogs away, fearing the tigers would be instantly downgraded from endangered species to vanished species if they met. At four and three pounds respectively, the cubs could make irresistible prey for their fellow carnivores.

Our dogs were not the only parties interested in the cubs. The tiger babies were even more of an attraction than the camels and zebras, and everyone who learned of the cubs' presence *had* to meet them. Totally smitten with the little tykes myself, I could understand the desire, and I enjoyed sharing the little dolls—but it did become a time-consuming burden trying to squeeze in all the visitors. Then an injudicious decision on my part, a few weeks after their arrival, catapulted the tigers into television stardom and they acquired more fans.

Not envisioning the aftermath, I bowed to the persuasion of Barbara Boyd, who does human-interest stories for WRTV, and agreed to a feature on Niki and Ivan in conjunction with "Be Kind to Animals Week," the first week in May. The next day, a jittery gentleman from the station, bogged down with cameras and light meters and film and skepticism, showed up with succinct instructions, "Get some film of Schaffer's two Siberian tigers." He was not happy with the assignment.

When I advised him that one of his subjects was four pounds and the other six, he was somewhat less apprehensive, but enthusiastic he was not. Visions of wild junglebeasts were still dancing in his mind. Parking his equipment in the entrance hall, he rambled about the house to determine the best location for shooting and decided on the breakfast room. It was bright and needed no artificial lighting. The fact that it had three escape routes might also have influenced his decision.

"What are you going to talk about?" he asked, setting up his bulky camera on a tripod.

"Whatever comes to mind, I guess. It's time for them to eat, suppose I feed them at the same time."

"Okay," he agreed.

While the bottles were warming, I donned my battle dress and dragged the lion skin out to cover the slick floor before I brought the babies inside. The photographer was visibly relieved at their diminutive proportions. He hung a microphone around my neck and then disappeared behind the camera, flicked a switch, and a green light came on. "I'm rolling," he said.

"These two Siberian tigers are brothers," I said, slipping Ivan his bottle as Niki began his harassment. "They were the only two in the litter, although tigers sometimes have as many as six. That little white spot on the backs of their ears is so their mother can spot them readily when she comes back from hunting for food."

Niki continued his ascent and bored into my neck; I prattled on. "I've heard Siberians called 'Death in a fancy dress,' but it's difficult to imagine anything so precious as these tiny babies being dangerous. But they get as big as six or seven hundred pounds when they're full grown."

Niki scored again, so I had to abandon Ivan to extricate the little runt from my shoulder. Then Ivan wandered off, having finished his bottle, and I snatched him back and held him out at arms' length in front of the camera.

"They still can't see, even though their eyes are open. In a few more weeks their eyes will start turning from the blue-gray they are now into a golden color."

I snatched Niki and thrust him toward the camera along with Ivan as I rambled on about how large cats purr differently from smaller ones, catching their breath between each purr while the smaller ones purr continually. My muscles began twitching and I feared we'd never run out of film.

"That'll do it," said the cameraman finally.

And he was so right. As soon as the program was over, telephone calls began coming in from people who wanted to visit the tigers. From all over Indianapolis and points north, south, east, and west, they called, people I didn't know and who didn't know me until moments before. For the most part, they asked to see the cubs, but some didn't bother with that formality. One woman informed me she'd be out with her entire Girl Scout troop on Saturday at 10:00 A.M.

It was impossible to acquiesce to all the demands, but I tried to squeeze in as many visitors as possible without disrupting the tigers' schedules and completely demolishing my own. Tiger-watchers were ushered into the family room and asked to refrain from any loud noises that would scare the babies, but a loud chorus of "Oh!" usually greeted the little guys. Occasionally, some kidnik squealed with delight and sent the frightened cubs, ears flattened against their heads, scurrying for cover.

Even so, the outbursts were understandable. To meet the tiger babies meant succumbing to their charms. Resistance was impossible. I always brought them inside for our playtimes, and before they could see they careened off the walls and bumped into furniture. When their vision improved, they became much more adventurous and, being innately curious, each new discovery required a thorough investigation. The two-way fireplace was explored regularly. I had but to glance away and they were in the middle of it, capering in the leftover ashes. When I dragged them out, streaked with soot, off they'd go, leaving trails clearly marked by little tiger toes dredged in the gray, powdery residue of winter. Usually they made a dash for our bathroom to dirty the tile floor and bathtub. They loved to jump up on the edge of the tub and race round and round, occasionally losing their balance and tumbling into the tub.

No one game held their attention for long, but they were adept at inventing new ones. Niki, in spite of being the runt, was the more aggressive of the two. Where he led, Ivan followed. Climbing the curtains in the family room was Niki's idea. The curtains were made of a loosely woven, coarse fabric and hung by rings attached to a wooden pole that ran almost the full length of the room. Both the cats loved to dig in and shinny up to the top where, like drunken tightrope walkers, they'd totter along the rod until they came to a dead end at the brick wall and were stymied. Reverse was not among their capabilities. They couldn't back up or back down, so they summoned me in strident terms until I leaped up on a chair and plucked them off. It was great exercise for them, but it was bad news for the curtains. Their shredded remnants still hang in tatters, mute acknowledgment to the action they've seen.

All of the potted plants came in for their share of attention, too, and one Jerusalem cherry tree got in a lot of overtime. Prior to the tiger era, it had sat undisturbed in a corner of the breakfast room on the floor; but the bright crimson baubles hanging from its branches were irresistible, so pretty soon there were no bright crimson baubles left. No tree either. A couple of palms in clay pots fared better. They survived, but not well. They were victims of the tigers' bulldozer game. The babies lunged at them, knocking them over with a strenuous crash that sent the battered plants clattering about the slate floor and the little cats tearing for safety.

Playtime with the tigers had a lot in common with a demolition derby, and Robert was appalled by my lack of discipline. He flew up ostensibly for a social visit and to see if the guest accommodations had improved since his bout with the fold-up bed, but I suspected his motives ran deeper. I've no doubt that had he found me an unfit tiger mother, he would have snatched the babies away and whisked them back to Florida. Fortunately, he was pleased with their progress and lavish with praise—except in the matter of their discipline, or lack thereof.

"No!" he barked at Ivan, and swatted him as the cub began his ascent of the family-room curtains. Then he barked at me, "Moselle, you have got to control those tigers before they get out of hand."

"I know, I know," I agreed.

Niki chose that inopportune moment to knock over a plant, and I felt compelled to take stern measures for the benefit of my mentor. "No, baby, you shouldn't do that," I said, tapping him on the nose.

"For God's sake!" Robert was exasperated. "You didn't even get his attention. Sometimes their mothers smack them so hard they knock them all the way across the pen. I'm not recommending you be anywhere near that forceful, but let them know who's boss. No, forget that. They already know. Convince them there's been a change and now *you're* boss."

"I'll try," I said contritely.

But the tiger babies' unruliness merely appalled Robert. Charlie Lama's behavior left him reeling in disbelief.

TWELVE

Llamas, for the most part, are an amiable lot whether they are llamas (*Lama glama*), alpacas (*Lama pacos*), or guanacos (*Lama guanicoe*). All three are members of the family Camelidae and, like their camel relatives, they do spit—but not without provocation. Usually. Our guys were guanacos, and from my prejudiced viewpoint they were more beautiful than any of their "cousins," with their finer features and shorter, less busy coats. In intelligence they all rank about the same, fairly low on an I.Q. totem pole. It's safe to say there are no Rhodes scholars in the group.

Linda and Lucy, our two females, were friendly and a little shy, but Charlie Lama was exceptionally outgoing, a real personality boy who loved to kiss. No one was more surprised than I when I received my first kiss, which I attributed to an attraction to my lipstick. Charlie soon branched out, however, and soon he was startling visitors by playing the field, bestowing his attention on men as well as women. The fellow simply liked to kiss. A dozen times a day he pecked me on the lips while I ran my fingers through the incredibly soft fur on his long neck.

Charlie Lama was the handsomest of animals, his rich caramel-colored coat contrasting with the white of his slender neck. His bearing was regal, head tilted back slightly as he looked down his nose and fixed his big brown eyes on his subject with a steady, unblinking gaze. Charlie was everyone's favorite.

Our routine rarely varied. When the weather was nice, I walked back and forth to the barn and Charlie was the first to hurry to the fence for a kiss. Then Reverend and Roxie arrived to reaffirm their status in the pasture hierarchy and sent him packing with a couple of nips to his short fluffy tail. Rev, his tongue dangling out of one side of his mouth, made a guttural gargling sound for a greeting before we proceeded toward the barn, then the zebras fell in behind them and the llamas brought up the rear. Somewhere along the parade route, usually coming down the driveway to meet us, the multitude of goats joined up with us. I was the Pied Piper of the quadruped set.

One evening, when I headed to the barn for the last of the day's chores, Merl Sorenson, a frequent visitor, joined me. Charlie came loping toward us, nothing unusual about that, but from then on the sequence of events changed radically. Charles and I were face to face when he stopped about a foot short, pasted his ears back against his head, and, a split second later, spewed out a glob of half-chewed grass held together with saliva that exploded in my left eye. The pain was intense, but so was the shock. As the tears rushed to the injured eye and washed the debris down my face, Merl and I looked at each other in dumb-struck silence. Then Merl was overcome by the humor of the situation.

"Your face!" he managed before he doubled up with uncontrollable guffaws.

Finally, when he began to pull out of it, he produced a handkerchief and dabbed at the disaster while I stood there puzzling over Charlie's bizarre behavior.

"My sweet Charlie Lama! He couldn't have done that intentionally. He made a mistake," I reasoned.

I made the mistake. Charles blasted me again the next day, the day after, and he continued to pummel me every time the opportunity presented itself, namely every time I appeared within range. With dilated nostrils and bulging eyes, back went the ears while his jaws worked feverishly to blend his missile into the proper consistency. His grass concoctions were painful, but the homemade shrapnel he devised from alfalfa pellets was brutal. The dark-green cylinders are about a quarter inch in diameter and three-quarters of an inch long, as compact as a .22 rifle shell and almost as lethal.

The fiend was a remarkably thorough planner, never spitting unless his victim, i.e., me, was within five feet, the limits of his capability. He maintained a record of a hundred percent accuracy. Although he preferred a full-face target, he'd settle for a profile if he couldn't do better, but he never reduced his standards by aiming for the back of the head.

My beautiful Charlie Lama turned into the ugliest animal I've ever known. Beauty may be only skin deep, but ugly goes clear to the bone, and in Charles's case right on to and through the marrow. As his behavior became more and more vicious, I gleaned a clear understanding of why ancient tribesmen offered male llamas as sacrifices to their gods.

For months I was his only victim, and I was on the receiving end of a great deal of harassment because of it. "What have you done to him?" "You did something to him." So ran the accusations. When the crumbum branched out and anyone at all became an acceptable bull's-eye, I was delighted. I was especially pleased when Merl got his baptism of fire.

"You S.O.B.!" he bellowed into the barn one splendid day, and I hoped I knew what had happened. Yep. Merl, too, had joined Charlie Lama's ever expanding list of undesirables.

Then Charles made a grave tactical error. He spit on Robert. He never should have done that. *ZAP!* and the side of Robert's face sustained a direct hit, lumpy rivulets of green goop dripping down his face.

"That is one mean animal," Robert said with slow deliberation. "He should produce handsome offspring, but if you want to keep him for breeding he needs discipline. And I will see that he gets it."

Robert departed for the nearest saddlery, purchased a leather whip with a loosely plaited "stinger" on the end, and returned to administer Charlie Lama's first lesson in deportment. When the teacher strolled nonchalantly to the fence, his student, true to form, immediately appeared. As soon as he let go his barrage, Robert and the whip swung into action. *Pow! Pow! Pow!* He made direct contact with Charlie's face, but the startled animal, taken completely by surprise, continued to spit. Five or six more lashes Charles received before the confused, enraged beast retreated.

"There!" Robert said with satisfaction. "That should be good for a start. It doesn't injure the animal in any way, doesn't bruise him, but it does sting."

During the second learning session, Robert was able to deliver only one brief blow before Charles departed in haste.

After that, whenever Robert approached, Charles turned his head in the opposite direction, adjusted his ears, and began working his mouth—all without spitting.

"Look at him! He's so mad he's talking to himself." Robert laughed. "That's a smart llama. He's learned."

Unfortunately, as soon as Robert left for home, Charlie Lama reverted to his old ways, and anyone was fair game. He *was* a smart llama and he'd learned, all right. What he'd learned was to mind his p's and q's whenever Robert, whip in hand, was on the scene.

THIRTEEN

I was both gratified and relieved that Robert was pleased with the tiger babies' progress. I felt a keen responsibility for my two precious charges, and they were an all-consuming concern. One could almost see the little cats grow. Ivan gained about one pound each week, and Niki trailed him by a quarter to half a pound.

Then Ivan got sick. He refused to eat and lay lethargically on the lion skin staring blankly at nothing and making no effort to move, not even to change positions. He was so listless he didn't bother to slap the bottle out of the way; he simply ignored it. When I took his temperature, I put in a frantic call to Robert.

"One hundred four degrees is a little bit high," he said

calmly. "From what you tell me, I think it's a virus. Put him on streptomycin. How much does he weigh now?"

"Eleven pounds."

"Ed can figure the dosage by weight. Give it to him twice a day. And don't worry, he'll be all right."

Ed loathed jabbing the sick baby with a needle, but he performed faithfully and Ivan didn't seem to mind the injections. He was completely disinterested in anything or anybody. I stayed with him almost around the clock, leaving him only to care for the other animals. When I went to bed at night, Ivan went with me. As I lay on my side encircling him with my body, he curled up into a ball and never moved, never wet the bed. He was a very good tiger, and a sick one.

It was three days and eight telephone consultations with Robert before Ivan began to improve, finally accepting his bottle and downing a few swallows. Gradually, his appetite improved, and when it did I sought to make up for the missed meals with supplemental feedings. At first, the little cat was weak and moved about feebly, but after another week he was his old, frisky, feisty self once again. But not for long. Before another week went by he came down again with all the same symptoms plus an additional one.

"He keeps licking the fur on the lion's skin," I told Robert.

"That's because of the fever, don't worry about that. Will he eat anything at all?"

"No, nothing."

"Did he eat yesterday?"

"Yes, every feeding."

"How many times did you feed him?"

"Eleven."

"Eleven feedings! There's your problem—you're feeding him to death!"

It was a classic case of the cure being worse than the disease, only in this case the cure was causing the disease. When I quit unwittingly gorging the poor fellow, Ivan's recovery was almost immediate. For another two weeks he was as fit as a tiger baby could be, and then yet another malady came upon him and my morale took a nosedive. Although Niki—seemingly the fragile one—thrived, it was one siege after another for Ivan, and I began to despair of the little tyke's ever growing up to become a fierce, ferocious Siberian tiger. My confidence in my assigned role, flimsy all along, became shakier yet.

This go-around Ivan's appetite remained good and his temperature normal, but he was listless once again, to such an extent he made his puddles on the lion skin, a highly significant development. Although the cubs disdained a litter box except as a pile of sand that was fun to play in, they were fastidious like most cats, always trundling off as far away as possible from their bedding for nature's necessities.

My diagnosis for Ivan's new illness, born of wishful thinking, didn't hold up for long. That morning, I tried to clip the cubs' nails but got only as far as Ivan's left front paw before his shrill objections so unnerved me I abandoned the project. He was off-balance, I told myself, that's why he wouldn't move around. So I pared the nails on the other front paw—over his vociferous protests—stood him on all fours, and he promptly collapsed into a heap as soon as I removed my support.

Ed thought the shag carpeting in our bedroom would offer more traction, so he propelled Ivan around the floor with both hands under his middle, with the same end result. The minute Ed let go of him, Ivan folded up, making no attempt to maneuver on his own.

Meanwhile, Niki kept interfering with the therapy, so I accidentally invented a game that became his favorite. Hoisting him up in the air with one hand under each of his armpits, I rocked him back and forth so his small body swung like a pendulum, and he adored it. He crinkled up his face as if he were grinning and was a happy swinging tiger as long as I'd provide the locomotion.

Niki's amusement was more successful than Ivan's treatment, hence the inevitable call to Robert for help.

"It sounds like a vitamin deficiency," Robert decided. "Have Ed give them some shots of vitamin-B complex. Are they getting any sunshine?"

"No, you told me to keep them out of the sun."

"I meant don't keep them confined in the sun. They need some sunshine. Take them outside for an hour or so a day."

With Niki skipping along at my heels, I carried Ivan outdoors several times a day for his sunbaths, and the minute I stretched him out on the ground Niki was ready to play. He backed off a couple of feet for a running start and pounced on Ivan, clutching him bodily, his smaller frame not quite eclipsing that of his larger brother. Then he batted Ivan with a right hook, a left. Ivan didn't seem to mind. When he felt more energetic, he retaliated, and soon both babies were rolling and tumbling in the grass like any other young kittens—most household models being considerably more petite, however.

The cubs took care to stay close to me and never intentionally wandered far from the security of their ersatz mama. Every now and then, one accidentally strayed and then he bleated a forlorn "Wah!" looking from side to side, obviously "lost." As soon as I spoke to him, he scampered back, and that called for a reassuring hug before he could dash off again for another daring adventure in the exciting new world unrestricted by walls.

Any new noise attracted the cubs' attention, and they stood

motionless, ears flattened against their heads, listening atten-
tively. If it were a menacing sound such as the bark of a strange
dog, they scurried closer to me. For the benign chirp of a bird,
no additional security measures were deemed necessary.

Our field trips became more fun as the cubs grew and their
eyesight continued to improve. A tall blade of grass jittery from
the wind held them transfixed, until something more dynamic
distracted them and they'd tear off in confused pursuit of the
moving target—a butterfly fluttering along at a low altitude or
a grasshopper popping suddenly into view. Flowers were a
special joy to them. They loved sniffing patches of wildflowers
that tickled their noses and made them sneeze, but the resilient
daisies were more amusing. Daisies were for batting, and the
little fellows delighted in swatting them, their big eyes widening
with enthusiasm.

Ivan responded well to treatment, and whether it was the
vitamin injections, the sunshine, or the combination of the two,
I could only guess. But even though the weather that May was
tiger-baby perfect, I hooked up a sun lamp in the mud room
for the occasional dreary day. When there were no therapeutic
rays outside, sunbeams were on tap in the tiger athletic club.
I was taking no chances.

As the cubs approached three months of age, I began their
weaning process as per Robert's instructions. First removing
the skin and fat from a raw chicken, I pureed the meat until
it was the consistency of wallpaper paste and added a quarter
teaspoon to thirty-two ounces of formula, gradually increasing
the amount until they were getting four tablespoons of solids
with each batch of Esbilac. The tigers accepted the change in
diet with no objections or ill effects. They did object to step
two, however. Having the undiluted chicken paste smeared on

their mouths went against the grain, so they hastened to rectify the situation by licking the sticky substance to clean themselves up. Mission accomplished.

"Now you can start them on solid chicken," Robert coached via the telephone. "Use chicken backs and be sure to chop them very, very finely."

I did better than that. I beat them to a pulp. Having been indoctrinated since childhood on the perils of chicken bones for animals, I was extremely apprehensive about this crucial step, particularly in light of Niki's tendency to choke. The first chicken dinner went off without a hitch. Niki chomped away happily while his brother shied away from eating the mutilated mess, batting it around the room instead. It took several days before Ivan accepted pulverized chicken as part of his regular bill of fare.

The tigers were still on the bottle, but after about ten days they weren't drinking any formula at all. Although they took the nipple and pulled on it strenuously, the results were negligible and I worried about dehydration. This, of course, called for another consultation. AT&T smiles on me.

"Once tigers are weaned they lose the ability to suck, that's all that means," Robert said. "It's nothing to worry about."

"But they're not getting any fluids."

"You have water there for them, don't you?"

"Yes."

"Then they're drinking. You just don't see them."

I couldn't buy that explanation, not with the surveillance-like attention the tigers received, but the "pro" was right as usual. I took to peeking in their windows and, sure enough, spied Niki lapping water in small, hesitant sips. The peeping Tom approach also shed a little light on Ivan's progress. I watched him dip a paw into the water dish and remove it quickly to shake off the few drops of water that clung to his toes. Even if he were not yet drinking, I knew his brother would show him the ropes sooner or later.

Now that the cubs were eating and drinking on their own, the most perilous phase of their development was behind them and I was both relieved and jubilant. The euphoria was short-lived, however.

"You can ship them back anytime now that they're weaned," Robert said casually.

Ship them back! Give up *my* tiger babies? Our understanding had been unmistakably clear, I was to care for the cubs until they were weaned and at that point return them to Robert. But I had filed that unacceptable prospect into a remote corner of my mind. Then as my two little loves gnawed, clawed, and burrowed their way deeper and deeper into my heart, I chose to ignore the possibility of ever being separated from them.

"Robert wants the tigers back," I wailed to Ed.

"This is as good a time as any. Before long they'll have to go in cages, and you won't like that. You can see them often at Robert's," he tried to console me.

"Not every day, I can't. At any rate, I absolutely refuse to ship them back like a crate of oranges. They'd get poked in some dungeon of a cargo bay and be scared to death."

"We'll take them back in my bus," Ed offered.

He had acquired a Travco recreation vehicle for business purposes. It was an auxiliary office where he could dictate and store charts and instruments and freshen up with a shower and a change of clothes on exceptionally long days. He also welcomed any excuse to crank up his new toy, so a trip to Florida was a thoroughly acceptable idea—but not to me. I grew increasingly more despondent over parting with Niki and Ivan, and when that gloomy day arrived, it was two little tear-splattered tigers we put on board the Travco.

Seeking to preserve the sanity of whichever of us was driving, Ed had gotten heavy-duty pet carriers for the cubs and they hated the confinement. Loud and clear they screamed their objections, until I let them out. Then the predictable pandemonium ensued. While Ed drove, I coped with them, distracting them when they decided to rip up the upholstery or shred the shower curtain. During my turns at the wheel they went back into solitary. It was a long, strenuous trip, one that did nothing to improve four shabby dispositions that only grew shabbier with each passing mile. By the time we reached the Compound, we were all growling.

"My, what a handsome specimen!" Robert declared, admiring Ivan after a few brief amenities. "Come along, let's get them in their pen. They'll follow you, won't they, Moselle?"

Niki's and Ivan's new quarters were in a large fenced-in area that encompassed one giant live oak and several lesser trees, an estate compared to the mud room. There was a great deal of jungle brush, too, and both little cats busied themselves with a tour of inspection, until a new playmate arrived on the scene.

Split was an eight- or nine-pound mongrel, white with an occasional splotch of black. When he was one week old, his mother adopted two baby leopards who had been rejected by their own biological mother and she nursed them right along with her own brood of three. Consequently, the pup grew up unaware of any difference between cats and dogs and had no fear of any of the Compound's felines. Split was six months old and not likely to get much older. So far he had evaded the claws of some of the more hostile cats as they reached out of their cages and took a healthy swipe at him, but he had had a few close calls and was still mingling with mortals only because of his agility. That was the reasoning behind his name, the fact that he'd probably get split right down the middle if he persisted in courting catastrophe.

Niki and Ivan were delighted with their new companion and raced up and down on the inside of their fence with Split keeping up the pace outside. Occasionally one of the little cats poked an arm through the mesh and gently swatted the pup, but that was strictly for kicks, no harm intended.

The plan called for us to remain at the Compound for five days, me taking care of Niki and Ivan in order to lessen the shock of the drastic change of environment. Since I was the only mother the cubs knew, ripping them from their familiar surroundings and placing them in a totally new situation would be less traumatic for them with "Mama" handy. They seemed to be adapting well.

"Niki and Ivan!" I called whenever I opened their gate. "Where are you hiding?"

Two little heads peeked out of the brush or around a tree before they bounced over to chat and be cuddled and grate my skin with their rough-tongue expressions of affection. A tiger kiss is comparable to a massage with a number-five grade of sandpaper, though infinitely more rewarding, and their conversation consisted of "Puh-puh-puh, puh-puh-puh." But it was easy to translate. Even though we hail from vastly different cultures, we had no difficulty understanding one another.

After we visited long enough to suit them, I removed any leftovers from their morning meal lest the chicken spoil; for the first two days I pittled them as a precaution, even though they actually needed no further assistance in that department. In four days' time, they became almost completely independent—except for loving. Tiger babies need lots and lots of loving.

I was almost sorry they were making the transition from Hoosiers to Florida crackers so smoothly. It meant my time with the babies was rapidly running out, and there was no need to extend my stay. Just before we were supposed to leave, Robert decided to move the cubs off the sandy ground, since fleas were a big problem in Florida.

"I want them in that cage right over there, Moselle," Robert indicated a large red circus wagon that housed a full-grown "working cat" when they were on the road. "Let me open the panel so you can put them inside."

I deposited Niki and Ivan on their old lion skin that Robert had thoughtfully placed on the floor and climbed in after them. Both babies jumped in my lap and I scooped them up, one in each arm, and hugged them tightly. There was a lot of chatter going on, but it was all on their part, I was having technical difficulties with a large obstruction in my throat and was unable to speak. Then my lacrimal glands went wacky and pumped a great deal more lubrication than my eyeballs required, the excess of which overflowed, spilled down my face, and splashed onto the tiger babies.

"Come on out," Robert said sympathetically. "You're just making it harder on yourself."

Reluctantly, I took his advice, looking back over my shoulder at the little cats as I walked away. They were staring at me through the bars, bewildered by this latest change of address, two miniature tigers pathetically lost in a vast new universe.

"Affairs of the heart always end in sadness," according to some sage. He was so right. Whoever said, "Parting is such sweet sorrow," was a nincompoop.

FOURTEEN

Our trip back to Indiana was considerably calmer than our southbound journey. Also soggier. I didn't dry up until Tennessee.

The first thing I did when we got home was check all the animals and, as I'd learned to expect with young Jack as "baby-sitter," everybody was fine. Calling to check on the tigers was the next priority, but a continual busy signal at the Compound prevented my getting through. Three hours later, I learned from the operator that the telephone was out of order.

It was still on the fritz the following morning, but it was no big deal, I told myself. I told myself a lot of things, such as, "Get yourself out to the airport and see if you can still remember how to fly." Following my own advice, I was pleased to discover everything from the preflight check to the landing sequence came easily, even though I had flown only once since the cubs' arrival at Camel Lot. Getting back behind the controls was a welcome distraction that helped fill the tremendous hole in my life left by the cubs' departure. The next day, I had another distraction far more compelling but most unwelcome.

On my first trip to the barn I was puzzled when neither camel arrived at the fence for our early morning rendezvous. The zebras, llamas, and goats were all present and accounted for, but there was no sign of Reverend or Roxie. Checking the barn, I discovered Roxie roaming around but Reverend lying on his side with a rampant case of diarrhea very much in evidence. The grain I offered him, hoping to coax him to his feet, failed to arouse any interest. Neither did a slice of his favorite oatmeal bread. Reverend was obviously ill.

Being unable to reach Robert now posed a real dilemma. I didn't know where to turn for help. The small animal veterinarian who took care of our dogs had understandably disqualified himself from treating "exotic" animals, as had several other vets I'd previously contacted. Even though Robert lacked the formal training required for a DVM degree, what he lacked in credentials he made up for by years of experience, and I relied heavily on his expertise. I was about to start through the Yellow Pages of the telephone directory seeking a veterinarian, the only course of action I could think of, when young Jack walked in.

"I know who to call. Dr. Herschler," Jack said decisively. "He's great. He cured the horse of a friend of mine once, and the horse was in a bad way, almost gone."

Dr. Herschler was quick to respond. Half an hour later, he walked into the barn and announced, "I want you to know I've never treated a camel before—but I can handle it."

The veterinarian exuded such confidence I felt assured he

could handle it, or any other problem with which he was confronted. A muscular six foot three with slightly graying dark
hair, he reminded me of a college professor, possibly because
of his gold-rimmed glasses and air of authority. As he slipped
a pair of coveralls over his street clothes, he rattled off
questions.

"What's a camel's normal temperature, do you know?"

"Between ninety-eight and ninety-nine degrees according to
the *Merck Veterinary Manual*," I answered. "But how are you
going to take his temperature?"

"Rectally, of course," he said, with a disdainful glance in
my direction.

Jack and I looked at each other, and without exchanging a
single word, exchanged identical thoughts: Herr Herschler was
about to have his complacency shattered—and quite possibly
the rest of him along with it. Reverend might be ill, but he
was still capable of expressing his wrath, and at the very least
he would be displeased by this course of action.

"Do you have a halter?" was the next question.

"No, I don't."

"I'll make one then."

He took a long nylon lead strap out of his bag, fashioned it
into a lasso that he placed around the still-docile animal's
neck, and handed the end of it to Jack to hang on to. Then
he put a "twitch" on Rev's ear that I got to hold. This device,
a wooden clamp that resembles an oversize clothespin, is com-
monly used on a horse's lip to keep the animal from moving
while something unpleasant is going on. But camels' lips are
not designed to accommodate a twitch, hence the ear for a
substitute.

As Dr. Herschler bent over, thermometer in hand, Jack's
and my eyes met once again, and this time the message we

conveyed to each other was, "Brace yourself, here it comes."
Seconds later the brouhaha was on. With a roar backed up by
his two thousand pounds of fury, Reverend lunged to his feet
and sent Jack and me both slamming against a wall and at the
same time he took care of his third adversary at the opposite
end of the action. The vet was inundated with a barrage of the
vilest substance in a camel's arsenal. And the man was un-
fazed. He calmly cleaned off the thermometer with a handful
of straw and squinted through his spattered glasses to read the
numbers.

"It's a hundred and five degrees," he said matter-of-factly.

My facial expression no doubt mirrored Jack's, one of wide-
eyed, openmouthed astonishment coupled with awe. Neither
of us said a word.

"I'm going to need some lab work, so I'll be back in a little
while to get a blood sample and also to give the camel an
injection. I'll bring Jim Lawrence with me, he's my assistant."

Jack and I got the message, one we were glad to hear. Our
inept assistance would no longer be required. It was especially
good news to Jack, who now had a sales career and, even
though his schedule was flexible, needed to devote some time
to his livelihood.

All day I stayed with Reverend, stroking his forehead and
trying to tempt him with food, but he was unresponsive and
made no attempt to drink or eat. He got to his feet only when
Dr. Herschler returned in the evening to administer another
injection, seven million units of penicillin plus two grams of
streptomycin, roughly seven times the dose for an adult human.

Reverend was worse the next day, so unresponsive he didn't
protest when the vet took his temperature or jabbed him with
a needle. Every two or three hours I tried to reach Robert in
hopes he might have some magic cure unknown to Dr. Her-

schler and also hoping for news of the tiger babies to lift my sagging spirits.

By the fourth day, my big friend was barely hanging on and I had little more than a fragile thread of hope and a constant stream of prayers to cling to. There was a brief moment of optimism when at last I got through to the Compound. But Robert had no other suggestions for Rev's treatment. To the contrary, more gloom was all he had to offer.

"How are the tiger babies?" I asked, anticipating little change in the week's time since I'd seen them.

"Not well, not well at all, I'm sorry to say."

"What's the matter?" I almost screamed.

"I don't know. The little one cries all the time, and neither one is eating."

"Oh, Robert. Could they be homesick?"

"I don't know what the problem is, Moselle. I've tried everything."

"They've got to come home, Robert. Can you bring them up?"

"No, I can't leave here right now. There's a tremendous amount of damage from that windstorm. It wasn't just the power lines it took down; there were a lot of trees blown over that wreaked havoc with some fences and cages."

"I can't leave Reverend, but I'll figure some way to get them and call you back," I said.

I knew Jack would go down for the tigers if it were at all possible. He was almost as devoted to Niki and Ivan as I was.

"All I need to do is change a few appointments and I'm ready to go," he said when I tracked him down in the late afternoon. "I'll be out as soon as I can."

I began calling the airlines. From two I got a flat and final no; they would not permit tigers to travel in the passenger section under any circumstances. The third would have to let me know. Soon afterward I received a call from some puzzled airline executive.

"How large are the tigers?" he wanted to know.

"About fifteen pounds, they're just a little over three months old."

"Are they vicious?"

"No, no, no. They're quite tame. They're just two little pussycats, really."

"Our luggage compartments are pressurized, they'd be quite comfortable there."

"Yes, but the tigers are ill and need special attention. They'll have an attendant with them. It could be a matter of life and death."

"All right. If you have any trouble, tell them I authorized it," he agreed.

Jack left for the airport amidst a flurry of instructions: where to get a rental car for the one-hour drive to the Compound, directions there from Tampa, what to do for the tigers under various circumstances. He was booked on a "red-eye special" that landed at Tampa International at 4:45 A.M. and a return flight that left there at 3:20 that afternoon. He was in for a long, strenuous day. We both were.

"And Jack," I called after him, "phone if you have any problems."

At least the next morning began with a bright spot. Reverend ate one slice of bread. One hundred calories wasn't much nutrition for an animal of his gargantuan proportions, but it was a positive indication he was feeling better. I was noting the development on his chart, 5:30 A.M., as the extension telephone in the barn rang.

"I couldn't get a rental car, Mrs. Schaffer, but I've found a taxi driver who'll take me to Robert's," Jack said.

"Good."

"It's awful expensive, though."

"Pay him. Just get there."

Jack called again when he reached the Compound. "Niki's awful sick, Mrs. Schaffer."

"Oh, no."

"*Awful* sick. I doubt if he'll make the trip."

"Try, Jack. That's all you can do."

"I just wanted you to know how sick he is."

He had not failed to get that point across and, as the morning wore on, Robert called to confirm Jack's glum assessment.

"The little fellow got a lot worse after I talked to you last night. Don't feel too badly if anything happens to them."

I barely managed a shaky good-bye and hurried back to Rev. Jack's next bulletin was from Tampa on his way back.

"They won't let me take Niki and Ivan into the passenger cabin with me," he said.

"Did you tell them you have authorization from the airline?" I fairly shrieked.

"Yes, but the captain says they smell too bad. They do smell pretty poor; they have awful diarrhea. They promised to load them last so they'll be the first off. They're already on the plane. I figured you'd want them back the fastest way possible. I had to sign a big long release form saying the airline isn't responsible, or they wouldn't take them at all."

There was a long pause before Jack added, "Niki's almost gone."

That time I couldn't say good-bye. The floodgates, shakier and shakier, finally burst.

Ed and I were at the airport for the last, long half hour of the grim vigil. Parked in front of the baggage sign as prearranged with Jack, I maintained a constant watch in that direction. Luckily the flight was early, and just before it was due to land, Jack pushed his way slowly through the revolving door, a pet carrier in each hand. One cage vibrated with action, the other was quiet and motionless. Jack, looking tired and forlorn, shook his head negatively from side to side. No words were necessary to convey the sad news. I knew the answer to my prayers, but it was not the one of my choosing.

"I think we'd better put them in the trunk, Jack," Ed suggested, getting out of the car to help.

"No! Just Niki," I objected. "I'll get in the backseat with Ivan."

"You'd better not let him out, Mrs. Schaffer. He's a mess, he'll ruin you," Jack cautioned.

"I don't care. Listen to that baby scream."

I didn't have to open the door for Ivan. He did that himself as soon as I removed the security clip. Out he raged, and around the inside of the car he roared, leaving his offensive pugmarks on the upholstery, the dashboard, the steering wheel, the driver, me, and everything else with which they made contact. Snatching him out of the air along about his third orbit, I hugged him to me while he continued to scream, but he did begin to settle down and his squalls finally tapered off to a mild "Wah!" Ed started the car as Jack cracked the back door slightly.

"I'll be a couple of minutes behind you," he said, and then he grew somber. "I'm sorry. I'm so sorry."

"You did everything you could. Thank you, Jack."

The full impact of Niki's death was delayed by Ivan's current needs, and I gratefully postponed facing that reality.

FIFTEEN

Ivan recognized his old home immediately, even though the lion skin was replaced by a pink wool blanket. Poking around the familiar objects, he sniffed the lingering tiger smells and lapped water eagerly.

"That's a good sign," Ed said. "He can't be too dehydrated."

I presented Ivan with a fresh chicken back meticulously hacked into fine splinters, but he looked it over, gave it one swift blow, and sent the meat skidding across the linoleum and under the washing machine. That was as close to food as he'd get of his own volition. Then he curled up in a ball and fell asleep, one tuckered-out little tiger.

My patient in the barn had been neglected for the past two hours, so I abandoned Ivan for Reverend and was rewarded with another encouraging sign from him. He had touched none of his hay or grain and drunk no water, but when I offered him bread he ate four slices, hand fed one piece at a time. I couldn't resist calling Dr. Herschler.

"I'm glad to hear that. I'm going to be away for a couple of weeks, but my assistant Jim Lawrence will take over. Please don't get your hopes up too high; the camel is still critical," he said.

Of that I was painfully aware. But Reverend did maintain a slow, gradual improvement while Ivan's health continued to deteriorate, and the mud room replaced the barn as the Intensive Care Unit. It seemed to me that at all times one of my furry friends teetered on the brink of eternity.

Ivan continued to refuse all food. His only nourishment was small slivers of raw chicken breast I slipped into his mouth and shoved down his throat for as long as he would tolerate the forced feeding. In spite of the medication pumped into him, his diarrhea continued unabated and he stopped drinking water altogether. A week passed and even with around-the-clock nursing care, medication, vitamins, and water squirted into his mouth with a plastic eyedropper, the little cat was going downhill at a rapid clip. Each day he became weaker and more emaciated. Big, sunken eyes occupied most of his face.

"Ivan gets worse every day," I cried to Ed. "If this keeps up we're going to lose him."

"I have one more idea—Harry Sanders. He treats a lot of children," Ed said. "Maybe he can come up with something."

Dr. Sanders concluded Ivan was a victim of deadly food poisoning, salmonella, and prescribed accordingly. He switched Ivan's drugs, and after two days on the new medication, the little cat began to show faint signs of improvement.

Although he still refused to eat on his own, I was able to stuff more chicken into him before he became unruly, and he drank water a few sips at a time. Still, his rate of improvement was much too slow and I began to wonder if we were overlooking a vital factor, treating the patient on the basis of an incomplete diagnosis. Niki and Ivan had shared every moment of their lives—eating, sleeping, playing together—until they were separated by death. Perhaps the longing for his lost brother, his constant companion, was contributing to his illness.

"Is that logical?" I asked Ed, after explaining my theory.

"You may have hit on something," he concurred.

"So, if we got him another cat for a playmate maybe that would work?"

"It would take some cat to hold his own with Ivan."

"Well, then, maybe a dog? Kozby's as tough as they come. What do you think?"

"What Kozby thinks is probably more important."

Being separated by only the garage door, their smells were familiar to each other and Kozby had seen Ivan many times through the windows. I felt they were sufficiently well acquainted, albeit remotely, to justify the risk. Placing a plate of table scraps for the dog and another one of Ivan's chicken five or six feet apart on the mud-room floor, we invited Kozby to join us.

Koz, never one to turn down a bonus, began stowing away the choice morsels as Ivan, his huge eyes even larger, ambled over and licked the dog's face. As soon as Kozby cleaned up his own dish and showed a definite interest in Ivan's, the little cat turned instant tiger. He pounced on his food and devoured it, simultaneously emitting serious threatening noises through his mouthful of chicken backs.

We stayed with the two new roommates for a while to reassure ourselves all would go smoothly, which it did, better than we could have hoped for. Kozby took a sip of water, Ivan joined him, lapping by his side. Koz lay down, and Ivan curled up close beside him and licked whatever was handiest, Kozby's face or a leg or an ear. And Ivan chattered incessantly. He talked the dog's ear off. It was the beginning of a friendship unmatched for sheer devotion. From the first introduction, Ivan adored Kozby, and as time went on the affection became mutual.

The cub's appetite took on such gluttonous proportions the two had to be separated at mealtime because Ivan gulped down his own carefully controlled diet and lit into Kozby's potpourri of leftovers before the poor dog could get started. Ivan bounced back to the picture of health, and in two weeks' time he'd made up the weight loss and was well on his way to becoming a fat Garfield look-alike.

It was a good while after Ivan's complete recovery before I had the heart to ask where Niki was buried. Ed had wrapped the small body in a terry-cloth towel and tucked him in for the last time, into the earth. The spot he chose was close by, in the woods next to a clump of white rhododendrons, a fitting memorial for a precious memory. It was July and there were no blooms anymore, but spring would come and they would bloom again.

Reverend's struggle with adversity was a longer one than Ivan's. There was a lot more of him to mend, about two hundred times as much in terms of body weight, and their maladies were of different origins. I was euphoric the day Rev consumed eighty-seven slices of bread doled out from an assortment of whole wheat, raisin, and oatmeal—Pepperidge Farm, of course.

"I think he's out of the woods now," Dr. Herschler agreed. "But I wouldn't have given a nickel for his chances in the beginning."

"Did you ever decide what his problem was?" I asked.

"In retrospect, I *think* I know. He did have pneumonia, definitely, but I think it was more than just one specific thing. He probably ingested a foreign body of some sort, possibly a piece of baling wire. All of the symptoms point to that.

"He's ruminating now, that's a good sign. I don't see the need for any more drugs. Keep pushing the food to him, and if you have any problem at all, call me right away."

"You can be sure of that," I said, hugging Reverend first, the doctor second. "Thank you for saving Rev's life, Dick."

"I'm glad I could help. And I want to thank you, too, Moselle. Now that I have Reverend for a patient, my camel practice has grown by more than one hundred percent," he joked.

Dick's llama practice soon increased by the same proportions when a baby arrived completely unexpected. Walking down to the barn one afternoon, I was alarmed to see an animal thrashing around on the ground, partially obscured by the tall grass. The other animals were standing around it in a circle, and a quick head count revealed only Charlie Lama was missing. I assumed it was Charles who was in trouble, so without the whip—my trusty Charlie Lama repellent—I leaped the fence to rush to his aid.

Then I was the one in trouble. When I was halfway across the pasture, I realized it was not Charles thrashing around on the ground, as he loomed up from wherever he'd been hiding and blasted me with a couple of rounds of his customized ammunition. That was merely a warm-up exercise prior to pulverizing me. As he reared back on his hind legs in order to knock me down, I ran around behind Roxie and used her two-thousand-pound bulk as a temporary shield while I tried to figure a way out of the perilous situation.

An attempt to outrun Charles would be futile, and probably fatal. Even with the strong impetus of the furious animal at my heels I couldn't make it to the fence ahead of him. My best chance was to fight back and hope I could intimidate him. Ripping off my shirt, I tied two knots in the end of one of the long sleeves and, swinging my lightweight weapon wildly, I rushed toward him. No doubt the element of surprise reinforced my bluff; Charles was not expecting a counterattack. While he pondered that sorry state of affairs, I was already backing up rapidly, and he didn't pursue me. I made it to the fence in time, thanks to my guardian angels. I need more than one— it requires an entire squadron, alternating the duty, to keep Charlie Lama at bay. Only when I was scrambling out of the pasture did Charles race over to make one last threat to terminate me.

By the time the skirmish was over, the object of my original concern had struggled to its feet. A small replica of her father, Charlie Lama, she was about fifteen pounds, most of which was legs with a tiny, wet body balanced on top of them.

Eleven months before, the length of the llama gestation period, Lucy and Charles had engaged in such a battle royal I was afraid one or both of them would be killed. The biting, spitting, and raking each other with their sharp-pronged hooves was accompanied by the high-pitched notes of a ferocious fight song that summoned me to the scene of the fray. Unaware that the course of true love could ever be this wild, I assumed they'd become mortal enemies and opened a gate to let Lucy escape to another pasture. For four months, thanks to my intrusion into their domestic affairs, the couple remained separated. Cupid does not regard me as an ally. . . .

Dick Herschler came over right away to examine the new mother and her daughter, the first "exotic" offspring at Camel Lot but by no means the first newborn.

SIXTEEN

Even when Ivan was a wee kitten, the sight of him was alarming to some animals, Jack the mynah bird for one. I doubt that Ivan's stripes identified him to Jack as a *Panthera tigris* with serious potential, and Jack probably didn't care. To him, a cat was a cat. Anticipating his distress should he have a close encounter with his bewhiskered adversary, I moved the bird from his breakfast-nook location to Ed's small den where Ivan was never allowed. What I failed to do was to take into account Ivan's ever-growing athletic prowess. He was a sizable cat, about twenty pounds, the day he put his big fat feet on the window ledge outside the den, pressed his nose against the glass, and sent Jack into flapping hysterics.

When I got to the bird, he was crouched on the floor of his cage, chest heaving and tongue hanging out of his beak as he gasped for breath. I moved the birdcage to a corner of the room and covered it in hopes he'd think it was night and sleep off the nightmare he'd just experienced. I didn't know anything else to do for him. In any event, Jack recovered rapidly enough to be in fine voice the next day and co-star with Ivan in another little melodrama that ended happily—I think.

I was away when a telephone repairman came to check out a problem of no incoming calls, but the cleaning lady was on hand to let him in. In her case, my standing instructions never to let Ivan out or admit anyone into his room were highly superfluous. Clair headed the list of those intimidated by the tiger.

"I'll need to get in there where the lines come in," the man told her, indicating the mud room where Kozby was barking nonstop. "Would you get the dog out?"

"You can't go in. A tiger's in there."

"Well," he became patronizing, apparently deciding to humor the deluded lady who thought a barking dog was a tiger. "Could you perhaps get the tiger out so I can go in there?"

"No, I'm sorry. I can't do that."

Ivan then chimed in to make it a duet, and the skeptic turned instant believer—and a shade or two paler.

"Er, uh, I need to call my supervisor. May I use your telephone?" he asked.

Up until then, Ivan's and Kozby's chorus had drowned out the mynah bird's contribution to the commotion; when they quieted down, Jack's raucous cackle and "Hello, Jack" came through loud and clear. But his long, low "wolf whistle" was the most damning of them all. It's a jungle call common to all mynah birds and sounds exactly like a two-legged wolf ogling an attractive girl. With that unfortunate background, the repairman got his supervisor on the telephone.

"Hello, Joe? I can't get in to check four-nine-six-five because a tiger's in there."

Clair could only guess what the boss had to say.

"No, I'm not, Joe. For God's sake, who the hell wants a drink at ten in the morning."

Pause.

"Joe, that's a bird."

Pause.

"Wait a minute, Joe." The harried man turned to Clair for help. "What kind of a goofy bird is that?

"Joe, it's a minor bird."

Pause.

"No, I haven't actually seen the tiger. Joe . . ."

Joe had hung up.

The distraught man returned an hour later when I'd gotten home and, though I sympathized with his plight and tried to commiserate with a straight face, I didn't succeed. To me, that one loud-mouth bird along with a pint-size pussycat could create such a furor was the height of absurdity.

"Mrs. Schaffer, my boss thinks I've been drinking on the job. Would you tell him there is a tiger in that room and that whistle does come from a daffy bird?"

"I'll do better than that," I said. "I'll snap a Polaroid of you holding the tiger."

If the road to hell is truly paved with good intentions, my offer added a couple of miles of concrete to it, along with one additional woe for the serviceman. Now, besides despondency, the poor guy had stark terror to contend with. I could sense the conflict swirling around in his head: Tangle with a tiger or look for a new job? *Was* there a lesser of those two evils?

He was difficult to persuade. Even when I trotted Ivan out, rigged up in his collar and leash, the man was still panic-stricken. In the eyes of the beholder, the little striped cat was ten feet tall. Although the man was greatly relieved to have the incontrovertible evidence of a snapshot, that had become secondary. Handing over the leash attached to a man-eating tiger was what brought the color back to his ashen face.

Kozby was Ivan's first choice as a playmate. People came second. Ivan would chew on the dog's ear, lick him, maul him—Kozby's patience was phenomenal. There was only one thing Koz would not tolerate: Ivan's batting at the uniquely male portion of the dog's anatomy. When that occurred, Koz bared his teeth and clicked them together as he growled an effective rebuke that prompted the little cat to cease and desist.

If they were outdoors, the games varied. Wrestling matches usually terminated with cat and dog tangled up as one entity tumbling down the slight incline of the backyard. King of the Hill was another favorite pastime, with a pile of leftover construction dirt for the hill and one tiger or one dog as a temporary king. Each reign was brief. The deposed monarch was quick to charge back up, shove the incumbent off the top, and reclaim the summit.

Ivan loved surprises, if he was doing the surprising. He'd crouch down, concealed in a clump of tall grass, and spring out to pounce on the victim of his choice. He preferred taking his captive unaware, but he was not averse to the attack if his subject was ready and waiting for it. People as well as Koz were eligible for that sport. When Koz was tired of—and sick

of—the little cat's rough antics, he streaked off out of sight
and whoever was available was the new target. It behooved
one to have a length of rope or an old tennis shoe handy.
Teasing kept Ivan amused for a while, but then he snatched
the new toy and carted it off to the bushes to add to his stockpile
of treasures: a baseball minus most of the stuffing, half of a
tattered blanket, countless shoes, and fragments of rubber
balls.

The five O'Sullivan sisters, ranging in age from six to sixteen,
came out often, and they were Ivan's special picnic playmates.
Ivan was big on picnics. They always stopped by a fast-food
outlet to load up, and the packaging was the part that Ivan
couldn't resist. As soon as he heard the crinkling sounds of
paper bags being emptied, he was up on the table slapping
over a Coke or making off with a sack of hamburgers, to the
accompaniment of delighted squeals and giggles. When one
of the girls gave chase, Ivan dropped his loot and turned to
pursue his pursuer, always overtaking her and sending her to
the ground with a thud. That called for quick action on the
part of the rescue squad. Ivan's tugging on a mouthful of his
prey's long blond hair clamped between his teeth was painful,
more so when he managed to remove a plug or two. None of
the girls wound up bald, but not because Ivan didn't give it
his all.

His intentions were innocent enough, all part of the fun.
Actually, he was a gentle animal, for a tiger, playing always
with his claws sheathed. But he did love to bite and chew,
and sometimes his enthusiasm caused small holes in the epidermis of his playmate. Swatting was another irresistible
hobby. Never once did he pass by me without taking a swipe.
Just for drill he'd bat at my ankle or calf, any handy part of
me—my derriere as he got taller and his range increased.

"Ivan's got to go in a cage," Ed announced when the little cat hit the forty-pound mark.

"Pen that baby up? He'd hate it," I protested.

"He's getting too big for you to handle as it is and he's not going to get any smaller. He can still come out to play but he needs an outside pen. He'll get used to it."

Despite my objections, Ed purchased a doozy of a cage, so heavy and cumbersome it required the assistance of two husky friends to assemble. Twelve feet square by eight feet tall, it had four sections of cyclone fencing. Its three-foot-wide door was too small to admit the four-by-four-foot doghouse that had to be hoisted up and over the side.

The new tiger's den was spacious, but nothing else favorable could be said for it. To defray the starkness, I tossed in some bric-a-brac, an old shoe of mine, Ivan's favorite pink blanket, and a couple of logs. I also included his rocking chair. Ivan discovered the joys of rocking when he learned to climb up on the patio furniture and urge the wrought-iron rocker to and fro with the forward-and-backward motion of his body.

With Ed badgering me, I baited the booby trap with a plate of goodies for Ivan and another one for Kozby and lured them both inside, clanging the gate shut on the two unwilling inmates. But they weren't inmates for long. Ivan zipped up one side of the cage and was teetering on the pole across the top when Ed hurried around to lift him off.

"See, he can't stay here," I said with relief.

"Yes, he can. I'll just add a top to the cage."

"He can still climb, and if he falls he could break a leg from that height."

"I'll take care of that, I'll lower the top."

Ivan's reprieve lasted only until Ed could lace twelve-inch

widths of chicken wire together for a roof, then Ivan and Kozby were ushered into their new domain on the patio, right outside our bedroom door. It was early evening, still daylight in the waning days of summer, and I watched anxiously as the cat and dog didn't adjust to their new confinement. Kozby barked his vehement dissatisfaction while Ivan busied himself more productively trying to shake the cage apart.

About midnight, Ed and I retired; Ivan and Kozby didn't. The racket of the rebellion was still shattering the normal quiet of the wee small hours when I finally got to sleep. When the first rays of sunshine awakened me in the morning, the ominous silence was the first clue something was amiss. Leaping out of bed, I hurried to the patio and was relieved to see Kozby snoozing peacefully, stretched out full length on Ivan's pink blanket. Ivan, nowhere in sight, was in the doghouse, I figured, also conked from the all-out efforts of the previous evening.

"Good morning, Kozby. Ivan, get up, you lazy pussycat," I said.

When I opened the door, Koz bestirred himself and ambled out, but there was still no sign of Ivan, so I went into the pen, intent on rousing the sleepyhead.

"Ivan," I called as I leaned over to peer into the doghouse. "IVAN!"

The tiger was gone. Looking around hastily for clues to his disappearance, I noticed two bent-up sections of the overhead chicken wire had been pulled apart and a tiger-size opening separated them. Obviously the persistent little cat had engineered the handy new exit and, project completed, was up, up, and away.

Assuming the escapee was lurking close by, I strolled around the edge of the woods and called to him, expecting any second to be knocked to the ground by a surprise attack. But when that exercise proved futile, I awakened Ed and we expanded the search, he heading one way, Kozby and I in the opposite direction.

By the time Ed had to go to the hospital, Wayne and Jeannie had already left the barn apartment, so Kozby and I continued our efforts alone, crisscrossing the five acres of woods more aptly described as jungle. It was dense with locust trees, man's dedicated enemies who thrust their rapierlike thorns impartially into all trespassers. Commanding the lower regions were the bramble bushes and spiny vines, and at ground level, sharp briars and prickly burrs. In the springtime, a brook babbled its way through the forest primeval, but it had degenerated into a marsh covered with thick green scum, irresistible for discriminating mosquitoes looking for an ideal place to breed. Frogs and snakes, too, considered it a splendid neighborhood for raising their families and multiplied there with complete abandon.

My lightweight pajamas and scuffs afforded little protection from the brutal forces of nature that ripped my flesh and the swarms of vampires sampling my blood. Bruised and bleeding and increasingly more alarmed after two hours of jungle warfare, I returned to the house to don more appropriate battle gear and recruit reinforcements. Jack, as always, was ready to lend a hand.

Having developed the Pavlovian reaction of calling Robert at the onset of any animal problem, I'd gotten him on the telephone before Jack arrived. Robert's comments, although realistic, were so disturbing I almost wished I hadn't reached him.

"The big danger is having someone shoot him," Robert informed me. "That's what happened to a three-month-old tiger of mine that got away. Some idiot shot him, skinned him, and sold the skin.

"You and Jack go to every house within a two-mile radius and explain to them the tiger is quite harmless. Be sure to make it very, very clear he's just a small tiger and nothing for anyone to be afraid of."

Jack and I carried out Robert's instructions and in every instance the response was the same. "A what? A *tiger!*" Admittedly there was such a Hans Christian Andersen aura about a Siberian tiger loose in Indiana corn country it made the facts sound like a freewheeling fairy tale. But the neighbors were all pleasant and cooperative and promised to call if they had any news of Ivan's whereabouts.

I was out of ideas, but Jack had a suggestion.

"You know David Sutherland, that guy who trains hunting dogs? Do you suppose they could hunt a tiger?"

"I don't know, but we'll find out."

David thought there was a possibility and sent out two men with trained beagles.

"Do you have anything with a strong tiger odor?" Roger, the spokesman of the two, asked.

I led them and their dogs into the mud room where the animals sniffed about, and then I took them to Ivan's vacant pen. His blanket, they agreed, reeked of tiger, so they tore off two corners and held a scrap in front of each dog's nose to give them the scent.

"Do you know which direction he took?" Roger asked.

"No, but I'd guess into the woods," I answered.

With a firm grip on his beagle's leash, Roger started for the woods while his teammate, Henry, released his dog and all

four headed out together. I'd thought it best to exclude Kozby
and the other dogs from the proceedings, so Jack and I waited
alone, pacing up and down the patio to vent our frustration.
From our vantage point we could see none of the action, but
from time to time we heard excited yips from the working dogs
as they went about their business. More than an hour went by
before the tracking teams reappeared.

"Red, here," Roger indicated his dog on the leash. "He got
onto the tiger two times, over where there's a big dead tree
down, but I can't let him off the leash. He'd kill the cat. The
other dog won't work this scent at all."

"Are you sure he saw Ivan?" I asked, doubtful but anxious
to latch onto a ray of hope.

"No, I think he did, but I can't be sure. I'll go back and
have another crack at it. Might as well leave the other dog
here, he's not worth a damn on this job."

The second beagle sortie ended on the same note and the
tracking team gave up and left. But I happened to remember
a friend with a talented bird dog and figured we had nothing
to lose with another attempt.

I accompanied Jim Norris and his English setter and pointer,
Mamie, to show them the area where the beagles had demonstrated some interest. Meanwhile, Ed got home and joined
the hunt, the four of us fanning out in different directions to
scour the entire five acres once again. And once again the
results were discouraging, more so because the sun was setting
and darkness would curtail any further activity. The long shad-
ows matched the long faces of the gloomy, weary group that
assembled around the breakfast-room table by a window with
a view of the woods.

"I can think of only one thing to do," I said. "Turn up the

volume on the outside speaker. That's how I found my way back this morning, following the music. Maybe it could help Ivan."

"I've got another idea," Jim said. "The Marion County Sheriff's Department has a team of German shepherds that are supposed to be magnificent. I've never seen them work, but they use them mostly for finding lost children. They don't bark and are quite gentle. Let me see what I can do."

The Marion County sheriff was more than willing to help if we could obtain permission for him to cross over into Hamilton County from the sheriff of that jurisdiction, a technicality that was easily resolved.

"And don't you worry, Mrs. Schaffer," the kind gentleman said when I reported his counterpart's being enthusiastically agreeable. "This is a crack team. If that little tiger hasn't been gone for more than forty-eight hours, we'll find him, you can be sure of that. We'll be there by eight o'clock in the morning."

We were so absorbed in our dealings with the law enforcement agencies we'd forgotten to watch Howard Caldwell's newscast. Ed had asked the Channel Six anchorman to mention Ivan's disappearance on the news, emphasizing the fact the tiger was a mere baby and quite docile. Before the program was over, calls began coming in from every segment of his vast listening audience, all expressing concern and offering to help. We manned our jammed "switchboard," rotating the duty among the four of us, until after midnight when we took the phone off the hook and officially called it a day.

I thought of one other possibility, but its chance of success was remote. Hoping a bouquet of tempting aromas might lure the little cat home, I heaped a plate for Ivan and placed it at the edge of the woods. Then I fell into bed exhausted and emotionally drained to do battle with the demons of the night:

a giant boa constrictor wrapping his clammy body around the cub; a pack of wild dogs mutilating the little cat; Ivan riddled with bullet holes.

Before the sun began to seep through the edges of the night, I went outside with a flashlight to check Ivan's dinner plate. It was untouched. When Ed awoke around five o'clock, Kozby joined us for another tour of the woods that ended with the same discouraging results.

"In that thick vegetation there are hundreds of places to hide," Ed pointed out.

"Why would he want to hide?" I asked.

"He could be frightened. Or he might be asleep, or we might not have come anywhere near him, particularly if he's moving around. The police dogs will find him."

I clung to that hope as a shaky bridge between me and total despair. After taking care of the dogs and all the barn troops, I put the telephone back on the hook and, with another hour to wait for the sheriff, stood aimlessly at the breakfast-room window gazing out toward the woods. When the phone rang, I recognized Joe Pickett's voice on the other end of the line.

Joe Pickett and Glen Webber had an early-morning radio show, a light program of bantering back and forth interspersed with news and music. Occasionally, they did a live interview with someone in the news, maybe a politician in Washington or an obscure citizen in Alaska. I had known Joe for many years, since we were on the staff of WISH-TV together, and being a frequent listener to the program, I was familiar with the format and not surprised by the call.

"Good morning," was Joe's cheery greeting.

"Hi, Joe," I answered despondently.

Five seconds of silence preceded, "How'd you know it was me?"

"It sounds like you."

More silence, then, "Tell me about your lost tiger, Mrs. Schaffer. How long has he been gone?"

Joe's manner indicated he thought he was talking to a stranger.

"It's Moselle, Joe."

"Mo?" he asked, obviously taken aback once again. "No, I had no idea it was you, old buddy. Schaffer was just a name and I didn't connect it with you."

"How did you hear about Ivan?"

"First from Howard's newscast last night and it's in the morning paper. How long has Ivan been gone?"

"Thirty-six hours. At least thirty-six hours since I saw him last. He got out some time during the night, I don't know exactly when."

"Did you—" Joe was in the middle of another question when suddenly there he was, Ivan! Covered from his head to the tip of his tail in a solid cloak of green burrs, he trotted along the patio toward the porch, puh-puh-puh-ing his way across.

"IVAN!" I screamed. "Oh, Joe, there he is!"

With no further word to the startled man, I dropped the telephone, tore outside, and grabbed up the burr-ridden tiger baby in my arms. Although I had stopped even trying to lift him ten pounds ago, I had no trouble that morning. He was as light as a sunbeam. Cheek to cheek, with his arms around my neck, I took him into the mud room, both of us chattering full speed ahead. Ivan was as glad to be home as I was to have him back—almost.

I don't know how much time transpired before I remembered Joe dangling on the line and hurried back to apologize.

"I'm sorry, Joe, please excuse—"

"Did Ivan actually walk in right that minute?"

"Yes, would you—"

"While we were on the air?"

"Yes. I've got to feed him," I answered. "Would you call the Marion County sheriff and tell him Ivan's back?"

"Sure, Mo, but—"

"I've got to go, Joe. Ivan's hungry."

Later on I heard about the conversation that took place on the air while Joe waited for me to return to the telephone. He and Glen discussed the fact nobody would ever believe that the whole episode of Ivan's return hadn't been staged, that he had actually come back at the precise moment when he did. The timing was too perfect to be credible.

Other than being excessively thirsty, Ivan seemed to be no worse off for his misadventure. He wasn't hungry, merely nibbling at his breakfast, but he lapped up a quart of water stopping only for an occasional puh-puh-puh. No scratches or cuts were visible, and no injury of any sort was apparent between the clusters of burrs. But he was extremely tired. His eyelids sagged as he rubbed against me while we conversed, and I removed the tenacious, prickly clumps from his fur. Finally, about an hour later, as I completed the job, he climbed up onto his Barcalounger, curled up into a ball, and dropped off into an exhausted sleep.

Where he had been and what had happened during those traumatic thirty-six hours, nobody ever knew. Except perhaps Kozby. I kissed him on the cheek and slipped quietly out of the room to resume telephone duty. It had been ringing incessantly.

Associated Press, United Press International, and what seemed like every radio, television station, and newspaper in the Western hemisphere wanted to know about Ivan. I don't remember what I said, which was just as well. It must have been absurdly incoherent. I do recall the astonishment in the voice of one reporter when I answered his question matter-of-factly.

"Where is Ivan now?" he asked.

"In his room."

"In his *room*?"

Déjà vu. Ivan was a celebrity again, which bothered him not one whit. But I, as his manager, found my new unsolicited job dreadfully time-consuming. In addition to the telephone calls and the requests to visit—plus the multitudes of droppers-in—there was Ivan's fan mail to answer. One air mail, special delivery letter arrived originally addressed to Ivan Schaffer, Zionsville, Ohio. "Ohio" was scribbled through with a note added, "Try Indiana," that was scratched out in favor of "Try Carmel," and finally altered with "Westfield," which happens to be our mailing address. The journey had been a circuitous one.

There were other more serious by-products of Ivan's thirty-six-hour hiatus, notably Ed's new lecture series. The fiasco of the cage provided him with a new topic.

"Moselle, you need to start thinking about Ivan going back to Robert's. He's outgrowing the mud room and eventually he's going to have to go into a pen."

"I know, I know. But not just yet. He's too little."

"He's getting bigger and more unmanageable every day."

Those facts were hard to dispute, especially when Ivan provided Ed with more ammunition. Concealing three gashes across the top of my hand, courtesy of Ivan, was impossible. Eagle Eye spotted them at fifty paces.

Ivan was fed on Royal Doulton china for practical reasons rather then esthetic ones. I had a few remnants that were discolored from our well water, and although they were un- sightly, they had no chips or cracks and were easy to sterilize in the dishwasher. That is, they had no chips or cracks until one morning when Ivan was overly enthusiastic about his break- fast. He jumped up and, with one well-placed blow, knocked the plate out of my hand and sent it crashing to the floor.

Anxious to retrieve the pieces before he cut his mouth or swallowed a sliver, I was reaching toward a fragment when Ivan lashed out and raked his claws across my hand, leaving his bloody signature indelibly carved in my flesh. I retaliated instantly. Reacting more from surprise and outrage than a desire to correct his table manners, I whacked the little cat on the side of his face and provided him with the shock of his young life. Flabbergasted, he sat back down shaking his head, put his paw up to the spot that had suffered the indignity, and stared at me in disbelief. Then he came over and rubbed against me, offering a series of puh-puh-puh's for an apology. It was the first realistic discipline I'd ever administered, and Ivan took it seriously. We had no more mealtime unpleasantness after that one isolated learning experience.

Ivan was extremely intelligent and quick to learn the bad along with the good. Before we had built the pen, Kozby taught Ivan to chase cars, a sport at which the dog excelled. It was a case of tiger-see-tiger-do, and after only one demonstration by his mentor they became a team, dog and tiger stretched out like greyhounds, racing down the driveway in pursuit of their mechanized quarry.

All things mechanical intrigued Ivan. He loved to climb up on the tractor and the riding lawnmower and hoods of cars— inside them, too, given the opportunity. If we were outside and someone arrived with a window down, they had a tiger in their lap. If he was in the mud room and I started my car, Ivan was at the window furiously trying to gnaw his way through the sill, or what was left of it. With Ivan in residence, the mud room absorbed some severe abuse.

When Ivan was incarcerated there without Kozby, he devoted his time exclusively toward the total destruction of his already disheveled quarters. Systematically, he removed the wooden inserts intended to make one large piece of glass appear to be twelve individual panes and chewed the wood into splinters. To personalize the doors and trim and cabinets, wood he couldn't get his mouth around, he diligently applied his claws. Nor were the walls overlooked. Besides the holes in the plaster caused by the heavy Barcalounger he shoved around, they were generously smeared with egg and Esbilac and chicken and beef, as were the washer and dryer and the now opaque windows. Ivan the demolitionist had no peer.

The bigger he got, the more destructive he became, and the little tiger was growing so fast his weight seemed to surge upward in ten-pound increments. Fifty pounds. Sixty pounds. When he hit the seventy-pound mark, the only thing that delayed his one-way trip to Florida was a series of abscessed teeth. The telltale symptoms—telltale to Robert—were one side of Ivan's face so badly swollen his eye was sealed shut and his inability to eat.

"It's nothing to worry about, tigers get abscesses a lot. Put him on antibiotics and he'll be all right," Robert said.

"He's frisky enough, but he won't eat," I reported. "He pounces on me like he always does, but you should see the surprised look on his face when he tries to bite me. It obviously hurts and he quits immediately, but then he forgets and does it again."

"He probably won't eat for several days, but it won't hurt him. He's plenty fat," Robert said.

Ivan *was* a fat cat. Even his tail was fat, and so long it dragged on the ground. It made a splendid handle, much to his distress, when circumstances called for immediate restraint. Those occasions arose mostly when Koz took a well-deserved breather and I was left to cope with the little cat by myself. The dog still had the upper hand when the tiger got to be twice his size. It took but one sharp rebuke from Kozby to shape Ivan up immediately; one rebuke from me and he did as he pleased.

Ivan's penchant for water was what brought on most of the crises after he got bigger. As a little tyke he loved to splash around in the puddles that collected on the patio after a heavy rain, rolling from one side to the other and pausing for an occasional sip of his environment. When he tired of the aquatics, you could watch him laying out his strategy for the next event on his agenda. Flat on his tummy, his neck extended, and his eyes widened, he flipped his tail back and forth, creating an arc of water with each trip. An instant later, whoever was closest found himself engulfed in a small, water-logged tiger's soggy embrace.

The metal water trough, when he was upgraded to it, was an Olympic-size facility by comparison. It did double duty as a toy chest for a while. Half the new toys acquired from his many visitors ended up in the watery depot, until eventually it became so congested with old hats and bedroom slippers and balls I had to remove the loot to make room for any water—or any tiger.

No such constraints were imposed by the pool of algae-covered stagnant water that ultimately proved to be our Waterloo. Ivan discovered it during his thirty-six hours at large and from then on took every opportunity he could arrange to indulge in its forbidden pleasures. He'd graduated to the big time. If Kozby went AWOL and Ivan got bored with the devilment-in-progress, he dashed for the woods and plunged into the mosquito-infested quagmire while I, still dry at that point, alternately yelled for Koz and pleaded with the wayward tiger.

"Kozby! Kozby! Ivan, please be a good tiger and get out of that awful muck."

Ivan usually did not choose to be a good tiger, he chose to get worse. When I got close enough to snap the leash onto his collar, he dragged me any place he pleased. I, in effect, was the one on the leash.

Just after one of our excursions to and through the marsh, our last one, Ed arrived in time to catch the finale. Propelled by Ivan, I came flying out of the woods, a Jolly Green Giant, panting from the exertion. That in itself was bad enough, but Ivan was prepared for an encore. When I dropped his leash, Ivan scampered ahead a few feet, stopped, turned around, and fixed me with the gaze that telegraphed his intention to "attack." I knew my one hundred pounds was no match for Ivan's eighty pounds, and experience had taught me to sit down quickly before I got knocked down. On that occasion, there was no time. In a demonstration that proved unequivocally that Force equals Mass times Acceleration, he decked me. Ed was appalled.

"I don't know if there's any point in discussing this," he stated calmly. "Ivan's going back to the Compound. You're no match for him. He knows it and I know it. You're the only one who doesn't, and I'm not going to wait around for you to be convinced the hard way."

Ed was right, of course. But that didn't make it any easier. This time the bus was awash in my tears all the way down to Robert's. And all the way back.

SEVENTEEN

Even though the better portion of five states separated us, Ivan was still a large part of my life. Robert and I talked on the telephone several times a week, and I seized every possible opportunity to hit the road or the airways to get down to the Compound. Even when I drove, the nine-hundred-mile trip wasn't drudgery—not with that striped pot of gold at the end of the concrete rainbow. Leaving him was always difficult, but with Ivan in Florida I had a lot more time for the other animals.

As it turned out, they would require a lot more time and attention than anyone could have foreseen. A catastrophe struck in the ice and snow of a brutal December.

I was a sound sleeper. But after being married to a doctor for fifteen years I could answer the telephone, write down a message or relay it verbally, without ever fully regaining consciousness. I was immediately alert, however, when our neighbor across the road sounded the alarm.

"The barn's on fire!" Margaret de Boer shouted into the telephone.

Without stopping to dress, Ed and I grabbed coats and boots and jumped into his car. We could already hear the sirens and see the flashing red lights of the fire trucks as we all converged on the barn in the early-morning darkness. Emergency equipment from three adjacent townships roared into the barnyard, and the firemen leaped from the vehicles, swinging into action before the trucks had come to a full stop. Some wrestled with ladders, others were dragging massive hoses into position. It was organized confusion, pandemonium with a purpose, as the skilled crews coordinated their efforts, shouting to each other over the noisy engines and blaring radios and the powerful jets of water that crashed against the building.

There was no wind, no slight breeze to dissipate the smoke. It hung in huge black lumps that obscured the upper portion of the barn, smoke so thick the high-powered beams of the search lights bounced off its impenetrable walls. To my great relief, one sweep of the maneuverable lights briefly illuminated a part of the pasture where an interested group of animal spectators had gathered to observe the proceedings. Thankfully they had gotten out, but I was frantic about Wayne. Jeannie was out of town, but unless Wayne had an early-morning class, he would have been asleep in the barn apartment when the fire broke out.

Hoping to get to the apartment quicker through the overhead door at the north end of the structure, I ran through the barn; but when I opened the door to the storeroom next to the apartment, I encountered a solid wall of fire. There were no flames, only an orange fireball that enveloped the entire room. Slamming the door shut, I wheeled around, intent on getting out as fast as possible, but already smoke had invaded the inside of the barn. I couldn't breathe. I couldn't see. Blindly running a few steps, I slammed into a wall—but which wall, I had no idea. Nor could I guess which direction led to the only remaining exit. I was completely disoriented. Everything was black. Tangible, three-dimensional black that extended to infinity. At that point I panicked. I didn't know what to do, and to make matters worse, I couldn't decide what to do, I couldn't think.

How long I stood immobilized, I don't know—probably a few seconds before I got a grip on myself. I've got to think, I've *got* to *think*, kept going through my mind.

I ran my hands over the wall, groping for some clue as to my location, and my fingers identified a door latch. That meant I was not inside a stall but still in the barn runway where one of two directions led to the way out. To the right or to the left? With both hands against the wall, I began feeling my way along it and, as the outside voices became louder, I realized my life-or-death guess was the right one. Time, I knew, was running out.

When I staggered outside, choking and gasping for air, I still didn't know if Wayne had gotten out in time.

"Wayne!" I shouted, as soon as I could speak.

"Here. Over here," Wayne's voice came from somewhere in the dark chaos.

I didn't see him until Herman de Boer rounded up Ed and Wayne and me and herded us over to his house when the firemen finished their work. Saving the barn had never been a possibility, not with a loft crammed full of incendiary hay and straw. Containing the fire was all they could hope to accomplish, and that in itself was a major feat. Were it not for those valiant firefighters and Margaret's quick action, it would have been worse.

Fifteen-year-old Margaret was getting ready for school when she saw an unusual glow around the big door at the front of the barn and she wasted no time. In rapid succession she called the fire department, then us, and ran across the road to rouse Wayne. He was in the shower when Margaret's urgent pounding on the apartment door alerted him to the danger. As soon as he jumped into his clothes, he rushed inside the barn and shooed the animals to safety—except for one. Our female zebra, Alice, in a panic I could relate to, refused to budge. Mac became a widower and remained one for three months until Robert could locate another female zebra.

It was a devastating experience for us all, but we had no time for "what if" regrets. There was too much to be done. Even before Ed allowed himself the luxury of a cup of coffee, he was on the telephone contacting prospective builders. Meanwhile, temporary shelter for the animals had to be arranged, and those antics provided some much needed comic relief.

Friends were eager to help and we gladly accepted their assistance. Katie and Merl Sorenson, Dick Herschler, Jack Dellon, and Jim Maloney hurried out to lend a hand. The first order of business was emptying the eighteen-by-thirty-four-foot storage building by the driveway so we could rig it up as makeshift accommodations. Out went the 1956 Ford tractor, tools, fence posts, lumber, and the standard collection of junk one must retain until it rots or rusts and can then be discarded in good conscience. Some of the old fencing and plywood was useful, as was the rope and baling wire that laced everything together. We partitioned the space into one side for the camels, the other for the zebra, with a small "gate" for each "stall" so I could slip in and out sideways to feed them.

Coercing the tenants into their new quarters was our next task, made more difficult by not knowing for certain where one of them was. Marsha and Howard Henderson, owners of the adjacent property, sent word the zebra was in one of their fenced-in pastures, or had been four hours earlier. How to get him back prompted a strategy conference.

"All we need to do is get him headed in this direction and 'spook' him, he'll follow the fence lines," said Dick-the-horseman, whose experience with zebras was limited to treating one sick camel in the same barn.

"It'll work," he continued when nobody said anything. "We'll drive him along the fence down the driveway and open up that pasture gate. Katie and Moselle can stand there in the driveway to block him, so he'll have to turn into the pasture."

"Er, Dick." I had an alternate suggestion, one infinitely preferable to me. "Why don't we just pull a car across the drive?"

"Because he'd probably go right through the car."

"Oh."

"This will work," he persisted.

"Why don't I call Robert? He might have some—"

"Mosie, zebras think like horses, like striped horses," Dick insisted—without citing any authority for that opinion.

The plan went into effect. Fanning out over the Hendersons' pastures after they spotted Mac, individual members of the posse stationed themselves at appropriate intervals to speed the frightened animal onward. Katie and I waited at our designated positions. Having acted alone in my previous roles as a zebra diverter, I thought it might add some small measure of comfort to have a partner in the action. It didn't. It wasn't a matter of diluting the collective anxiety, it was a case of two people independently intimidated waiting side by side for the stampede.

When somebody shouted, "There he comes!" we'd already gotten that news direct from the source and had spontaneously gone into our act, jumping up and down and waving our arms frantically. As the zebra's hooves pounded the asphalt, he streaked down the driveway, skidded to a halt just before he flattened the two raving maniacs in his path, made an abrupt ninety-degree turn right on cue, and entered the pasture. The rest was easy. Using the same fear technique, the rescue squad chased the frightened animal into his new "stall," and I got to perform my other specialty, shoving the sixteen-foot metal door across the entrance before he had time to escape.

The camel caper did not go as well. It developed into a three-hour endurance contest, since nobody knew how to think like a camel . . . not at first. Time and again I lured Reverend and Roxie to the edge of the driveway with a bucket of grain, but that was the end of their forward progress. Each time Rev put two toes of one foot on the hard surface, then quickly retreated, and Roxie was even less adventurous. She accepted Rev's findings without question and kept all four feet planted on familiar territory. Neither one had ever set a pad on an asphalt surface and had no intentions of undertaking so bold a move now.

Their timidity necessitated more haphazard construction. We had to fence off the dangerous debris littering the other side of the barn before we could begin the long detour around it. Sloshing through the ice and snow that had been churned into slush by the heavy fire trucks, we made it to within twenty feet of our destination before Rev balked. Nothing could induce him to go through a three-foot-wide puddle of water ahead of him. Pleading, coaxing, and attempted bribery were all to no avail. So was covering the water with a section of plywood camouflaged with a layer of straw. Reverend refused to budge and it stalled progress for an hour.

"I've got it, I've got it!" Jack cried out excitedly. "He knows the water's there. But we put a pile of straw behind him, he looks back and thinks he's already in the middle of the water, and he wants to get out of it so he goes on through it."

That rationale brought on a chorus of hoots and derisive comments but nobody had any better ideas. Cold and wet and exhausted, we were to the point of trying anything with the remotest possibility of success. And it worked. Cheers went up from our small, weary band as Rev glanced back over his shoulder, noted the straw, and strolled nonchalantly through the puddle that had caused him so much consternation.

The llamas and goats had a small outbuilding for their temporary shelter, but there were still a few more problems to be resolved. Wayne and Jeannie moved into the house with Ed and me, which took care of the most urgent problem, and replacing Wayne's eyeglasses then took on top priority. While he was getting the animals out of the barn, a zebra had kicked him, knocking off the glasses he was wearing and his extra pair went up in flames along with virtually everything else, including his books and notes. Wayne can't read without corrective lenses, and to complicate things, semester finals had just begun. With no precedent for a guideline, I took pen in hand and wrote notes, which Wayne delivered sheepishly, to each of his law-school professors.

Dear Professor:
Please permit Wayne Sturtevant to take his examinations as soon as his glasses are replaced. One pair was

broken when he was kicked by a zebra and the other was destroyed in the barn fire.

Sincerely,
Moselle Schaffer

All four professors were cooperative, and their verdict was unanimous: Wayne's was the most creative excuse they'd been subjected to in all their collective years of teaching.

In the interest of both time and money, we contracted for an unsophisticated "pole barn." Although the new structure lacked the elegance of the old one, nobody cared, certainly not the camels and zebra, who didn't give a fig for the esthetics. After six weeks in their cramped quarters, they would have been happy with a lean-to.

The new barn was more spacious, with extra stalls—for almost a week. Then began the influx, starting with the primate invasion.

A South American couple I knew received a promotion contingent upon a transfer to England, where it was impossible, ostensibly, to take their pair of cottonhead marmosets. Being devoted to their pets, the couple could only accept this opportunity for advancement if they could be certain Flopsy and Mopsy had a happy home. So they said. The fact that this couple has been spotted frequently in Indianapolis and its environs since then makes their story somewhat suspect, but I bought it at the time.

As the term "cottonhead" implies, these small monkeys have a shock of white hair that juts straight up from their scalps and gives them the appearance of being in a perpetual state of fright, which they are. The rest of them is brown, including their furless, wrinkled faces and long, stringy tails. They look like six-inch-tall withered old men. Extremely high-strung, they leaped around their cage chattering excitedly at the slightest disturbance and, like zebras, almost anything disturbed them. But unlike our zebras, they never became friendly.

Here they received almost total privacy, by their choice and mine. In the morning, they got a continental breakfast consisting of monkey biscuits soaked in orange juice and spiked with vitamins. Then I cleaned their cage and checked the temperature to make certain it was the prescribed 75 degrees, and that was it. They didn't see their fellow primate until they received their animated dinner, fresh fruit generously sprinkled with fat, live, wiggly rainbow mealworms. The worms were the *pièce de résistance*. Dextrous little monkey fingers grabbed them by the handful and, chirping with glee, crammed them into their mouths until their cheeks bulged.

Mealworms were the link between the pair of marmosets and the trio of their kinsmen who brought on this plethora of primates. I'd gone to the pet shop for a supply of that popular commodity when the owner beckoned me.

"Come in the back room," Jason said with a grin.

"No, thanks," I declined, suspecting a trap.

"Aw, just for a second." He continued the pressure until I succumbed.

The three monkeys were in separate cages and, with malice aforethought, Jason opened the first door.

"This is Biddy," he said, handing me a cuddly young woolly monkey. "She's shy and very sweet. She loves to snuggle."

Biddy settled down in my arms and gazed dreamily into my eyes, one finger coyly poised on her lower lip.

"And this is Buddy."

Rambunctious Buddy, a capuchin, bounded from his cage to my shoulder where he parked, wrapped his eighteen-inch-long tail around my neck, and began shopping around my scalp for items of interest. Removing Buddy and his itchy tail resulted in his voluntary relocation to my other shoulder.

There was nothing shy about Biddy's brother, Joe Joe. The tallest of the three at two feet, he could reach my coat pockets, and he rummaged around in them claiming everything he found as his own. When I retrieved a package of matches from his mouth, he reacted like a spoiled child, jumping up and down and clicking his teeth together as he shrieked in protest.

"Okay, Jason, they're cute," I said, handing back the drowsy Biddy.

"No, no," he said smugly. "They're yours."

"No, no," I mimicked him. "They're all yours."

"Now, wait a minute, Moselle. Let me explain the situation."

The explanation was handkerchief-wringing material fit for the prime-time soaps. The monkeys belonged to a little old spinster schoolteacher, who at that very moment lay on her deathbed clinging to life in spite of her *dire* pain because of Biddy, Buddy, and Joe Joe. They were the only family she had, and she couldn't let go until she knew they would be cared for.

"All three of them, Jason?" I asked, hoping to strip off a layer of guilt by taking just one of the group.

"All three of them. They're brothers, they can't be separated."

"Brothers? Different breeds and they're brothers?"

"I'll tell Miss Walker she can let go now." He ignored my question and started out the door with one of the cages.

"Do that, Jason."

Flopsy and Mopsy were not happy with their new roommates, and for good reason. The minute I released the new threesome, they zeroed in on the marmosets and clambered all over the cage, poked their fingers through the mesh to steal food, and so unnerved the little guys that they huddled in first one corner and then another to escape the terrorists.

The newcomers' diet was much the same as the marmosets', with the addition of shredded lettuce and hard-boiled eggs. They were given their own rations of mealworms, but they arranged for additional supplies, the ones delivered to Flopsy and Mopsy. I caught Joe Joe committing the felony. He crawled up under the marmosets' cage, reached through the mesh, flipped over the saucer, and he and his two confederates gobbled up the additional shower of mealworms. Having the five together was an unsatisfactory arrangement, but that was the only heated, enclosed stall, and it made an ideally spacious cage for the active acrobats. Biddy, Buddy, and Joe Joe would settle down, I figured, as soon as they got used to their new domicile.

What I never have figured in retrospect is how I could have been so deluded.

The monkeys' new next-door neighbor was docile by comparison but, short of a bull elephant in rut, anybody would be. When our friends Katie and Merl decided they had to have a pair of kangaroos, the restrictive covenants in their residential area presented something of a stumbling block, although kangaroos per se were not excluded. Fences were prohibited and pets allowed outdoors had to be leashed at all times. Envisioning a few problems when the "big reds" reached their seven-foot heights, Katie and Merl elected to board the "Australian rabbits" at Camel Lot.

None of us knew much about "roos," so I did some research on the species. The embryo has a thirty-eight- to forty-two-day gestation period in the mother's uterus, after which the baby, about the size of a pinto bean and weighing one gram, magically appears in Mama's pouch. For years, scientists disagreed on how the youngster arrived at that destination and there were four schools of thought. One contended it was placed there by the mother, using her lips as the vehicle; another maintained the hand was the transportation. Some naïve soul who doubtless flunked anatomy decided the baby was born through the mother's nipple. The theory given the most credence was the mama roo's licking a path on her stomach to provide a roadmap for the newborn's first journey.

Only recently have zoologists definitely established the method by which the "joey" manages the three-minute trek from the uterus to the pouch, which is actually an open womb. The little guy climbs unassisted through the fur up his mother's middle. Although his head, tail, and rear legs are not fully developed at that time, the arms are strong—complete with claws—and the jaw muscles and tongue are functional. Having nostrils quite large in proportion to the rest of him, it is presumed the joey's sense of smell aids his navigation. The mother, busy cleaning herself up after the birth, licks herself and in so doing sometimes licks ahead of the baby's path, providing unintentional assistance.

Once inside the pouch, which serves the same function as an incubator for a premature birth, the baby attaches his lips to one of four 1- to 1½-inch-long nipples, and there he remains. Because of special breathing passages peculiar to his anatomy, he can nurse and breathe simultaneously as the milk is squirted into his mouth by rhythmic contractions of the mother's mammary muscles. The reason for his having to move to the new location is that Mama can get but a limited amount of oxygen and nourishment to the fetus while inside the crowded uterus.

Mother kangaroos are meticulous housekeepers, and the pouch is cleaned daily while the joey is in residence. It's actually a matter of necessity, since as soon as the baby is on solid food he develops the messy habit of snacking on hay— the kangaroo equivalent of eating crackers in bed. Joey becomes a real pain in the pouch for Mama K. before the 190 days are up and he goes on his first outing.

Another unique feature of the versatile pouch is a "rubber" ring around the edge composed mainly of sphincter muscles that enables the mother to open and close the "crib" at will. Mama is standing by with the "door" fully expanded when Junior solos. At the first hint of trouble, Junior hightails it back, dives in head first, and turns a somersault to right himself; Mama contracts the muscles and the babe is tucked safely away. At twelve or thirteen pounds, when he comes hurtling back to his refuge, it gets to be a real jolt for his patient mom. Understandably, if he hasn't departed for good at the end of 235 days, she begins eviction proceedings. She relaxes her muscles, leans over, and the hefty baby tumbles out onto the ground. Joey's joy ride is over.

For approximately eighteen months, the offspring is known as a "joey at heel," never leaving the presence of his mother. When he grows older, he's a "young at heel." The baby rarely strays far, but when he does, he is recalled by his mother's soft, sucking noises, the language of love. Kangaroos have no voice, hence they express feelings of pleasure in that manner. A harsh coughing sound indicates the situation is not quite kosher and steps are underway to put it right. A bad cough is bad news.

Finally, the youngster grows up and is identified as a "doe" or a "buck" for the mature years. There are no terms for a female senior citizen, but when a buck gets a little age on him he's referred to as a "boomer." That's roo-ese for "dirty old man."

Expecting a "big red" to be red, I was surprised when we opened the crate and out bounced a fifty-pound, gray-colored joey about three feet tall. He reared back on his stalwart tail, rocking to and fro, and eyed the four of us, Katie, Merl, Ed, and me, with a singular lack of concern. For one who had just completed a long, cramped flight from Oklahoma, the animal was amazingly calm.

Anxious for us to become friends, I established a daily routine designed to win Harvey's confidence. Each time I went into his stall I curried favor with an irresistible Seasoned Ry-Krisp. At first I had to extend the cracker at arm's length, and Harvey, neck outstretched, grabbed a quick bite before taking off for a brisk thump, thump, thump around his stall. Little by little he came closer, and eventually he was waiting by the door for me—or more than likely for the cracker. Very gently, he took my hand and held it between his two paws, nibbling away with his small Bugs Bunny–type teeth. Eventually he became daring and allowed me to stroke his soft velvety fur, but only his back, not his sides. I think Harvey was ticklish.

Harvey wasn't bright. In fact, it would be impossible to underestimate his I.Q. That was no handicap for Harv, how-ever, only for me. It took me three days to teach my backward student how to return to his stall from his outdoor playground, a fenced-in area adjacent to his quarters. Harv simply couldn't master the rudiments of going back through the same door he had come out of. Down on my hands and knees I crawled—in and out, in and out—until Harv finally got the hang of it.

Robert was scouring the country for a female kangaroo, but meanwhile, concerned about Harvey's lack of companionship,

I experimented. My first choice for a roommate, a young kitten, had Harvey rocketing around the room in a frenzy, but a two-month-old goat met with his approval. It was a huge hit with the little kid as well. The posh garden apartment with the wall-to-wall sawdust carpeting and reliable room service appealed to Walter's taste for high living.

Goat and roo became devoted friends, sleeping side by side and simultaneously eating and drinking from the same dishes. The only friction occurred whenever Walter tried to snatch Harv's Ry-Krisp from him. That displeased Harvey, and he either gave the offender an effective shove or placed his paws on either side of Walter's neck and shook him.

Harvey had built-in entertainment when Walter got tall enough to jump up on the big wooden box that served as the kangaroo's hideaway. Walter danced, gyrating and pirouetting with a discernible rhythm, while his appreciative audience sat back quietly and gazed transfixed. When Harvey tired of the one-man show, he rang down the curtain by pushing the performer off the stage and rolling him around in the sawdust and occasionally—an added insult—tugging on Walter's short, wiggly tail.

After four or five months of their close association, there were a couple of developments I feared might give rise to psychiatric problems somewhere down the line. Walter began spending half the day staggering around drunkenly on his two hind legs trying to imitate his big friend's modus operandi. The second difficulty was of a more delicate nature. I caught Harvey making improper advances to the little goat and Walter struggling to escape the unwanted attention. Harvey, I'm afraid, had fallen in love.

EIGHTEEN

It had been six months since I'd seen Ivan. With the barn rebuilding plus getting the new animals acclimated, it was impossible to get to Florida, and I was afraid my little cat had forgotten me. But Ivan's greeting, his high-pitched bird-chirping sounds of delight, quickly allayed my fears. I slipped one hand under the gate, placing it flat on the floor of his pen, and he covered it with a large paw. Repeatedly stacking a hand and a paw one on top of the other was a game of ours, and Ivan hadn't forgotten that either—or the all-important rule of keeping his claws sheathed.

My "little" tiger was over two hundred pounds, and I was no longer allowed to go into his cage without Robert, but we were having a splendid visit nonetheless. Then I answered the telephone. It was a call from a zoo in California and Ivan was the subject of the ensuing conversation between Robert and the zoo director.

"No question about it, Ivan is the most perfect specimen I've ever seen," Robert informed the man. "Yes, I can ship him within the next thirty days. . . ."

That's all I heard before I grabbed the phone out of Robert's hand and rudely interrupted the negotiations. "Ivan is not for sale. Not now and not ever. I hope I'm making that unmistakably clear," I said and rushed out of the room.

"Mosie, you can visit him in California." Robert tried to console me.

"No, I can't. And you gave Ivan to me. Remember?"

"Yes, of course. And you gave him back. Remember that?"

"Yes, but it was for Ivan's good. We didn't have a large-animal vet then or the facilities for a big cat."

"And you still don't have the facility."

"No, but we will. We'll build a place for him. Can I have him back?"

"Certainly."

"Promise?"

"I promise."

For the first time I could remember I was eager to leave the Compound. Building a suitable place for Ivan would require a great deal of work and I was anxious to get him home for good as quickly as possible. It had been a close call and some other unforeseen development could whisk my precious tiger out of my life forever.

"Open your suitcase," Robert said as I was leaving. "I have a present for you. Here are two ostrich eggs. They may not be fertile, but I think they are. See if you can hatch them."

"How?"

"As soon as you get home, maintain them at a constant one hundred degrees and turn them a quarter turn every four hours for thirty-nine days. Stop turning them on the fortieth. They should hatch, if they're going to, on the forty-second day. Be careful they don't get broken on the way home."

With little confidence that any feathered creatures would emerge from those portable wombs, I set about the hatching farce with a notable lack of enthusiasm. First, I tried a heating pad, but the temperature was impossible to regulate, surging to 100 degrees and then dropping to 85. An improvised heat lamp was more consistent: I covered the metal skeleton of an old lamp with heavy-duty aluminum foil and clipped it to a shelf in the guest-room closet so it dangled upside down. Experimenting with different bulbs and adjusting the contraption's height, I finally settled on a hundred-watt General Electric light bulb suspended about two feet over the "incubator"—a cardboard box lined with bath towels. Plus or minus 5 degrees, the temperature hovered about 100 degrees.

I did turn the eggs but only from a feeling of obligation, as if I'd be an accessory to murder should I fail to jostle those pockmarked calcium containers at the prescribed four-hour intervals. No sense of anticipation guided my footsteps to the guest-room closet, not when there was an exciting project to lure me to the backyard. Construction was underway on Ivan's new domicile, a much more secure one than our original effort that Ivan had tested and found wanting.

There was a great deal of emphasis on the strength and height of the fencing, even though Ivan had outgrown the tiger climbing phase. Superior Fencing set two-inch metal posts into three-foot poured concrete supports before stretching the heavy-gauge cyclone fencing around the thirty-by-sixty-foot playground. It was a comfort to have professionals in charge of the outer defenses. When it came to the prospect of chasing an AWOL tiger, I had a long memory.

The rest of the work force was skilled labor, too, but friends whose skills lay elsewhere. At times, the cast looked like "Our Gang" comedy as thumbs were smashed or two roofers working in opposite directions staged head-on collisions. Understandably, progress was slow.

Meanwhile, back in the guest-room closet, there was no action at all. On the forty-first day of the haphazard incubation, I checked on the ostrich eggs only once, having been relieved of the rotating duty. The following day it was early afternoon before I remembered to look in on them, expecting more of the same—nothing. But a wave of goose pimples broke out all over me when I observed activity in one of the eggs. A jagged hole about the size of a half dollar had appeared. To get a closer look, I knelt down and detected two little red specks, two small "ruby chips" I assumed to be eyes. Unprepared for this blessed event, I hurried to the telephone to get instructions from Robert.

Robert was ecstatic. "This is really something. It must be a zoological first. I can't get over it—this is really something!"

"That's all fine, but what do I do?"

"Wait for two hours. Then if the bird hasn't gotten out by himself, help him out. Crack the shell and peel back the membrane, but don't use any tools—you might injure him. If he's positioned correctly, he'll be rolled up in a ball with his beak next to his feet. Be sure to call me afterward."

I paced nervously, hoping my crash course in ostrich obstetrics would not be put through a rigorous exam. But at the end of the two hours allotted for labor there was no discernible progress in the birthing process. I scrubbed for delivery.

Ostrich shells are a brittle porcelain type of substance, about a sixteenth of an inch thick, that snapped with a loud crack each time I broke off a fragment. The almost-bird flinched, I flinched, and then I paused for a minute until both the infant and his obstetrician regained some degree of composure. Following Robert's instructions, I peeled the membrane with my fingernails—until I ripped off a section with some feathers still attached and decided to disregard my orders. A slightly wounded fowl seemed a better risk than a bald one, so I opted for a pair of manicure scissors for snipping the tenacious covering. It was similar to the membrane of a standard chicken egg, only thicker and stronger. The shell itself weighed three pounds with the embryo still inside and was about the size of a small football, approximately eight inches long and six inches in diameter. I peeled and peeped, peeled and peeped, and halfway through the ordeal was relieved to note the bird's proper, if uncomfortable, position of nose to toes.

Transition from potential omelette to full-fledged ostrich took over an hour, at which point an awkward, wet bird rose to his feet, shook himself, and looked me over briefly. Then, staggering forward so rapidly I thought he'd topple on his face, he covered the length of the closet—about twelve feet—and smacked into the closed door. When he turned around he simply stood there, wobbling on two spindly little drumsticks as he stared at me, and I stared back. What had been a dormant glob encased in crockery was transformed into a living, breathing wonder of nature thrust into the great adventure of life. I was awestruck.

This method of birth has it all over the delivery system the stork devised for human babes. Mama O. never had the first twinge of a labor pain. Nor would she have had any immediate responsibility had she been on hand after the birthing. In a remarkable demonstration of advanced planning, the newborn ostrich arrives with his own supply of nourishment and is quite self-sufficient for the first three days in his new environment. In Watts's case, that feature was especially practical since I, a Doubting Thomas disciple, had laid in no provisions for this unexpected guest.

As Watts and I continued to scrutinize one another, I discovered the two red dots I had mistakenly identified as eyes were actually his nostrils. His eyes were brown, surrounded with long, curled eyelashes, and the two small round holes on either side of his head were ears. Covering the one-pound bird's body was a mixture of soft tan and brown underfeathers topped with bristly white quills—except for his bottom. The most amazing thing about the ostrich, other than his having been hatched at all, was his bare bottom. Not one single feather decorated his derriere.

After twenty-four hours, there were no developments with the other egg, so I acted on Robert's advice and investigated. With a small tack hammer I gave the shell a series of delicate taps that produced no results, followed by one healthy blow that brought on instant, catastrophic results. The rotten egg cracked into two jagged pieces and the overpowering stench that engulfed Watts and me left both of us gasping for air.

Shoving the pieces back together as best I could, I ran out of the house with the dripping disaster, heaved it into the woods, and watched it splatter against a tree. "All the king's horses and all the king's men" wouldn't be able to put that fiasco together again either, not unless they'd improved a whole lot since Humpty Dumpty's fatal accident.

After Watts used up the three days' worth of groceries he'd brought along, I prepared the elaborate smorgasbord Robert recommended for him: one hard-boiled egg yolk, grated; one teaspoon each of Alpo dog food and ground oyster shells; two tablespoons of dry oatmeal; some finely chopped raw green pepper, cucumber, green beans, and lettuce; a bit of freshly clipped grass; and a smattering of construction gravel. The last item was donated by a local builder, although the donor was unaware of his dark-of-night contribution.

Sprinkling each separate dab with manganese dioxide—a trace mineral to help prevent perosis—gave the food an unappetizing gray cast that could discourage even the hardiest of gluttons, and it discouraged Watts. He turned up his beak at everything but the grass and ate that only if I hand fed him blade after monotonous blade.

"He doesn't have anybody to learn from. Get another, more mature bird and put them together," was Robert's analysis and solution.

I thought of Watts as a "he," but there is no simple way to determine the sex of an ostrich until it matures, at which time the males turn black. Some experts can distinguish between males and females, taking specific measurements, and also with chromosome tests, but the most accurate method requires surgery in order to check the bird's gonads. That drastic procedure was hardly warranted, since "he" needed a teacher, not a spouse, so I bought a white leghorn hen and hoped Annabelle also had the maternal instincts attributed to mother hens in general.

Watts was an apt student. After Annabelle taught him how to run through their plate of food and kick the contents onto the carpet, he did a commendable imitation of her pecking lunch up off the floor. His unkempt appearance he must have come by on his own, since Annabelle was respectable looking after a meal and Watts was invariably a mess. In addition to the crud he managed to smear all over himself, his beak was gummed up with a mishmash of everything he'd taken in and not quite gotten down his gullet. Always there was a scrap of cucumber rind or green bean protruding from the side of his face that gave him a rakish, smart-alecky look.

The china I used for the Ostrich Hilton's room service was the same Royal Doulton that had done tiger duty, and it also doubled as Watts's bed. Not for him the cardboard box lined with soft towels where he spent the forty-two days prior to hatching. He preferred a hard, shiny dinner plate for sleeping. It was a spartan choice from my point of view, but there's no accounting for taste. What can you expect when your mother's a one-hundred-watt General Electric light bulb?

A closet barnyard has more drawbacks than meet the eye. One of them meets the nose—with a wallop. The birds resisted my efforts at paper training and, with the stepped-up production upon Annabelle's arrival, the guest room as well as the closet became offensively pungent in ten days' time. It was fowl in every sense of the word.

In spite of Watts's haphazard hatching, he was doing so well I was reluctant to rock the boat, but he did need fresh air. So did we. It required no persuasion whatsoever to get a stall remodeled so Watts and Annabelle could have a secure paddock right outside the barn with those congenial herbivores for neighbors, Harvey and Walter. Ed and the tiger-pen crew temporarily diverted efforts from their major project to make the essential modifications. It only usurped one Sunday afternoon and then they were back sloshing around in concrete as they poured the floors for Ivan's and a girl friend's side-by-side condominiums and stacked the concrete blocks that formed the walls.

The construction team was diligent and dedicated, but each

member's time constraints, plus amateur standing in a new field of endeavor, precluded any records being set, except perhaps for bruises and abrasions. Wayne had the most experience and that wasn't much. One of his part-time jobs wedged in between classes was that of apprentice carpenter. Ed was titular foreman, but his medical practice demanded more and more of his time, so the foreman-in-fact was whoever happened to get to the job site first. I was not conscripted. To the contrary, nobody trusted me with a hammer, so my duties, by popular demand, consisted of running out for more nails and staying clear of the four-by-fours being heaved about.

Ken Kawata, a curator of the Indianapolis Zoo, acted as a consultant and came out often to recommend a change here, an addition there, and collectively we could think of nothing that had been overlooked. Almost four months after the project got off the drawing boards we were down to the finishing touches. Ed and Merl were putting on the exterior veneer and, in deference to Ivan's eardrums, Jack Dellon was oiling all the gates and other moving metal parts; there are no abrasive scraping noises in the wild. Completing their custom-built chaise longue for Ivan's catnaps, Wayne and Jack Owen were sanding away at the huge wooden contraption. No tiger tenement this.

Then came a jolt that sent me reeling and caused the conscientious construction gang to lay aside their tools dejectedly. Ivan was desperately ill. Using a new drug, Robert had wormed four tigers, and three of them were dead. Ivan was comatose, responding to nothing.

"Could you get hold of that veterinarian you think so much of and have him call me immediately?" Robert asked.

I conveyed the alarming news to Dick Herschler, who promised to get back to me as soon as he had talked with Robert.

"Mosie, we need all the expert advice we can get," Dick reported. "I'm going to call Merck Laboratories."

"They aren't the pharmaceutical company that made the drug," I told him.

"I know. But they have top-notch veterinary medicine specialists."

Dick set up a three-way conference call and, with Robert supplying the symptoms, Dick and the Merck doctors combined their expertise to map out a course of treatment for Ivan. Theirs was a formidable undertaking. Not one of them had ever treated a tiger and being unable to examine the patient was an additional handicap, but they tackled the problem without hesitancy. We could only hope and pray that it was possible to counteract the effects of the lethal drug.

It was late afternoon when Robert informed us that all the doctors' recommendations had been carried out, but there was no change in Ivan's condition.

"I'm coming down, Robert," I told him.

"*No!* I don't want you here. There's absolutely nothing you can do for the tiger. Everything that *can* be done is being done. Ivan's unconscious, Mosie. It would only distress you to see him this way. Don't come down here!"

Robert's insistence on my staying put reduced my choices to one, the telephone vigil, with which I'd had far too much experience. Two excruciatingly long days went by before Ivan began to respond slightly, then three more with no further improvement. In frequent contact with Robert, the little cat's far-flung medical team made continual adjustments, modifying a dosage or changing a drug and, after a week, Ivan began to show marked progress. But it was almost a month before I quit bombarding heaven with my tearful entreaties and switched to calmer prayers of thanksgiving.

It was yet another month before Robert allowed me visitation privileges. With my first glimpse of Ivan I could understand why. His battle for survival left him frail and emaciated and I readily agreed his move to Indiana should be postponed. The trip itself would be stressful, and with winter approaching the drastic change in climate would be an additional shock to his system. Ivan would not be home until spring.

Unwilling to risk a cold snap during Indiana's predictably unpredictable early spring, we waited until late May for the big move. Ed and Merl flew to Florida, rented a truck, and with their enraged passenger confined in a big circus cage in the back, headed north. At every weigh station they presented the documents listing their cargo as one four-hundred-pound Siberian tiger, an unnecessary formality under the circumstances. Ivan assured everybody within a two-mile radius there was one disgruntled cat on board.

Only once did Ivan's chauffeurs have to introduce him as evidence. Outside of Atlanta at 2:00 A.M. when Merl was pulled over for running a red light, he gave the policeman an honest excuse for his offense: "I'm sorry, officer, I didn't want to slam on the brakes because of the tiger in the back. I was afraid he might get hurt."

"I see. And what else do you have back there, a dinosaur maybe?" the officer asked sarcastically.

"I'll show you," Merl replied, anticipating events to unfold exactly as they did when he raised the rear door.

All that could be seen of Ivan was two golden eyes glaring hostilely out of the darkness, but the Siberian roar that assaulted the policeman's eardrums was unmistakable. The officer's sarcasm was gone, and probably his voice, too. Without a word—no threat, no lecture, no comment—he indicated with one authoritative gesture that the truck should proceed with all deliberate speed.

That image, still foremost in Merl's mind, prompted him to warn me when he and Ed pulled into our driveway later that same morning. "Don't go near Ivan," Merl shouted as the truck rolled to a stop. "He can reach out between those bars at least eighteen inches, and that cat's so damn mad he could kill you!"

I climbed up into the back of the vehicle, and before I could say a word my docile pussycat greeted me with his familiar chirping sounds followed by "Puh-puh-puh, puh-puh-puh," and I knew his wrath didn't include me. Slowly, nonetheless, I approached the cage and slid one hand in on the floor. It was covered immediately by a giant paw, and then I got a lick on the cheek from that rough sawblade of a tongue.

Herman de Boer and another neighbor, Ken Rust, came over, and with the aid of a block and tackle the four men maneuvered the crate and Ivan emerged, slowly surveying his surroundings as he sauntered around. The tiger went over every inch of his property, sniffing, pawing, rubbing against the fence, and marking his territory with spurts of urine. Then he lay down, crossed his arms, and looked casually around at the scenery. Ivan was home at last.

Envisioning a joyous reunion similar to my own, I'd confined Kozby to make certain he'd be on hand to greet his old friend. But Koz was a dud as a member of the welcoming committee. He took one brief look at the four-hundred-pound tiger, streaked off with his tail between his legs, and we didn't see him for three days.

Although Ivan was not exactly friendly to the men he knew well and saw frequently, he managed to be fairly civil—at first. But as his dislike for men gradually escalated into a phobia, there were no exceptions. Ed and Merl and Wayne were *persona non grata* along with anyone else who was masculine.

A few months later, when Ivan's roommate joined him, she was pleasant and agreeable to male and female alike, but he soon put a stop to that. In a matter of weeks she was hurling her four-hundred-fifty-pound frame against the fence right alongside her mentor. Deutchka, Russian for "little sweetheart," remained just that as far as women were concerned, but like Ivan, she made no secret of her antipathy for the opposite sex. Even so, she couldn't match his awesome display of hostility. Deutchka was one year older, but Ivan rapidly outgrew her in size and at five years of age, when she was a relatively wee 550 pounds, Ivan bordered on 700.

When Charles Frace, the noted wildlife artist, wanted to do a portrait of Ivan, I warned him what to expect. Unless he painted with the rapid, choppy brushstrokes of a Goya, it would be difficult. Charles ended up using a telephoto lens to snap hundreds of photographs of Ivan and used them to work from. Frace's painting understandably depicts Ivan with his serious, all-business look.

Nancy Noel, another outstanding artist, spent hours socializing with the tigers, and the cats reveled in the attention. Consequently, the Ivan emerging from Nancy's canvas is a pussycat with never an aggressive thought to cloud his countenance.

Although the other animals were popular subjects for both canvas and film, they all played second fiddle to Ivan, as did even Deutchka. In descending order of popularity, they ranked: tigers, zebras, camels, llamas, kangaroo, monkeys, ostrich, and goats. Babies, any babies, were exceptions to the rule. Regardless of the species, they became favorites and *always* there were new little pygmy goats to fill the bill. With their prolific breeding tendencies, the population of Camel Lot varied from week to week.

Whoever coined the phrase "breed like rabbits" was obviously unfamiliar with goats. They are stellar producers. It requires only 151 days from the assignation to the inevitable, and then the cycle repeats itself. Our herd of five doubled in size almost as soon as they jumped off the truck, when we were blessed with two sets of twins, about as commonplace as single births.

The kids are adorable, unique little creatures and amazingly precocious. They're vociferous and alert with their eyes wide open immediately after they're born; only the horns are missing to distinguish them from their mature counterparts. Springing around like small wind-up toys, they pause only to sleep or to fall down on their knees to take nourishment from the mother. Within one week's time, they're supplementing Mama's milk with solid nourishment, and in six weeks they're weaned.

Female goats are the victims of a bad rap. Nanny goats don't smell bad. The same cannot be said of the opposite sex, however. Billy goats urinate on their legs and, if for no other reason, are decidedly rank. One of our guys, Grumpy, turned that unfortunate habit into a full-time hobby, with people as his targets. He'd run over as fast as his stubby little legs could carry him, plant his two front feet on his victim's thigh, and drench them. Man or woman, large or small, it made no difference to Grump. He was afraid of nobody, except Ivan, which led me to believe he had more sense than he sometimes demonstrated.

NINETEEN

Camel Lot's census underwent its most drastic change when my husband and I came to a parting of the ways. As Ed's medical practice grew, it became ever more time-consuming and our interests veered off in opposite directions. Little by little, we drifted apart. Ours was a marriage that gradually eroded, and almost twenty years after we'd skipped down the aisle together, we were no longer in step with each other.

There is no ideal season for divorce with its inevitable mental and emotional turmoil, but there is a worst possible time of year. Winter. Winter at Camel Lot is an ongoing battle for survival. When the temperature drops to 20 degrees below zero and an icy wind snarls across the snow-covered fields, the chill factor can plunge to 85 degrees below zero, a brutal cold that

causes frostbite—or worse. Adding to the misery index is the
blowing snow that collects in four- and five-foot drifts, mon-
uments to adversity that turn my pilgrimages to the animals
into white nightmares.

Although the tigers are only fifty feet from the house, the
journey down that thirty-five-degree incline takes on shades of
an arctic expedition when everything is parallel to the ground—
the blinding snow, the trees bowing in submission, and me
alternately face down or flat on my back when I slip on the
treacherous ice. In addition to resembling a defensive tackle
for the Indianapolis Colts with all my cumbersome clothing, I
am juggling two trays of food that weigh at least twenty pounds
each, and every time I fall the meat is strewn about in a five-
foot radius. The landscape looks like the site of a full-scale
battle, Bull Run on the morning after.

The hungry cats, whose appetites escalate in inverse proportion to the temperature, race back and forth impatiently
while they watch my clumsy performance. When I finally step
inside their shelter, they're waiting for me, whiskers sheathed
in ice from the condensation of their warm breath and a mantle
of snow covering them from their heads to the tips of their
tails. Ivan, exasperated with the slowness of his inept waitress,
takes matters into his own paws as soon as I set down his tray.
He reaches out through the five-inch opening, hooks his claws
on the metal rim of the tray, and gives the dish one swift jerk
so it slides all the way across the floor of his condominium
well out of my reach.

This means in order to retrieve it I will have to confine the
tigers in the other pen, an ordinarily simple task turned formidable in this the era of the ice age. The cables that control
the guillotine doors are frozen into immobility, as are all the
locks and chains and, short of a blowtorch, nothing will thaw

them but hot water. Another struggle up to the house and schussing down the perilous slope again is in store for me. Then there's a third round trip to procure the cats' drinking water after I chisel their dishes loose from the concrete to which they're frozen.

Once the tigers are squared away, it's time to tend to the barn contingent, a chore I postpone until I check the weather forecast for the fifth or sixth time that morning. It's a delaying tactic, all that lies between me and the next battle against the powerful forces in nature's conspiracy. One lane of the frontage road, plowed by the county, is usable, but no vehicle can make it down the driveway until a front-end loader dips the snow bucket by bucket and dumps it over the efficient fences that retain each flake that lands there. Until then, sometimes for several days, each harrowing excursion to the barn is made on foot. Hanging on to the fence when I can find it and struggling through and around the drifts, the quarter-mile distance takes an exhausting hour or more to negotiate one way.

The barn troops, bored and restless in their confinement, clamor for attention, and I employ the squeaky-wheel approach, catering first to the most obstreperous ones, the goats. A handout of Seasoned Ry-Krisps keeps them in line until I can serve their entrée. Like Charlie Lama's whip, Seasoned Ry-Krisps are standard equipment. Since all the herbivores are hooked on them, I always have a pocketful of "crisis crackers," an infallible bribe that lures any animal anywhere I need to move him or her.

Drinking water for the animals is a cold-weather problem that intensifies when a blizzard rages. The stubborn pump handle becomes next to impossible to budge and wrestling with it once brought on the severe chest pains of a "heart attack" that prompted an emergency visit to my doctor, Fred Hendricks.

"I don't know what in the world you've been doing that could cause a sprained chest." Fred laughed as he brushed aside my diagnosis. "The cure is simple, though. Stop doing it."

His prescription worked—until the next blast of arctic weather. Samuel Coleridge once asked, "When winter comes can spring be far behind?" Yes.

During my first winter as Camel Lot's lone caretaker, lessons were plentiful. I had a chance to learn one of them over and over again: Always expect the unexpected.

Roxie was behaving strangely. Although the temperature was a comfortable 40 degrees and the other animals frolicked in the pastures, the camel was in her stall performing some weird sort of dance I'd never seen before. With her nose about two inches from the blank wall she faced, she swayed from side to side, lifting first one front foot and then the other in a distinct rhythm. Her tail was raised and in her rectum was a dark, round "marble" that appeared to be stuck. I watched her for a while, waiting for the collection of marbles to tumble out in a normal bowel movement, but nothing happened.

An hour later when I checked on her there was no change in the dance routine and no progress on the part of the marble. She was obviously feeling all right so I didn't call the vet. Dick Herschler, Supervet I, had moved to California, but I had lucked into another superb veterinarian, Don Steen, who had also become a good friend. Instead of soliciting Don's advice, I pondered on the problem and concluded Rox was constipated. And what could be better for a common malady than a common cure? I fed her an entire box of seedless prunes. Twenty-four hours later Roxie was no longer constipated and no longer pregnant.

Over a year before, I'd observed some hanky-panky, a commotion of riot proportions as Rev, swinging his powerful neck, knocked Roxie to the ground and forced his attentions on her. Excited over the prospects of a baby, I kept a close watch on Rox, but after eleven or twelve months gave up hope. I didn't expect to pinpoint a natal day, since experts' estimates of a dromedary's gestation period range from 360 to 420 days. Nor did I expect to detect a seventy-five-pound bulge—less than five percent of the mother's body weight—but I did anticipate some indication of pregnancy.

When that "indication" appeared, it was a wet, forlorn-looking little waif huddled in the corner, rejected by the mother who had just brought it into the world. Each time the newborn staggered to its feet and approached Rox, it was met with a forceful kick that catapulted it across the stall back to the same corner it had left only seconds earlier.

Before I called the vet, I dried the baby with towels and covered it with a blanket, hoping Roxie wouldn't consider my actions an affront to her motherhood. She didn't. A far cry from the usually doting camel mother, she couldn't have cared less.

"Go ahead and milk Roxie and feed the baby," were Don's instructions.

Milk Roxie!

"But Don I—"

"I'll get there as soon as I can, but it's important to get some milk and some colostrum into the baby right away," he cautioned.

Go ahead and milk Roxie. That's what the man said. Just like that. Luckily, it was early enough to get Wayne on the telephone before he left to pursue his law practice. I had something else for him to pursue.

"Do you know how to milk a camel?" I asked, without any preliminaries.

There was a short pause before he answered, "No. Are you asking merely out of curiosity, or am I about to learn?"

A few minutes later, Wayne and I squatted down on either side of Roxie with a bucket on the floor between us. Peering under the camel's gargantuan belly, our eyes met for a second, but neither of us spoke. I was glad Wayne didn't. He is a low-key, soft-spoken man, except on the rare occasions when he's exasperated—and I thought this just might be one of those occasions.

Finally I said what was foremost in both our minds. "You know we're going to get our brains bashed in, don't you?"

Wayne didn't answer. A study in concentration, he began to pull on one of Roxie's teats, and a thin stream of milk zipped into the bucket. Here it comes, I thought, Roxie's going to let us have it now. But she didn't. She turned her head, glanced casually at Wayne and, instead of decapitating him, stuck her head back into the feed bucket to resume her munching.

"How are you doing that?" I asked, impressed by Wayne's success.

"Just like I've seen in the movies," the attorney replied.

Observing him carefully, I tried to imitate his technique, but not so much as a squirt came from my efforts. When I switched to the other teat, the results were the same.

"I think I'm doing it like you are but I'm not getting anything," I commented, continuing to tug as hard as I dared.

Wayne was so absorbed in the task in hand he said nothing, and we both worked away steadily for twenty minutes before there was a cupful in the bottom of the pail. During the whole ordeal Roxie remained calm and cooperative—why, we could only guess. She may have been so uncomfortable from the excess milk she welcomed the relief; or she may have figured if she kicked up a ruckus the two clods trying to get milk would most likely ruin her. Whatever her reasons, her mood changed radically when Don hove on the scene.

"Look!" I said, proudly displaying the fruits of Wayne's labor.

"For God's sake, is that all you've got?" Don answered disdainfully. "Let an old farm boy show you how to do it. Moselle, get me a pail of hot water."

Wayne and I were ignorant of such fine points as warming the hands to keep icy shock waves from surging through the milkee. Not so our man of experience. He rolled up his sleeves and dipped his hands in the water, but as soon as he applied his properly warmed appendages to Roxie's appropriate appendages the rhubarb was on. The camel reared, kicked, spit, roared, and snapped simultaneously as we all cleared the walls of the enclosure as a well-synchronized trio, but not before Rox impartially distributed an assortment of bruises.

"Well, old farm boy, how *do* you do it?" Wayne asked sarcastically.

"With restraints, I think," Don decided.

Prior to round two, Don and Wayne moved the baby out of the ring into another stall where we made a bassinet of straw for the little beauty. She had a mop of reddish brown ringlets on top of her head—just like her mother's—a soft, curly coat, and the suggestion of an arch in her back that would gradually fill out into a hump.

Don, in his cowboy role next, twirled a lasso over his head and dropped it on the protesting target, after which a muzzle discouraged Roxie's nasty inclination to bite. For further measures against her antisocial behavior, Cowboy Don wove a network of ropes around the camel's legs. By then, all two hundred pounds of Don was soaked with perspiration and a gray hair or two had sprouted in his dark mustache. There is a great deal more to a large animal practice than the professors in veterinary school let on, I think, otherwise we'd likely have an overabundance of poodle pamperers.

"Wayne, hold the ends of these ropes, and Moselle, I want you to lift Roxie's left front foot off the ground and keep it up," said our leader.

This act of heroism on my part was supposed to keep the camel off-balance. It did not. Roxie's foot was off the ground for one second before it made contact with solid stuff, my shin. If ever I am a candidate for a camel-milking squad, I hope my record will be held against me. I'd like to lose that election.

This utter insanity never did proceed smoothly, but the results of Don's "stripping action" were significantly better than Wayne's and mine. I noticed during the process that the pair of teats I had tackled produced no milk even with Don's businesslike approach and found out why later, when Don treated Roxie for mastitis.

"Well," Don said, after he had wrenched a couple of quarts from the unhappy mother. "That should be enough for now."

He transferred the hard-come-by nourishment into a two-liter plastic bottle, capped it with a large rubber nipple, and the baby downed her first meal eagerly.

"I'll milk Roxie a couple more times, and that should get enough colostrum into the baby camel. Then we'll start with the milk substitute Calf Nip—you can pick it up at the feed store. I'll be damned if I'm going to turn into a full-time milkmaid," Don declared.

TWENTY

The birth of Rebecca brought a lot of problems into sharper focus, one in particular. Money. Originally intended as a profitable business, a breeding farm makes no dollars and not much sense since I fall in love with all the four-footed merchandise. As opposed to the FIFO method of inventory of first in–first out, I worked on the FISH principle, first in–still here. Cash flow per se was no problem, it was the direction of the flow that was becoming ever more critical. Outward, ever outward it gushed, like an uncapped geyser.

The animals were my family, but they're not the type that grow up, leave home, and return once a year for Christmas dinner. Most of them stay. They do grow up, and their appetites along with them, then they give birth to adorable little new appetites that also grow—rapidly. Meanwhile, so does the Consumer Price Index. My pocketbook doesn't. Camel Lot was a small slice of paradise, but paradise with a heavy overhead. Having extremely limited funds made generating income crucial, and I weighed possibilities carefully.

College had equipped me to read and write French, but conversation was of secondary importance in the courses. Consequently, I'm big on French grammar, a relatively unmarketable skill. It doesn't take a finger-walking trip through the Yellow Pages to learn there's little demand for verb conjugators, whether in French, Spanish, or Swahili.

Getting back into flying seemed like the logical step to take. Although I no longer had an airplane, I'd had discussions with a fixed-base operator in the metropolitan area and planned to fly for him. Then along came the baby camel, and stirring up formula at three- and four-hour intervals put a flying career on hold. I was looking through the want ads in search of something more lucrative than addressing envelopes when an ideal opportunity presented itself.

As a guest at the Black Curtain Dinner Theater one evening, I was chatting with its genial owner, Randy Galvin, a friend of long standing. For reasons that escape me now, I felt compelled to offer him some totally unsolicited, irresponsible, and erroneous advice.

"You know, Randy, you'd sell a lot more drinks if the waitresses came around more often," I advised him. "We were here at least twenty minutes before anyone took our order."

"Do you think you could do a better job?" he asked, a sly grin on his face.

"Yep, as a matter of fact I do," was my spontaneous, illadvised answer.

"Then Mosie, baby, you're on. You can start tomorrow night."

The offer didn't require much thought. Conversely, I wondered why it had never occurred to me. Evening hours would leave entire days free for the animals, and I was aware good waitresses make excellent money. The key word here is *good*, but at the time that evaluation was insignificant. In my estimation, being a good waitress required nothing more than delivering drinks and remembering to smile a lot—even at fuzzy-brained drunks with a proclivity for pinching.

That misconception was my first goof, the second was showing up for work in a long white dress. All the waitresses at the Black Curtain wear floor-length evening gowns, and I was careful to dress appropriately, I thought. What I hadn't noticed was the color—black—and my white attire was not only inappropriate, it was also instrumental in assuring my own double jeopardy. When the dissatisfied customers complained about the waitress in white, it eliminated any possibility of my passing the buck.

The next error of a record-setting night was neglecting to wear an apron, another detail I'd failed to observe. Aprons are worn not so much for absorbing spills as for the convenience of stashing away checks. On a tray the size of an ordinary dinner plate it is a logistical triumph to transport an order of drinks to a table of eight even without an additional handicap. Clutching a handful of cumbersome cardboard at the same time relegates the feat to the realm of the impossible. Consequently, I poked the checks in any convenient spot I was likely to remember, and kept Randy busy gathering them up and delivering them to me.

"These were under Beethoven's bust in the foyer," was a particularly annoying find for him.

House rules at the Black Curtain are probably the same as at any other drink-dispensing emporium. Numbered checks, for which she is accountable, are issued to each waitress; drink orders are scribbled on the checks and presented to the bartenders, who mix the beverages and stamp the tickets "filled." It's the waitress's responsibility to determine the price of each drink, total the bills, collect them, and turn in the exact amount at the hour of reckoning. If she forgets to collect from a table, she has just given the party. She also pays if she neglects to add the tax or if $19.00 plus $34.50 adds up to $37.50.

The major stumbling block at a dinner theater is the frantic timing. Instead of one table wanting drinks now and another group needing attention at a respectable interval, it's pandemonium on cue. As soon as the curtain goes down, six tables insist on ordering from the same waitress at once, ten waitresses simultaneously storm the bar, and two harried bartenders hurl out drinks as rapidly as they can slosh the ingredients together.

Adding the proper garnish to each drink is also among the duties of the waitress, I learned the hard way. It was brought to my attention by a picky customer who received an oliveless martini and was bent out of shape by the oversight. I didn't consider it a monumental tragedy but he unfortunately did.

Gibsons get onions, cherries belong in Manhattans, and a gin and tonic is topped off with a slice of lime. That much I knew. But when it came to something offbeat like a tequila sunrise or a Harvey Wallbanger, what to park on top was a dilemma. To solve the predicament, I took a sip of each mystery drink, only a small sip and always discreetly with my back to the customers, and if it were sweet with a pinkish tinge, in went a cherry. Sweet with an orange cast naturally called for a slice of orange. Because it is impossible to distinguish between Bourbon and Scotch in a dim light, highballs, too, re-

quired the taste test. The fact that I was still sober at the end
of the long evening supports my contention that the sampling
was done on an extremely small scale.

Then there was the matter of distance to contend with. Randy's assigning me the area farthest from the bar might have
been his policy for newcomers, but I think not. I suspect his
motives. An Olympic track star in Reeboks would be hard
pressed to make that run successfully, and I discarded my
high heels after the first heat. Even so, by the time I arrived
in my stocking feet at my destination, the tray was awash in
most of what had begun the trip *inside* the glasses. I was so
glad to get there and technically fulfill my responsibility, removing the empties didn't cross my mind until one sarcastic
oaf made a point of it.

"I wonder if the bartender is experiencing a shortage of
glasses," he wondered out loud, with a sweeping gesture across
the cluttered table.

By the end of the second act I had a whole new concept of
good waitresses as well as a complete understanding of surly
ones. As soon as I was secure in the knowledge that Mr. Bloody
Mary was sitting next to Miss Bourbon and Water who was
beside Mrs. Whiskey Sour, Bloody Mary changed to Kahlúa,
Bourbon and Water switched to Courvoisier and Whiskey Sour
became Velvet Hammer.

Confusion reigned, and immediately prior to the last act it
accelerated into chaos. When the tab was presented along with
the last round, the conversation deteriorated to the interminable
interrogatories: "Betsy, did you have the crème de menthe?"
No, Eileen was the culprit. Therefore Mike's portion came to
$4.50 more than had originally been determined, because Ei-
leen's thirst was Mike's responsibility, not Leslie's, whose
share consequently came to $4.50 less. I miscalculated one

tab by $10.00 and it had to happen to the same bozo who'd pointed out the error of my ways in the matter of the missing olive.

"Is this your first night?" he wanted to know.

"My last," I replied—without the mandatory smile.

There's no doubt that cocktail waitresses who make money earn it. Table hopping is tough duty. The only training available to ladies in waiting is the dear school of experience Benjamin Franklin spoke about, and he was right about it being dear. Tuition for my one night in the classroom came to $28.50. I presented a check to a table of four that was actually intended for a "deuce"—as we say in the trade—and the foursome, pleased with the modest bill, paid it hastily and left just as hastily. The same cannot be said of the "deuce" when they got their check. They got testy.

I wasn't sure who complained to Randy about me, it would have been easier figuring out who didn't, but the one detractor he mentioned by name was not entirely justified. He misquoted me. I had inadvertently gotten him a Bourbon instead of a Scotch when he informed me stuffily, "I never drink anything but Scotch." I was merely trying to help him broaden his horizons by persuading him to branch out, and I did *not* say, " 'Foolish consistency is the hobgoblin of little minds.' " I said it *could* be.

Out of a job, if that label can be applied to a one-night stand, I looked around for more economy measures to add to the ones I'd already initiated. About the only thing I could think of was a less-expensive source for fruit and vegetables, primarily for the monkeys, so I visited the grocery store where I often shopped in hopes of making a deal. My cousin, Kathy Reagan, who had just graduated from medical school, was with me and stood by quietly as I explained my needs to the manager. I didn't have to have top-quality produce but would be happy to purchase discards such as bruised oranges and blemished apples unsuitable for sale to their regular customers.

"Why certainly," he said, smiling and nodding agreeably. "But I wouldn't think of charging you. Just be at the loading dock each morning at eight and help yourself to anything you like."

Pleased over this real coup, Kathy and I arrived at the appointed hour the next morning but were puzzled to find no crates or boxes on the dock. Our puzzlement was of brief duration.

"Oh, I'm sorry," the manager apologized. "Let me show you. The dumpster is right below the loading dock, not actually on it."

Kathy behaved well. Not until the man was out of earshot did her laughter get out of control. Inside the dumpster was a bubbling cauldron of garbage. Smashed oranges and grapefruit, innumerable packages of coleslaw mix, strawberries turned purple, four or five rotten bananas, and one identifiable artichoke comprised the top layer. I can't vouch for what might have been present at lower levels.

"Well, here goes," I said, gingerly reaching for the mangled artichoke I could pick up by one leaf.

"Are you crazy!" was Kathy's reaction. "What are you going to do with that?"

"Pitch it as soon as we get away from here. We've got to fill up at least one of our plastic bags, the man thought he was being nice."

"Oh, my God! Botulism here we come," she said, retrieving a flattened banana for our collection. "I noticed eight or nine garbage cans on the way over here. Can we stop and root around in them on the way home? That would probably be a lot of fun too."

Before we got our bag filled, one item at a time, she was jokingly belligerent: "I don't know how you talked me into this. I've known you to have some pretty bad ideas, but this is by far the worst."

If it wasn't, it was close to it. That was my last attempt to cut corners on any of the wildlife's provisions, but I always kept an eye out for bargains.

The bulk of the tigers' diet comes from Bausback Corporation, the only outfit in the state licensed to sell meat not for human consumption. A large source of their beef is cattle and milk cows that have to be destroyed for some reason—a broken leg or an entanglement with a fence—and though it's bad luck for the farmer and the animal, it's good news for my pocketbook. Bausback picks up the animals, butchers them, and packages the frozen beef in fifty-pound blocks. But weather governs their supply. Icy roads or fields curtail operations; intense summer heat causes the meat to spoil if the animal isn't discovered promptly.

When I can't get beef, chicken is an agreeable substitute to the tigers, but it's unpalatable to me, costlier in the outlay of time as well as dollars. Quantities are limited to three chickens per customer when they're on sale, which means an average meal for the cats requires four separate, undetected trips through the check-out lanes. But years of chicken runs and a few refinements have elevated this mundane task to the ranks of artistry. My now practiced eye can spot the plumpest fryers at a glance, and I grab up my paltry allotment of three, depart via the farthest of the twelve check-out lanes to deposit my purchases in the car, and go back for more.

On the next trip, I patronize the checker at the opposite end of the store. Experience has taught me to shun the express lanes. The clerks there are less harried and more apt to spot a repeat offender, so I weave back and forth, slinking through the longer lines until the clerks do a double take, as if mine is a face they've seen before—and recently. When that occurs, I crank up the car and take my business elsewhere. Gathering up one poultry meal for two tigers, about thirty-six pounds, can take several hours.

Ground meat of any sort is unacceptable to the cats. Because it's always available, I tried a commercial product used by zoos, but Ivan and Deutchka staged a hunger strike. I formed it into meatballs studded with chunks of chicken, drenched it in homemade chicken soup—which they love—and tried every conceivable gourmet disguise, but they refused them all.

"Stick with it," Julian Duval, a curator at the Indianapolis Zoo, encouraged me. "When they get hungry enough they'll eat it."

I also offered them frozen rats Julian provided me with, but the tiger reaction to ratcicles was the same as mine would have been.

After three weeks of lean times, Deutchka snared a bird in flight—right out of the air—popped him into her mouth, and sent him down the little red lane to the hereafter faster than I can relate the event. I capitulated. It was back to chicken and beef and uncertainty again.

Nowadays I'm in an ideal situation, blessed with a meat procurement team on twenty-four-hour alert. Brad Thurston and Todd Kogan are avid ecologists and any deer, horse, or cow they hear about that meets an untimely end, they claim for Ivan and Deutchka. A plastic surgeon, Brad is an artist with a scalpel and equally talented with other forms of cutlery. Todd is handy with a chain saw and also volunteers his Closet

Camel Lot

Percy and me

Zero, Zulu,
Xerox, and Zip

Zero and baby Zulu

Zero, Zulu, and Xerox

Zero, Zulu, and Xerox with Lucy, Larry, and Lori Lama

Jack Leer and me bringing back Jeremiah and Jeb, after the two wolf pups escaped

Ivan as a baby

Robert Baudy and me with Ivan, after his escape

Reverend and Roxie

Jane Doe

Brad Thurston
feeding Bucky

John Deer

Hamlet

Company's van for transporting animals to other locations. In deference to the sensitivities of the owner should the victim be a pet, they take the carcass elsewhere for the filleting process. That's no small accomplishment when dealing with a 1,500-pound horse.

Unfortunately, there are some repercussions from this worthy enterprise. Brad's wife, Karen, was understandably nervous when her horse Samson sprained an ankle and began limping around like a candidate for recycling. Nor is Susan Danner, Brad's scrub nurse, enthusiastic about the program. I received a joshingly irate phone call from her:

"You know Brad has standing orders in the office that when anyone sees a road kill they're to haul it off into the bushes and call him. So there I am on busy I-465 at six-thirty this morning, dressed for work, dragging a ninety-pound doe off the highway."

Other friends provide Ivan and Deutchka with special treats from time to time. Candy and Ken Worman, who raise a lot of the meat they feed at their breeding farm, drop off huge shank bones when they butcher, and the tigers all but turn handsprings with excitement. My favorite murderer, who chooses to remain anonymous, presented them with his "pet" geese who went beserk and attacked him, two thirty-pound bullies I dragged into the tiger's pen and served whole—except for the small wedge missing from their throats. Ivan took his trophy, tossed it up in the air, and bounced it on the ground several times, then waited for it to get up and play. Anything served in its original wrapping, be it feathers or fur, Ivan considers uncouth and unacceptable. The chief carnivore prefers the high-priced entrées. But Deutchka rushed to her condominium with hers and plucked it, a mouthful of feathers at a time, before she devoured it.

The only "treat" ever unappreciated by the tigers was a whole side of pork presented to them by my friend Ruddy Edwards. Deutchka bored a half-inch hole about the size of a quarter into the flesh and that was it. They didn't eat it, play with it, or even touch it again. The cats keep a kosher den.

The extra delicacies I provide are limited to small stuff. Every now and then when a barn cat drags in a chipmunk I snatch the body for the tigers' beef *à la mode*, but for the most part I specialize in other types of accident victims, rabbits and squirrels, those who've collided with a four-wheeled adversary. I much prefer back roads for this activity since body snatching is embarrassing. When I spy a target, I slam on the brakes, glance around furtively, jump out and grab the deceased, and pitch it in the car. In a matter of fifteen seconds the dastardly deed is done. It used to take twice as long, but I've fine-tuned furtive glancing.

One ghoulish side effect has resulted from this rather macabre activity. Like the alcoholic who can't get by the entrance to a bar or the gambler who succumbs to the sight of a casino, there's no way I can close my eyes and cruise on by a suitable-looking prospect.

Providing treats for the other animals is easy, even dull by comparison. There's not a whole lot of melodrama in opening a package of Seasoned Ry-Krisp. The hoof stock's self-service pastures are accessible around the clock, I grow all the hay they eat, and nearby Zionsville Grain keeps an ample supply of corn and oats on hand. The feed store also handles the various powdered formulas I'm frequently in need of, such as the baby camel's Calf Nip.

Two new llamas and a baby zebra were born shortly after Rebecca's arrival, and I was both pleased and relieved when their mothers assumed responsibility for the care and feeding of their offspring. It was becoming even more imperative that I find work, the sort that paid in cash and not merely in the pure delight that was my current compensation. As soon as Rebecca was weaned, I accepted the flying job I'd already been offered four months previously. It had been several years since I'd flown regularly, so I practiced, took a check ride, and studied company policy carefully in order to get off on the right foot.

The airport I became affiliated with disdained the devil-may-care blue jean–type image, preferring the gray-flannel look for its pilots, so I dressed according to code in tailored suits complete with stockings and high heels. I think that was a hindrance. At least I like to believe that was the reason my first charter was canceled on the spot as we were about to board the aircraft.

There was one female in the party of three that staggered out to the single-engine Cessna 172 and she had obviously partaken too generously of the juice of the grape—not the kind that goes directly from the vine to the consumer. Pointing at me, she brayed, "Is that the pilot?" Upon being informed by me that yes, I was, she advised her companions in a voice that could summon every hog in four adjacent counties, "Then I'm not going. She can't fly. She can't even see over the dashboard."

Had I thought I could penetrate the air space between the lady's ears, I would have pointed out that I intended to fly the airplane, not wrestle it, but I didn't. I just waved good-bye as they stumbled back toward Operations. So much for getting off on the right foot.

My next passenger was braver, more so than I, in fact. He was the traffic reporter for a local radio station that broadcast live during rush hour. Wanting a closer perspective, Mr. Traffic continually badgered me to "get lower, lower!" when we were almost grazing the tops of vehicles that streamed along the Interstate.

He got worse when we were terrorizing downtown Indianapolis. I wanted to climb up to avoid the pigeons we were scaring off the rooftops, so I cited an FAA requirement of five hundred feet above people or property. Mr. Traffic didn't care. "They'd have to catch us first," was his response.

"High in the sky over downtown Indianapolis . . ." went his spiel. High in the sky? We were so low I could count the cigarettes in the ashtrays as we careened by the upper floors of the office buildings.

I flew that harrowing assignment on a regular, daily basis for a few weeks, until out of the blue my big break came along. When one of the other pilots hinted he'd like a crack at show biz, I graciously relinquished my kamikaze commission to him, unaware I was simply abandoning the frying pan and was now poised for a precipitous leap into the fire.

Harry, the pilot who flew the cable lines for the telephone company, was a good buddy of mine. I'd noticed he was a chain smoker and that his hands shook so badly he had trouble holding a match steady. I'd also observed each time he set a coffee cup in its saucer there was an inordinate clatter before the cup finally settled down for good. The tic in his left eyelid and the fact that he could never remain seated for more than three consecutive minutes were other symptoms that should have been significant. They were, immediately after I flew right seat on a cable run.

"You might like to be my replacement," Harry said, explaining he'd had the job for almost a year and it was time to move on to other things. "Come along and ride shotgun and I'll show you the ropes."

Instead of ropes I saw a lot of treetops from a perspective of two and three feet. When a hill loomed up in our flight path, Harry jerked back on the controls and aimed at the sky, providing us with a brief perpendicular view of the heavens until we approached stalling speed, that critical point at which you either do something about it or drop out of the sky. Harry chose to jam the yoke forward, and we hurtled toward the ground before he leveled off—but not for long. *Wham*, and I was pasted against the side of the cockpit as the cable made a ninety-degree turn and Harry threw the airplane into a steep right bank.

To check the cable lines, it's essential to fly low, because only when the supposedly buried cable is visible is there a problem. This usually occurs when a farmer unfamiliar with the territory plows too deep, but there are other causes as well. When a break in the line is spotted, the pilot duly pinpoints the location on his map and reports the trouble after he completes the inspection flight. As soon as he can talk again. Weather is no deterrent to the citizens of questionable sanity who fly these runs. They go unless the visibility is so cruddy they can't tell the runway from the parking lot.

Cable runs make crop dusting, a notoriously dangerous occupation, seem like a leisurely ride on a merry-go-round. By the time we landed, I had contracted all of Harry's nervous afflictions and originated a few of my own. I declined his generous offer to recommend me for the job. There had to be a better way to put grain in the feed buckets than rubbing elbows with angels.

Flying commercial photographers with suicidal tendencies can also play havoc with one's central nervous system. Fearless Fred, who specialized in aerial photos, always removed the door on the passenger's side so he could lean out for unobstructed shots while I circled the target in a forty-five-degree bank. "Steeper! Steeper!" was his battle cry as two hundred pounds of Fred, plus camera, dangled over the terrain. He had a lot more confidence than I did in his seat belt, all that kept Fred from becoming as one with the landscape.

I'm partial to straight-and-level flight, taking the shortest distance between two points with no hair-raising incidents en route. But even trips from Indianapolis to another city and back again proved impractical. I never knew when I'd be detained, where, or for how long. One steady client, steady in terms of frequency, attended weekly, well-lubricated business meetings in Chicago, and while he met—and guzzled—I paced the terminal at Meigs Field. Never once did he return at the agreed-upon time. Usually he showed up two hours late but sometimes as much as four, always clutching a fistful of swizzle sticks to substantiate his claim he'd been tied up.

My erratic schedule was defeating my purpose, the welfare of the animals. I was constantly imposing on some friend to drop what they were doing and parcel out hay or check the tigers' water or be sure the llama babies hadn't gotten themselves separated from their mothers. It was an impossible situation.

I wanted to stay in aviation, but only one other possibility—and it was a long shot—seemed feasible. United Airlines was running full-page ads recruiting pilots. The only prerequisite, so it said, was a commercial license.

Although airline crews spend days at a time streaking around the country, they know their schedule way in advance and the pay is good. I could hire someone to care for the animals during my absences, and there was also the appeal of long stretches at home. But there was an enormous stumbling block between me and an airline career. I'd learned to love small airplanes, but I was still deathly afraid of airliners, those behemoths of the sky. I'd have to take up George Mikelsons's offer of a "quick fix" before I could even apply.

George and I were student pilots together, but he far out-shone me in ambition as well as talent. As the founder and sole owner of American Trans Air, he went from a $3,800 Piper Tripacer, his first airplane, to a fleet of multimillion-dollar aircraft that includes everything from 727s to L-1011s. And not only is ATA the largest charter airline in the United States, it boasts a phenomenal safety record, never one in-flight accident, not even so much as a nicked runway light. That comforted me.

Several years before, George had invited me on a flight and was shocked to learn I was still gun-shy of big airplanes.

"Come take a few flights on the flight deck with me and I'll cure you," he offered.

I'd thanked him and said I would. Someday. Maybe. Now the time had come. I was no less fearful but the motivation was compelling.

When I finally called George, he said, "Great! Be at the airport Sunday afternoon at three o'clock."

"Where are we going?" I asked.

"Bermuda."

"Oh, no! I was thinking of something like making a couple of trips around the traffic pattern at Indianapolis International."

"Mosie. Be at the airport at three on Sunday."

Having a buggy-whip mentality in the jet age is a severe handicap. I was hostage once again to the anguish that pre-ceded my first flying lesson, hoping desperately for some jus-tifiable way out of the ordeal I'd arranged. When I climbed into the jump seat of the Boeing 707, I was stiff with fright. The flight engineer handed me a box of crackers and a jar of cheese and all the way to Bermuda I spread cheese crackers, a mild form of beadcraft. If it helped, I wasn't aware of it. George patiently explained all the instruments and procedures, but he might as well have been lecturing to an empty jump seat.

The return flight was a bit less traumatic, but I was a long way from cured. That one trip was scant preparation for my interview with United. Filling out the employment application before I was ushered into the personnel director's office, I was so jittery I could hardly hold the pen steady. Why I kept the appointment I'd made I couldn't explain even to myself. Apply for a job I wanted in the worst way not to get? Temporary insanity was the only logical explanation. Although the pleasant gentleman tried to put me at ease before he got down to business, it was an impossible undertaking.

"I see you're multiengine rated," he said, looking over my application. "Have you had any jet experience?"

"No! None at all," I blurted.

"That's no problem. We'll fly you to Denver for your preliminary jet training and . . ."

The rest of the conversation was a blur. I felt as though I were being shanghaied, about to be whisked off to a grim fate from which there was no escape. Making my getaway was the one thing on my mind. Somehow the interview was concluded and I might even have said "thank you" or "good-bye."

United didn't Express Mail my rejection. There was a decent interval of forty-eight hours before I received their form letter. They were dreadfully sorry, but they had no openings and anticipated no openings and good luck elsewhere.

I did go back for more of "Dr." Mikelsons's therapy, and he did effect a cure. But it was a cure with a catch. Now I can fly on an airliner and whether it's a 727 or an L-1011 makes no difference at all—as long as it's American Trans Air.

It's just as well I didn't go to work for United, since finding someone to help with the animals was a remote possibility. I couldn't even write a job description, let alone hire someone to fill a job I couldn't describe. I could provide a clothing guideline, but that in itself might discourage applicants: no fluttery garments (the zebras are nervous); no hats whatsoever (Ivan hates hats); several changes of clothing (Ivan sprays—accurately); bulletproof vest optional (comforting during confrontations with irate, shotgun toting farmers); running shoes (recommended for llama chasing).

Three of the llamas became afflicted with wanderlust: Lucy, Larry and Left Turn, who got his name from one ear that jutted out horizontally as though he were perpetually signaling his intentions. With effortless grace they hurtled the fences any time they chose and rambled any place they pleased. It was impossible to keep them at home. I couldn't even keep them in the same zip code. It got to the point that I recognized the voices of the law-enforcement officers calling to report the animals' whereabouts and knew which county they were in before the officers identified themselves.

Unlike their father, Charlie Lama, they were friendly and most of the neighbors enjoyed their visits. The problems they caused stemmed from their unusual appearance. When the large, strange-looking creatures loomed up, horses went berserk. So did a few people. One time the boys, who always toured together, ambled into a house under construction, tiptoed up behind a carpenter engrossed in his work, and scared him so badly he abandoned the job, permanently. Lucy Lama caused *me* such a fright I, too, thought it was all over but the obituary.

Lucy took off on a day when the mercury looked up to zero and the wind whipping across the snow-covered fields stirred up a secondhand blizzard on its own. With the usual pail of grain to lure her home, I tracked her for over two miles until I found her in a field with high fences and an open gate through which she'd apparently entered. But this time the standard coaxing, begging, and attempted bribery were to no avail— she refused to budge. Eventually I gave up. Closing the gate behind me, I trudged home at dusk, certain she'd be secure there until I led her home the next morning.

But it was more of the same on the next day and the day after that, and I couldn't understand why. There was no food available to her, no grass, no leftover corn to scavenge. Surely she was hungry.

A week went by and Lucy still showed no interest in the grain that had never before failed me. Pondering the mystery and how to alter my strategy, I latched the gate and turned to leave only to confront the business end of a sinister-looking double-barreled shotgun. I was so startled, and frightened, I gasped involuntarily before my eyes moved slowly upward to meet the menacing gaze of the bearer of the bad news. It told me this was no joke.

"Is—is—this your land?" I stammered.

"Yes."

"I'm sorry. I realize I'm trespassing, but I didn't think you'd mind," I apologized to the large, hostile stranger.

"I do," he stated, quite unnecessarily since the shotgun had already suggested as much.

"Th—th—then I'll try to get my llama and we'll be going right away," I said.

"Your llama?" he asked, and his grim expression changed to a look of confusion.

"Yes, my llama," I reiterated.

"Ha, ha, ha, ha, ha." He doubled up laughing at the joke I didn't know I'd made. "I've been feeding that 'deer' all week, not knowing it was really a llama that belonged to someone, and I thought you were up to no good."

Cut off from the sweet feed to which she'd become addicted, Lucy was glad to get back to her regular grub, plain old corn and oats and hay. I was glad to get back period.

TWENTY-ONE

 The fence-leaping lla-
mas were indirectly responsible for the only evictions ever
carried out at Camel Lot, right after I starred in another cross-
country event sponsored by my athletic friends Larry and Left
Turn.

Stepping inside the monkeys' quarters afterward to warm up
in their controlled 75 degree temperature, I was surprised—
although I shouldn't have been—when it felt exceptionally
chilly. It was: The thermometer read 45 degrees. When I turned
the thermostat to 90 degrees and the furnace didn't kick on,
my suspicions were confirmed. Once again the furnace was on
the blink, for obvious reasons, and the reasons all had names:
Biddy, Buddy, and Joe Joe.

The monkeys were cute and smart and adorable. And bad. And busy. And trouble. Give my guys three screwdrivers and two hours and they could dismantle a Titan missile down to the last bolt.

I first became aware of the trio's interest in heating and air conditioning by accident, Buddy's accident. He wasn't around one day when I went in to play, and I assumed any minute he'd come swinging down from the rafters and land on my shoulder. But his arrival was a lot more dramatic than that, and faster. The furnace clicked on with a loud pop and out of the flue came Buddy like a circus performer blasted from a cannon. In one flying leap he landed on top of the marmoset's cage, frightened but unscathed except for a small scrape on his forehead.

I immediately had an additional safety guard attached to the furnace, hoping that would quell their interest, but it didn't. They couldn't crawl inside anymore, but dexterous little monkey fingers stayed busy turning, poking, and pulling any part they could move. On three different occasions they put the furnace out of commission.

It was increasingly embarrassing to call Bryant Heating for emergency service, and the fourth time was the finale. I was cold, tired, and irritable from Larry and Left Turn's latest excursion as I picked up the telephone to dial.

"I don't have any heat again. I know you can't believe it," I said to Bryant's service manager.

"Oh, but I can," he cooed facetiously. "The monkeys again?"

"Yes, but I promise you it will never happen again."

"They're gone?" he asked, a ray of hope in his voice.

"Not yet, but they will be by the time you get here."

As soon as the car was warm, I grabbed a jabbering monkey

and shoved him under my coat, dashed out, and hurled him into the car and went back for the next protesting passenger. When I got in the driver's seat, the monkeys became hysterical. They were all over me, scuffling amongst themselves to get closer, first one and then another putting a stranglehold around my neck as they clung to me in terror.

I drove, peeping through the ever-shifting mob of monkeys, and was about to go back for cages when Buddy, the ringleader, spotted the groceries still on the back seat. Marshmallows to the rescue. Ripping open a cellophane package, he began cramming them into his mouth by the handful and his gleeful chattering attracted Biddy's and Buddy's attention. By the time we'd covered the ten miles to the pet shop, all three of them— and the upholstery—were smeared with gobs of sticky stuff and the white powdered sugar that frosted their fur.

Jason, the manager, was not there to greet his three slightly used monkeys and the one frazzled Homo sapiens returning them. I didn't wait for him; I repeated my earlier performance, reversing the procedure. Storming in and out of the store, I thrust a screaming monkey at whichever dumbfounded clerk happened to be in my path. All the while the rest of the employees, the monkey-less ones, and the customers stood around gawking at the totally deranged creature with the seemingly endless supply of monkeys.

Not since that historic day has my path crossed any of the awesome threesome's, but I've heard about them. Biddy was adopted by another schoolteacher, Buddy went to live with a magician who very likely has by now made him disappear, and Joe Joe is gainfully employed. Joe Joe is a model, working in a haberdashery that caters to a "discriminating clientele." Or used to.

———

Three less mouths to feed didn't make an appreciable improvement in my steadily worsening financial status, so I was receptive to an idea cooked up, literally, by my friend, Martha Owen. We should get into catering, she decided. We'd create exquisite desserts for restaurants whose patrons dined on pompano en papier, sipped Chateau Lafite-Rothschild from crystal wineglasses, and never flinched at a bill with three figures and no decimal point.

No matter that we lacked Board of Health kitchen approval, she'd already solved that problem. A friend with a restaurant would allow us occasional use of his kitchen after he closed the place at 1:00 A.M., so we could truthfully reassure any squeamish customer we had access to an approved facility. Sweet Talk, Inc., was launched with high expectations.

It fit in well with my other responsibilities. While date-nut tortes spent their allotted time in the oven, I could clean the tigers' pens; cheesecakes permitted me to shovel one zebra stall.

Martha and I alternated delivery duty, mostly because of the mad Frenchman. Pierre had a highly volatile personality, never more then two centimeters away from an explosion. Luckily, he had an escape valve, *la bouche*, located directly under a pencil-thin mustache and immediately above his Vandyke beard. Out of *la bouche* poured a continual stream of "darling" and "sweetheart" as he grabbed the victim of the day—Martha or me—clasped her to his ruffle-shirted bosom, and shoved her out at arm's length before smashing her against his chest again. The "darlings" and "sweethearts" were interrupted only long enough to plaster kisses on first one cheek and then the other. It was a strenuous workout when he was pleased with us. When he was not, he erupted with shrill invectives laced with *"Mon Dieu!"*

"*Mon Dieu!* What can I do with a dessert that looks like it survived the San Francisco quake. The last cheesecakes cracked. *Mon Dieu!* You will ruin me!"

"Pierre, if you'd—"

"Not *one* cheesecake, all of them!"

The tirades were unsettling but preferable to the calisthenics. It was with mixed emotions we solved Pierre's problem by slicing the cheesecakes prior to delivery, thus allowing them to be shoved in and out of the refrigerators sans cracks. This show of genius seemed to add tone to Pierre's muscles, and the Gallic demonstrations of pleasure took on new vigor. Martha and I considered relinquishing his account while our rib cages were still intact, but he was the only paying customer.

Although we stirred and baked and delivered, what we didn't do was collect. As novices, we were unaware of a time-honored tradition of this business—handing over the product with one hand, the other outstretched for payment. To our way of thinking, that would be insulting. We sent out monthly statements, but of our seven customers, only one other shelled out money, and he only at the direction of Small Claims Court. In discussing our collection difficulties with a friend who owns a furniture store, John Kirk, I received little sympathy but a lot of advice.

"Damn it, you ought to collect the money when you deliver the merchandise. Now who owes you and how much?"

I reeled off a list of names, one of whom John recognized from his own dealings.

"I know that fat jerk," he said. "With him you have to get right to the point like I did. I walked into his office and told him, 'I've come for my money or your hide and I don't care which.'"

While Martha and I recognized the merit of John's approach, neither of us had his six-foot-three physique to pull it off. Our accounts receivable continued to grow as we acquired additional customers, so the more business we did, the more money we were out. But success is a relative thing. Obviously the less money Sweet Talk lost, the more successful it would become. According to generally unaccepted accounting procedures, by ceasing operations altogether we could achieve the ultimate. Our accountant agreed. He thought in our case that premise was sound.

Camel Lot was a hotbed of unemployment. Nobody who ate here worked here, except me, and I proposed to alter that unsatisfactory state of affairs by putting my furry friends to work. There is a great demand for "exotic" animals for special occasions, particularly camels. I receive numerous requests for my guys to appear in a manger scene, or give rides, or lead parades, but heretofore I'd always declined, explaining that if my unmannered hooligans participated there would be no parade—or manger, or birthday party. But what if they were trained . . . Rent-a-Camel? It had promise.

Since Robert had badgered me for years to discipline the animals, I knew I could count on him to coach me; and I already knew the first thing he would require, "slipping" halters on the camels. I'd previously made one aborted attempt at it and discovered—among other things—just how loose Robert's terminology is. But finding a camel trainer to do the job was not among my options. It's possible to let one's fingers walk through the Yellow Pages until they're arthritic and still not locate a board certified camel trainer. I called a horse trainer I know and put the proposition to him a little differently, altogether eliminating the word "slip."

"Do you think you could manage to get halters on my two rowdy adult camels?" I asked Gus Maxwell.

"Of course," he answered cockily. "Camels are nothing but horses with a hump, and I never met a horse I couldn't handle."

Ah, yes.

Rev and Rox performed in the expected manner, that is, the manner expected by me. They effectively demonstrated to Gus the differences between camels and horses, which added up to three cracked ribs, an untold number of bruises, and one lump on the head about the size of a lemon. After two hours of unabated mayhem, during which I tried to convince Gus to quit, he staggered out of the stall bloody and bowed but victorious. When I tried to pay him his fee, he refused.

"Forget it, honey, you can't afford it. There ain't that much money in Fort Knox."

I waited two days before the first session of Camel Training 101, rationalizing that the camels needed time to recover from the halter ordeal.

"Attach lead ropes," Robert told me. "Let them dangle for a while until the camels get used to them. Then hold the lead rope taut in front of the camel and give it a brief, slight pull. When the animal takes a step forward, give him a reward. Then just keep repeating that process."

The first part of the operation was uneventful. Neither trainee objected to the lead ropes. Nevertheless, with cowardice tempering my ambition, I let the ropes dangle for a week before reentering the classroom. Then I continued the course precisely as Professor Baudy outlined it. But one severe setback cropped up immediately. Reverend did not approve of the curriculum. When I gave him a small, insignificant, and extremely brief tug, he sent his right front leg—along with his foot—to convey his disapproval. Temporarily parked on his ankle, I soared rapidly up into the air until he suddenly removed his appendage, at which point I descended at the standard rate of thirty-two feet per second per second, and school was out. For good.

When I look back on my career as a camel trainer, I cannot in good conscience describe it as distinguished. I can say it was brief.

But I was not yet ready to scuttle the Rent-a-Camel business, not while there were unexplored avenues for Rev and Rox and Rebecca, as well as the other animals. An opportunity soon arose to check out another possibility. My friend, Michael Bechert, wanted a new composite for the modeling agency that represents him and thought unusual animals in the background would add oomph to the photographs.

The "shoot" began well. As Michael in sports clothes casually propped one foot on the fence and Rev and Rox peered over for a closer look, his photographer, Jimmy Mack, snapped away. Next, Michael posed in a black tuxedo with a background of zebras for an equally effective picture. It was when they got to what was intended as a series of photos with the tigers that things deteriorated. These shots called for sophistication, with the debonair model impeccably attired in a business suit, pouring champagne with glass in one hand and bottle in the other.

As the two men got closer to the tiger pen I cautioned them again, but Michael brushed aside my warning. "I know Ivan. I know what he's going to do, so he won't scare me," he said.

I tried once more when Michael proceeded to *lean* against the cyclone fencing, "I think that's too close."

Ivan did too. Bullet fast, he shot across the pen and hit the fence with a 6.3 Richter-scale thud and a well-timed roar, and sophistication went by the wayside. Only one photograph captured the epic event and it is a blurred one. Michael, open-mouthed and levitating about six inches off the ground, was still bravely hanging on to his props, but the glass was upside down and the champagne was shooting straight up out of the top of the bottle.

A second request for the camels' services came from a fashion photographer promoting camel's-hair coats, a booking I readily accepted since I was now experienced in the business. One of the models was unnerved by the close proximity of the big guys, so I sought to put her at ease.

"They won't bother you, Beth, just back right up to the fence," I assured her.

Beth did, with her frozen smile growing a bit wan. She was an attractive-looking young blonde, I thought, in spite of her short, straight hair that reminded me of a bleached-out haystack. It must have done the same for Roxie. Rox clamped her jaws on the top of the model's head, removed her scalp from the hairline up, spit it out on the ground, and stomped on it. There was a moment of horrified silence until we all realized the bloodless scalping only separated the model from her wig.

The time had come to scuttle Rent-a-Camel.

As Alphonse Karr aptly pointed out back in the 1800s, "The more things change, the more they stay the same." My businesses may come and go, but regardless of the career *du jour*, my days all begin the same. Always I'm up by six or an hour before daylight, whichever comes first. Then it's off to the DoNut Den, nearby Zionsville's early-morning "country club," where the dues are a cup of coffee with or without a warm, fresh doughnut. For its regular customers, the Den is a mandatory stop on the way to the workaday world, and for some it *is* the workaday world. Jim Russell, a plumbing contractor, sold sixteen furnaces three sips into his first cup of coffee one morning. A residential builder happened to pull up a chair to the same table. Gerry Patton's clients don't have to wait until his office opens if they want to buy some radio spots. They know where they can find their account executive, doughnut in hand, at 7:00 A.M.

The DoNut Den functions as a branch office for a good portion of Zionsville's early risers. Kris and Ed Wilkinson, the gregarious owners, don't limit their activities to dispensing doughnuts and replenishing the do-it-yourself coffeepots. Taking messages and making certain they're delivered promptly is all part of the daily routine.

Butcher, baker, candlestick maker—doctor, lawyer, merchant chief. Every conceivable occupation is represented by the DoNut Den's clientele, I'm happy to say. There's a wealth of wisdom and expertise right at the rim of my coffee cup: Dick Carr can reduce to my level some baffling term such as a "dedicated circuit," before I go off on a wild goose chase. When I have to fill in a low spot in the pasture, Joe Hicks translates my "about this high and maybe from here to the wall" into trade jargon with: "Here"—he scribbles on DoNut Den stationery, a paper napkin—"call this guy and tell him you want a single-axle load of topsoil." Outdoorsmen Greg Lacy and Clyde Milligan, adept at locating wild blackberries and raspberries, let me in on their secret finds, and Tad Krajewski does the same with his forte, the highly prized morel mushrooms.

If I need an insurance consultation, Keith Settle or Lloyd Hughes are ever obliging. And, in the unlikely event there's no specialist around to solve a specific question, County Commissioner Sam Dodd will handle it—or know who can. Coffee hour for me is a must. It's the equivalent of a daily conference with my unofficial board of directors.

The goods and services committee is extremely important,

too. Michael Bechert keeps a sharp watch on my car and points out when the tires should be rotated or the engine sounds as if it needs a tune-up; sporting goods rep Steve Bluestein is my couturier and winterizes me with insulated snowsuits at cost. As an expert on things mechanical, B. J. Martin can assemble any diabolical device that carries the warning "Some Assembly Required"—the most ominous phrase in the English language.

Reliable Barb Mundy is goods *and* services. She never fails to procure my weekly lottery ticket and never fails to inform me I didn't win again. The full-service coffee shop is also a transportation hub, ideal for bumming a ride or borrowing a vehicle. When Bausback has beef, Jack Leer lends me his Wolf Run Golf Club truck to pick up a thousand pounds of meat rather than cram it in my car.

Almost any business that has to await standard office hours in Indianapolis can be transacted at the Den before sunrise. Although there's no major surgery performed there, so far as I know, Brad Thurston can be persuaded to whittle a splinter out of my thumb with his ever-present pocketknife—properly sterilized, of course.

When I get back home, the sun has nibbled off the edges of the darkness so I can check all the animals and socialize a bit before feeding, the routine that precedes stall and cage cleaning. Before my neighbor, Herman de Boer, pointed out the error of my ways, I thought shoveling was simply a matter of getting the straw, and other things, from point A to point B and how it got there was of no consequence. He caught me jabbing the pitchfork down to pay dirt and straining to lift the heavy load and set me straight.

"No, no, no. That's not the way to do it," he informed me. "Take a little at a time off the top. Like this."

He demonstrated briefly, much too briefly to suit my Tom

Sawyer inclinations, but long enough to teach me the de Boer approved method. I lost my amateur standing but reaped one immense benefit in terms of physical well-being. My "manure elbow" symptoms improved markedly with the new technique. Known in more glamorous circles as "tennis elbow," the maladies are essentially the same and extremely painful.

Herman was helpful in the mechanical category as well. Although my 1956 tractor looks like something put together by a bunch of Neanderthal men, it runs well once I jump-start it. He taught me how to get it going without all the fireworks I usually generated. When both participating batteries are of the same voltage it altogether eliminates the Fourth of July effect.

Every chore at Camel Lot is made more time-consuming because of the preliminaries. The actual vintage of the manure spreader is unknown, but it predates the tractor by at least a decade and is held together by the universal farm cure-all, baling wire. Before it can limp around the pasture to disperse its payload, more temporary-permanent repairs are always required. I long for a new manure spreader. I covet them. I dream about them. My idea of pure joy is finding a bright, shiny new one parked under my Christmas tree—that or a Rolls-Royce I could trade in for a manure spreader.

The riding lawn mower also demands its share of attention, for which I keep a bottle of soda pop and my golf clubs handy. Both battery posts require one solid whack with a two iron and a dousing with the carbonated beverage before it can be coerced into performing.

The Table of Organization at Camel Lot is simple—the age of specialization hasn't come within shouting distance. Mowing, shoveling, feeding—all the departments and department heads are me. Other than Erin Shannon, a fifteen-year-old high-school buddy who's here for four hours a week, I have no employees. But to say I have no help would be a grave injustice to the numerous friends who generously volunteer whenever the need arises. Some don't get a chance to volunteer now that I've become a highly successful con artist. A visitor who responds to my "How are you?" greeting with "Fine" has automatically passed the physical and qualified for a number of events in the barnyard Olympics, my choice. He may get to unload ten fifty-pound bags of grain from the trunk of my car or wrestle with a gate that's fallen off its hinges. Camel Lot is woefully short of full-time muscles.

TWENTY-TWO

There was one brief interval of real prosperity when I had live-in muscle power available. It belonged to Steve Trott.

Dick Herschler sent me a magazine clipping on California bed-and-breakfast businesses, on which he'd scribbled, "This is something you ought to try." Bed and breakfast is an old established custom in Europe—private citizens opening their homes to overnight guests, primarily travelers, and serving them breakfast before they go on their way the following morning. Until recently, they were unheard of in the United States.

I did think about it. It was an interesting idea to lean on, but I had one serious reservation. Just how awkward might it be living under the same roof with a total stranger, or strangers? When a classified ad in the *Zionsville Times Sentinel* attracted my attention, I decided to find out. A graduate student wanted to rent a room in the Zionsville area for three weeks.

Steve Trott explained he was finishing up at Indiana University Dental School and the room he currently rented would only be available for the next month. He came out to look over the accommodations I offered, a bedroom, bath, and den in a separate wing of the house, kitchen privileges, and garage space for his small sports car. With Steve anxious to portray the unobtrusive student who'd be cloistered with his books and me trying to present the picture of a quiet, conventional household suited to the pursuit of higher knowledge, we were both reserved and formal during our first meeting. By the time he moved in four weeks later, there had been some developments that made any pretense on my part impossible. Steve couldn't use the garage after all, because the car would frighten Jane Doe, and cooking was out of the question for the present with a baby marmoset warming on the kitchen stove. It wasn't necessary at the moment to mention March Hare, who had taken up residence in my bathroom.

The marmoset was the only one of the three whose arrival I was directly responsible for. One morning when I opened Flopsy and Mopsy's cage, I noticed what appeared to be a dead, featherless bird on the floor. Upon closer scrutiny, I realized it was a baby marmoset, still breathing but obviously discarded by its parents. I picked up the clammy little body and hastened to call Ken Kawata at the zoo for consultation. Ken stressed warmth as of the foremost importance, so I hastily transformed a cast-iron skillet into an incubator, and after a few adjustments the baby was warming at 85 degrees. A dish towel folded over several times made both a king-size mattress and a blanket for the two-inch-long *enfant*. Attempting to feed the little tyke with a doll's bottle failed, so I resorted to an eyedropper, hoping the baby's inability to nurse was temporary.

That same afternoon, Ruddy Edwards, riding high atop his commercial lawnmower, leveled a rabbit nest hidden in the tall grass and bunnies scattered in all directions. Mama Rabbit was abroad at the time and Ruddy, realizing she'd never be able to reassemble her brood, tried to rescue them all. The only two he managed to catch he tucked into his jacket and brought to me.

The brothers rabbit were both wild as March hares, healthy and lively specimens. One was so lively, in fact, he leaped out of Ruddy's coat and disappeared forever. Although we searched with the fervor of two obsessed—moving furniture, emptying drawers—we never found so much as a telltale bit of fluff.

His two-ounce sibling we consigned to my bathroom, an excellent nursery for small creatures. Radiant heat beams down from ceiling coils to warm the easy-to-clean tile floor, and there's plenty of room for an active fellow to run around. March Hare settled in, but he never settled down. I had to pounce on him, capture him for each feeding, and fight him to work the nipple into a mouth the size of a mosquito's footprint. The only physical contact the bunny enjoyed was being tucked inside my sweater, where he'd snooze contentedly as I rambled around the house attending to various chores. Perhaps motion had the sedating effect of a lullabye, or possibly it was the additional warmth and the close proximity of another being without the restraint of being held. Maybe it was a combination of things. One rabbit does not an expert make.

Jane Doe was also unsolicited. I have trouble saying no to any endangered animal, whether or not it's a member of an officially designated endangered species. It was impossible to turn down a baby deer whose mother had been gunned down with one blast of a shotgun while the little fawn, a day or two old, stood helplessly by her side. The "sportsmen" who murdered the mother kidnaped the baby and crammed her into a small cage where they proudly displayed their trophy, careful to keep her alive, barely, with a bottle of milk—cold, straight out of the refrigerator—whenever they happened to think about it. Becky Havlin, a young woman I didn't know at the time, heard the horror story and ransomed the little fawn for a hundred dollars. Having no facilities to care for her, Becky called me.

"Bring her out," I said. "I know virtually nothing about deer, but I'll do my best."

Within the hour, Becky and her friend, Morris Riskin, arrived with the little seven-pound spotted whitetail cradled in Becky's arms. When she placed her gently on the grass, the baby struggled to stand and, failing that, flopped over into a bed of irises where she lay frightened and helpless, panting from the effort. She was so malnourished, her small cloven hooves turned under, leaving only the bloody joints of her legs to support her body; all of her extremities were covered with oozing sores from attempts to stand up on the bare concrete where she'd been confined. With one look at the pathetic beauty our roles were reversed. I became the captive—a willing one, to be sure.

Morris, Becky, and I partitioned off a large section of the garage with cyclone fencing, filled it with fresh straw, and Jane Doe seemed pleased with her new quarters, opulent compared to what she'd known. She had plenty of company, too much for her liking until she got used to the comings and goings of the multitude of garage cats. For the first five days, I fed her around the clock at three-hour intervals, and her gaunt little frame gradually began to fill out. In ten days' time, she could bear weight on her hooves and manage one or two feeble steps before her wobbly ankles gave way and she collapsed.

Several times a day I carried her outside to enjoy the fresh air and sunshine, but I was relieved of that pleasant duty when Steve moved in. Before he'd finished unpacking, the real Steve Trott emerged, a sensitive, caring young man who was a delightful companion. Naturally, his having biceps appropriate to his six-foot-five frame detracted not one whit from his charm. At first, Steve asked if he could give Jane Doe her bottle, and when I leaked the news of March Hare's presence, he wanted to feed him too. In time he'd inform me, "I've already fed Jane and March. I upped the ante for Jane, she seemed like she wanted more."

The baby marmoset didn't make it, but the twin brother I was slow in discovering thrived. It was three days before I detected a small, furry head that seemed to emerge from the middle of his father's back, its tiny body well camouflaged in Dad's fur. In the marmoset family the father does almost all of the baby-sitting. The baby cruises around on Papa's back, handed over to Mama only for feeding. After a tough night, a put-upon daddy gets thoroughly fed up with junior's antics, turns to his spouse, and grumbles, "Get this monkey off my back." That's how the age-old expression originated. Maybe.

The room-rental project was not the objective experiment I anticipated. With Steve around it was more like having a brother I didn't know existed walk into my life and begin sharing many of my joys and anxieties, and responsibilities.

"I'm kind of dragging my feet at the dental lab, do you mind if I stay on for a while?" he asked when the first three weeks raced by.

Mind! Never—particularly when Dolly Lama was rejected

by her biological mother and we acquired another baby to bottle-feed.

Steve was an extremely permissive ersatz mother and spoiled Jane Doe unmercifully, before I had a chance to. Morris and Becky built her a veritable estate that encompassed almost an acre, and Janie loathed it. At least, she thought she did. She never spent enough time there to really find out. The minute she began running up and down the fenceline "honking" her displeasure, Steve let her out. His bringing her into the kitchen for just one bottle spelled the end for Janie's al fresco meals. She staged a hunger strike. No more eating in the garage like riffraff, she'd dine inside or forget the whole thing. Then when she got to the weaning stage, nibbling on weeds and small branches, we discovered her affinity for sweets. Snatching a bag of doughnuts off the kitchen counter, she devoured one of those jelly-filled concoctions and then licked off all the raspberry goo I'd gotten on my fingers trying to retrieve it.

As she grew taller, nothing could be left on any table or countertop. Orange juice was a special favorite with her, and she'd swill down an unguarded glass before its rightful owner could stop her. She liked lemonade almost as much. I don't know about her taste for alcoholic beverages, but I almost found out when I caught a guest about to offer Janie a Manhattan. I daresay she'd have liked that too.

Having Steve for an ally was Janie's great good fortune. It was at his insistence that I finally stopped confining her at night. She was losing her spots, the random splashes of white indicative of immaturity, and she cut down on her formula feedings in favor of browse. But I'm so overprotective, had I been blessed with two-legged children they'd likely have been restricted to the playpen until they were big enough to over-power me or old enough to vote. I was as nervous as a mother sending a child off to the first day of school when I permitted Jane Doe her first overnight.

My worries were somewhat alleviated when I heard her funny little squeal at the patio doors the next morning. She'd come for her bottle. Janie was remarkably punctual. In addition to visits at various times during the day, she always appeared about nine in the morning and five each evening. Were I not immediately aware of her arrival, she kicked on the door impatiently to announce her presence. Where she was and how she was, most of the time I could only guess at and fret over. But as a little creature of the wild who was capable of fending for herself, she must be allowed the freedom to which she was entitled. Jane Doe was the only animal I'd ever raised and subsequently relinquished all control over; learning to love loosely was difficult.

The minute I heard of the market for doe urine, seven dollars per ounce wholesale, I looked at Jane Doe in a different light. Here was an ideal business partner. Obviously the enterprise lacked any get-rich-quick potential, but it had indisputable growth characteristics. As Janie grew, her contributions to the business would increase, and if the venture proved successful just one additional deer could double production.

Studying Janie's habits carefully, I learned the best time to transact business was between thirty and forty minutes after a bottle. The close scrutiny also disclosed one minor drawback I hadn't anticipated. According to my calculations, warm weather when fluid intake was greatest would be the time of highest volume, but I hadn't taken nature's cooling system into account. Tiny dots of perspiration popped up on the top of Janie's nose, merged into droplets, and there went part of our profit trickling down Jane Doe's cheeks.

That minor cyclical aspect of the business, however, was not its greatest drawback. Jane had a mind of her own and apparently she lacked ambition. She refused to cooperate. The one time when I was properly prepared, at the right place at the right time after stalking her for half an hour, she made her intentions clear. She gave the bucket one swift kick while the cash flow kept right on flowing—flowing right on into the ground.

Unsuccessful though it was, the experiment did alert me to other possibilities. Llama manure as fertilizer is far superior to most waste material, I'd heard. If so, my pastures were rich with a black gold I had but to strip-mine, merchandise, and *voilà!*, prosperity was upon me. It seemed important, however, to put the product to the test before extolling its virtues and accepting money for same. Something about misrepresentation and false advertising lurked around in the corners of my mind.

From a nursery's fall closeout I bought a puny assortment of leftovers with little foreseeable future, twelve Shasta daisies, eight delphiniums, and a half-dozen hollyhocks. My investment wasn't much, but neither were their prospects. With no idea of the proper amount of fertilizer to apply, I put a half cup of llama uglies into each newly dug hole, inserted one scraggly survivor from my $3.60 purchase, and not until the first whisper of spring did I check on them. Surprisingly, twenty-three of the twenty-six plants were stretching up out of the ground.

Continuing the noble experiment, I applied the Moynihan technique of "benign neglect" and didn't water them, cultivate them, or provide them with any assistance whatsoever, and they thrived. Delphiniums, usually two to three feet tall, peaked out at four feet, the daisies' fat blooms were of sunflower proportions, and the hollyhocks approximated Jack-in-the-beanstalk quality.

I was excited about the project and ready to forge ahead with a chemical analysis, another precaution. Finally locating a laboratory in Memphis, Tennessee, that would accept the assignment, I sent along a supply of camel and goat uglies as well, hoping they might also have commercial potential. They didn't, and the numbers established for the nitrogen, phosphate, and potash content in the llama manure didn't mean anything to me. As far as 1.69 percent nitrogen is concerned, it could have been 83.7 percent and still not prompted any dancing in the streets on my part. But a nurseryman explained to me the real merit of llama manure. Its slow nitrogen release provides a steady supply of nutrients without danger of "burning" the plant. No overzealous gardener could scald his prize-winning peony with my exotic fertilizer, and that was the reassurance I needed for a go-ahead.

Prowling the pastures, I began to harvest the plentiful crop, an easy job because llamas are a cooperative lot. They select one spot and gravitate to it, stockpiling my wares in the same place for days at a time before they move on to another easily accessible location. There is nothing offensive about shoveling llama uglies. They're odorless, self-contained units about the size and shape of a multivitamin capsule. I collected six bushels of raw material, sealed it into individual quart-size plastic bags, and stored them in the garage. Printed labels listing the nitrogen, phosphate, and potash percentages added a professional touch to my exotic fertilizer, and I was sure I was on to a winner.

What I hadn't reckoned on was the effect of the sealed dung in moisture. Before I could peddle the little nuggets of black gold, they became splotched with a fuzzy white mold, a repulsive, diseased-looking collection more likely to prompt a bum's rush than an order. I regrouped.

The next harvest was spread out on newspapers and allowed to dry in the sun for three days before packaging and, as an added precaution, I poked holes in the plastic to prevent the unsightly fungus. Somehow the effect was not the same with the serrated packaging. It looked slipshod and amateurish and sales were commensurate with the eye appeal of the product. Five calls to five garden shops resulted in five firm no's.

Still convinced the product itself had merit, I gave it more thought and came up with a lulu of an idea, the Organic Man. Basically he was a three-dimensional "stick man" design with a body about six inches tall composed of llama uglies, hands and feet contributed by goats, and the head courtesy of the camels. Ideal for any potted plant, the Organic Man would be a guaranteed conversation piece in addition to an ever-present source of nutrition for the plant.

After experimenting, I selected a wire strong enough to be stuck into the potting medium and yet narrow enough to thread the uglies onto without shattering them. Then the wire was clipped into the proper lengths for the long straight body and shorter arm pieces, and the two were soldered together. Trial and error established the drying time for the camel portion of this endeavor as seven days, four for the considerably smaller llama components, and two for the goats. With any less time interval, the recycled grain and grass split, and too long a period caused them to flake off as they were being strung. Also, the harvesting procedure had to be modified now that quality control was a factor: Shoveling mutilated the specimens, so they had to be selected one at a time. Down on my hands and knees in the pasture, I plucked them individually, carefully collecting only those in prime condition and as close as possible to a uniform size.

I tried to gather the essentials when no one was around to

observe that rather questionable behavior, but there was no way to avoid the watchful eye of Herman. Farmers miss nothing. One day when I was involved in the somewhat suspect activity, I noticed through my peripheral vision a large pair of work boots and rightly concluded it was my neighbor. How long he had been watching I didn't ask, but the expression on his face told me it had been long enough to reach some unfortunate conclusions. Herman never did understand my explanation. It's difficult to convince a farmer who thinks of manure as manure that there are esthetic qualities to it—indeed, it is quite impossible.

The painful part of production was threading the uglies onto the wires. It's not the same as the gentle art of bead stringing. A slight miscalculation meant an eighth of an inch of wire punctured another finger, and once again blood dripped onto the work in progress. Sore appendages were an occupational hazard, as was boredom. There is *nothing* so excruciatingly dull as pushing thousands upon thousands of uglies onto skinny little strands of wire. Construction of six prototypes was laborious, time-consuming, and painful.

Once the bodies were assembled, the rest was easy. For a face I glued on store-bought roll-around eyes, stuck in two small white pins to simulate nostrils, and a tiny clay pipe to represent the mouth. A few strands of camel fur on the Organic Man's head were topped off with a wee little straw hat, and a bit of red plastic ribbon tied around the middle concealed the solder joints and provided a spot of color. The finished product, in a cardboard box with a transparent lid, had real pizazz, and I was eager to get on with sales, especially after tabulating costs and estimating profit at an exhilarating six hundred percent.

Once again I batted a thousand with the sales calls, but this time on the positive side of the averages. All seven potential customers placed orders, and with enthusiasm.

"Give me a dozen of them," one florist said after he recovered from an onset of laughter.

"How do you know you want them?" I asked the highly amused customer. "You didn't even ask the price."

"I don't care," he replied, still chuckling. "I've gotta have 'em."

I was elated. Obviously this barnyard bonanza would cure all my financial woes. The only thing I had to fear was an epidemic of diarrhea putting me out of business. Outside of that, it was a matter of keeping up with demand. Slightly euphoric, I began work on the fifty-four orders.

Streamlining the operation, I did all the wire cutting at one time, then all the soldering. That saved some time. When it came to stringing the uglies, it was a different story. To build fifty-four Organic Men required 2,160 uglies and sixty interminable hours punctuated by brief intermissions to stem the flow of blood. I was two weeks delivering the first batch and the reorders that quickly followed I accepted with reluctance. When one merchant doubled his purchase, I was downright depressed. But the real downer was a rush job for thirty that plunged me into despair and engulfed the entire house with a pungency it had never before been subjected to. Because of the urgency, all the components had to be dried in the oven, and there is nothing to compare with uglies baking at 200 degrees for three hours. Not even Gertrude or a rotten ostrich egg could match the stench.

To meet the deadline, I pressed into service every unwary individual who stumbled across my threshold, among whom numbered my friendly veterinarian now turned sullen.

"Lucky I went to veterinary school, isn't it?" Don Steen

grumbled as he extracted a piece of wire from his bleeding thumb. "I wouldn't be able to handle a job like this otherwise."

There were no volunteers for this hazardous duty, and no one conscripted was happy in his or her work. After a frantic ten-day siege, I filled my last order, *the* last order. A little basic arithmetic indicated my time, excluding deliveries, harvesting, and time out for bandages, netted fifty-five cents an hour. Looking up from that lowly vantage point, a bare minimum wage was clear out of sight. Had I but donated all the red corpuscles spilled in production to the local blood bank, I'd have been better off by three boxes of Band-Aids, two cookies, and a glass of orange juice.

TWENTY-THREE

The entrepreneurial flame still flickered, but it was sputtering badly. Had time permitted, I might have become morose over another failure to shore up my shaky finances, but Percy was so demanding there were few spare moments for reflection. Janie's old quarters in the garage were vacant only a few weeks before they acquired a new tenant, a baby zebra whose future was ordained before it even got born. My already having two hostile males vying for the favors of one female caused such problems that the two males had to be kept in separate pastures, and a third contestant would create an intolerable situation. So it was decided the baby, should it too be a male, would go to Robert's place in Florida.

Zulu, the segregated zebra, first called my attention to the arrival of the new zebra when I met him excitedly clippety-clopping up and down the driveway. He'd jumped the fence to get a closer look at the new kid on the block, a ninety-pound striped miniature of its handsome mother.

The vet came over with binoculars, and for the next forty-five minutes we stared at the newborn on the far side of the pasture, trying to determine its sex. Any attempt to examine a zebra with its mother present—assuming the baby could be caught—would spell suicide. Mama Z. would guarantee it. Unscientific though it may be, the most practical way to sex the offspring is by watching it urinate. The direction of the flow and its point of origin are significant because of the anatomical differences between the sexes.

"It's a male," Don Steen said confidently when the baby finally cooperated. "Now, before you try to catch him, be sure he's nursed several times so he'll have gotten some colostrum."

Don and I held a strategy conference whereby Wayne or Jeannie, unbeknownst to them at the time, became the designated kidnappers. In the late afternoon I isolated the other animals, put a bucket of grain at the far end of the barn runway, and left the stall door open for the zebras. They could be counted on to come in for the feed and they could be counted on to flee the minute the door of the barn apartment opened. The unpredictable element crucial to the success of the snatch was timing.

The plan worked perfectly. When Wayne heard the zebras come in, he let them become engrossed in the feed before he "spooked" them and, with a mad dash, he got the stall door closed before the baby, bringing up the rear, could get away. The trip down to the garage with Steve, the baby zebra, and me in the back of a borrowed van went equally well. Then we hit a snag. The baby wouldn't take his bottle. For the next hour, Wayne, Jeannie, Steve, and I took turns coaxing and pleading—to no avail. Even an attempt to pry apart his tightly clamped jaws and wedge in the nipple was futile.

"I think we're going to have to give up and take him back to his mother," I said after another hour.

Thoroughly discouraged, I propped one foot up on a bale of straw and rested an elbow on my knee—letting the bottle dangle from my hand—and instantly the little guy responded. He maneuvered his way under my bent knee, latched onto the nipple, and chugalugged the entire bottle. I had accidentally allowed the baby to assume his instinctive nursing position, and the battle of the bottle was won by chance.

I might have learned from his first demonstration that we would do things Percy's way. In any event, Steve and I both *should* have learned from the precedent Jane Doe set. We didn't. We brought Percy into the kitchen for ostensibly one feeding, and from that point on we had monumental problems. Percy was the handsomest zebra I've ever met. He looked as if he'd been gift-wrapped in artful swirls of black satin ribbon, and nature, heavy handed with wide bands of "eyeliner" and thick fringed lashes, also gave him a wide-eyed, innocent look. Underneath that deceptive packaging hid a young tyrant, one who ruled with an iron hoof.

After he scraped his forehead on the sides of his pen, I let Percy have the freedom of the whole garage, but that didn't suit him. Whenever he wanted to come in the house, which was most of the time, he kicked the door to the mud room so forcefully I raced to let him inside lest the next sound be that of splintering wood. Down the brick hallway he'd clatter, rounding the turn into the family room and across its slate floor to the more secure footing of the kitchen carpet. It took him no time at all to learn that the refrigerator was the source of all good things, and he'd nudge the handle in an attempt to open the door. He never mastered that trick, but he learned to turn on the kitchen faucet. Still too young to drink, he loved to stick his head in the sink and let the water splash on his nose and run down the sides of his face.

Answering the door was another of Percy's diversions. One jingle of the bell sent him hustling to the front door, and he was always delighted by the ensuing attention he received from a guest, once they got over the shock. He didn't actually attempt to answer the telephone, but every time it rang he pushed his way between me and the phone to be conveniently available for loving. Percy's craving for affection was boundless, and he reciprocated generously in the same fashion as a dog, nuzzling up close and licking incessantly.

He also liked for me to sit on the floor so he could rest his head on my lap for a short nap. Percy couldn't purr his contentment, but he snored. I often woke him up when I could no longer stifle a laugh. There was something overwhelmingly comical about an animal the size of a young pony who fancied himself a lap zebra, especially one who snored.

A zebra capering around the house was a bit unhandy even at a relatively diminutive ninety pounds. By two hundred pounds, an additional problem arose: discipline. But it wasn't a problem for long. A simple change in command restored order. As long as everyone did what Percy pleased, when Percy pleased, peace and harmony prevailed—to a degree. There was no question that Percy was extremely intelligent. That was established matching wits with him. Who was the smarter, Percy or I, that was the question. Bets favored the one with the powerful jaws and the striped complexion.

That he was more forceful, considerably more obstinate, and infinitely more ingenious went uncontested. He also had it all over me with size and agility, which he used to his advantage. Whenever I did anything that displeased him, such as rapping him on the nose when he chewed on the furniture, he was quick to retaliate. He flipped his ample rear end into position, lifted his left rear hoof, and waited—like a football player poised for the kickoff—fixing me with a defiant stare. Percy never once kicked me. He didn't have to. The mere threat was enough to get his wishes carried out. Forthwith.

The zebra baby was a delightful playmate. He loved romping outdoors, but only if Steve or I were along. If we ditched him, which was tough to do, and sneaked into the house, his anxious little face appeared at a window and he tried to gnaw his way back in.

Having a zebra attached to my apron strings led to the inevitable. I became increasingly more reluctant to part with my rambunctious little shadow and bemoaned the fact to Don.

"I thought your agreement with Robert only applied to a male foal," he said, casually dropping a blockbuster.

"It does," I answered, incredulous at the implication of his remark. "Are you telling me Percy's a—"

"For God's sake, Moselle, haven't you examined her?"

"You said—"

"I know what I said, and I was looking at her through binoculars all the way across the pasture."

Don is always positive. Even when he's wrong he's positively wrong. And I was positively elated. Percy could go into the pasture with her brother Zulu as soon as *she* was weaned, both from the bottle and her naps in my lap. Weaning was easy. Lap napping is tough to kick.

Steve's three weeks that stretched into six months' tenure was such a pleasant experience it resolved my doubts about sharing my home with "strangers." A bed-and-breakfast business was worth a try since I had nothing to lose, I figured. Most of my friends figured otherwise. The silverware would be the first thing to disappear, according to them, followed shortly by the television sets and any other portable object with a ready resale value. That was for starters, before their imaginations soared past the outer limits of reason. By the end of the first week I'd have been robbed, raped, and murdered; or possibly raped, robbed, and murdered. In any event, I'd only last a week—which would be longer than some of my other, less-illustrious careers.

I settled on the first of March to begin the B&B operation. The snow and ice would be succumbing to warmer temperatures then, making it less likely for a guest to get snowbound, and I needed the next three months for preparation. Although genteel shabby would probably be acceptable, not many people would be pleased paying for shabby shabby. The guest suite needed fresh paint, and I am an abysmally slow painter, swabbing every square inch with three or four strokes and inspecting the effect before moving on. A new bedspread and curtains were also essential, and I sew the same way I paint.

The only construction I planned was the addition of a wall in the hallway to set off the suite from the rest of the house. For a greater sense of privacy, visitors could close a door and lock it if they chose. Thinking my place should appeal to business travelers, I bought a desk for the den and added a telephone. A few other incidentals needed to be taken care of, but the major project was to whittle down the unmanageable mob of cats who camped out in the garage so that Percy would be comfortable there.

They all stemmed from one female who was dumped here four or five years previously. Crazy Cat was a gorgeous Persian, a femme fatale with long black fur and golden, almond-shaped eyes. Extraordinarily affectionate, she cranked up a purr that sounded like a motorboat whenever I held her, simultaneously caressing my face with the soft pads of her front feet. Then she'd bite my nose. Her routine never varied, including one assignation after another with some transient Tom, proof positive of which she always delivered in the garage.

As soon as the kittens were weaned, Crazy Cat was long gone before I could have her spayed, and the current crop of little furry faces were all mine to tend. Those I couldn't find homes for grew up trying to emulate their mother and they were diligent. And successful. I always had an ample supply of kittens to bestow on friends and neighbors.

Though I was in no danger of running out of neighbors, my tactics did jeopardize some friendships, those with small children as members of their households. When I arrived on the doorstep with a wicker basket in which there were three little puffs of fur—always three—wearing blue satin ribbons (always blue to suggest they were males), I was invariably greeted by a chorus of shrieks. Some were from the parents, some from the children, but for different reasons. Usually a compromise was reached and the squalling little people were allowed to keep just one, which was all I hoped for in the first place.

I was accused of being unscrupulous. I was even accused of removing competitors' FREE KITTENS signs posted on telephone poles in the area. I was innocent, although I did have some prior knowledge as to exactly when the signs would disappear.

The all-time high cat count was twenty-two. Things were so hectic, I inadvertently shut one in the freezer and luckily discovered him some fifteen or twenty minutes later, while there was still time to thaw him out.

Since Jane Doe seemed to enjoy their company when she was mistress of the garage, I didn't make a concerted effort to reduce their number until Percy moved in. They made Percy nervous. Casting aside the scruples I had left, which didn't take long, I found enough homes to reduce the census to eleven kittens and three adults. Then opportunity didn't just knock, it almost battered down the door.

Mary Flick from the Phoenix Theater in Indianapolis called in hopes of borrowing a few camels or zebras for a new stage production. "The director wants some animals in the opening scene," she explained.

"My camels and zebras can't go anyplace, but I have eleven kittens that can, and they wouldn't have to be returned. The only stipulation is that good homes be found for them," I told her.

Mary would check with the director and I feared that would be the end of that. But she called back to ask how soon they could pick up their bewhiskered thespians.

"No, no. I'll deliver them," I insisted. "This afternoon."

Was she kidding? Risk them changing their minds? I called a college student who lived close by, Steve Simmons, and together we rounded up all eleven kittens, tucking them one by one into an aged plywood traveling cage. As we congratulated ourselves on our success, Steve picked up the cage by its handle, whereupon the rotted bottom fell out and our captives tore off in as many directions as there were kittens.

Our second time around we could only capture nine of the wary fugitives, but that at least reduced the population to a less formidable number, five felines. The unruly cats liked to gather en masse at the sheltered entrance to the house to bask in the sunshine, and they became disagreeable when disturbed. For any stranger having to run a gauntlet of hissy-faced, arched-back cats, numbers do make a difference. Five is better than twenty-two.

The other wildlife presented no problem. Bismarck had gone to the Happy Hunting Ground and the rest of the canine contingent were a friendly lot. March Hare had graduated to the outdoors, and nobody inhabited the guest-room closet. Tranquillity reigned. All week.

TWENTY-FOUR

" 'Twas the night before Christmas and all through the house" echoed the squeals of a baby pig. Hamlet appeared and tranquillity's reign came to an ignominious end. Hamlet was an inedible Christmas ham, a Yuletide "gift" thrust upon me by Jack Dellon, whom I had long regarded as a friend.

For the gift exchange at their annual Christmas bash, Jack had drawn the name of a young lady in the office who hailed from Piggott, Arkansas. His co-worker's geographical origin naturally stimulated Jack's hyperactive sense of humor, and he scoured the countryside for a unique gift for her. He found it in Hamlet, a four-week-old, seven-pound calico pig. Most of Hamlet was strawberry blond with splotches of black sprinkled at random over his plump torso; short, stubby, white legs and brown eyes comprised the rest of nature's color scheme. A green satin ribbon was added by Jack in an attempt to make the little porker irresistible, which it did. The lass from Piggott was enchanted with the piglet, but the same could not be said of her husband.

"Either the pig goes or I go," he said, more or less. Actually he said more.

Hamlet was repackaged and returned to the donor. But resourceful Jack, mindful of my low threshold of resistance to animals, was not dismayed. He knew I was out for the evening and he also knew where I hide the door key. Subsequent events prove once again that a little knowledge can be a dangerous thing—for somebody. Still gift-wrapped, Hamlet was napping in front of the fireplace in the family room when I walked in shortly before midnight. Since it was Christmas Eve and 21 degrees below zero, nobody but a direct descendent of Ebenezer Scrooge could initiate eviction proceedings. The piglet would have to stay overnight. "Overnight" was inappropriately optimistic.

I turned up the heat in my bathroom to what I hoped was baby-pig warm, 78 degrees, and unpacked the little guy. Immediately Hamlet demonstrated his version of how to eat like a pig. Plunging his front feet into a dish of the "Tail Curler Rockets" that accompanied him, he buried his snout in the dry feed and propelled the cereal bowl around the slick tile floor, his two back legs providing the locomotion. Hamlet did have slovenly ways. In addition to stomping around in his food, he loved water, except for baths. Blowing bubbles in his water dish just prior to turning it over was great fun. Then he'd splash around in the puddles to stir up a thick gray paste of the previously spilled Rockets. Hamlet was a messy pig, but not as messy as my bathroom.

Hamlet was also destructive. There is a ledge around the bathtub that serves as an ersatz greenhouse for plants that cannot otherwise survive the harsh Indiana winters. Only the hardier ones survived Hamlet. The smaller ones were sent crashing into the tub, and the ones he couldn't budge, he ate. He gobbled up one entire camellia bush, a whole pot of tulips, and enough miniature oranges to send Kaopectate stock soaring. Turning over the wastebasket, pulling towels off their racks, and shredding newspapers were more of his specialties.

My bathroom looked like the pigpen it had become. Even though it's large, there's no such thing as a bathroom large enough to share with a real, live, honest-to-goodness pig. After three days of this mandatory togetherness, all my goals in life became consolidated into just one burning desire: having my own, personal, private pigless bathroom.

Efforts in that direction were discouraging. The few people I thought of as ideal candidates for a pig pet would "think about it after the holidays" or "consider it when the weather breaks" or "maybe" their way into what amounted to a "no." There were some interested parties, but their motives, I feared, were long-range plans to turn Ham into a has-been. Being the feature attraction at a neighborhood barbecue is not conducive to longevity.

Time and the weather were on Hamlet's side. Bit by bit he became an incredibly affectionate little clown, as smart as pigs are reputed to be. Sitting at the dressing table meant having a small pig in my lap or a small pig trying to climb on to my lap; once he settled into a comfortable position, he grunted with satisfaction and dozed off into a contented sleep. Should I refuse to pick him up, he squealed until I scratched his ears then immediately went limp and crumpled into a heap on the floor. As soon as the attention stopped, he was on his feet again. If it were the best he could do, he rooted around until he managed to wedge his snout into the side of my quilted bedroom slipper and snuggled in to snooze.

Hamlet was also managing to root his way into my heart. Whenever I came into the room, whether I'd been gone ten minutes or an hour, personality pig squeaked his delight and executed two quick 360-degree turns in place then, like a broken field runner, zigzagged across the room before skidding to a halt for two more pirouettes. The petite, economy-size pig was really a ham.

Pigskins are highly elastic commodities. No matter how small they start off, they're capable of expanding to accommodate as much as five hundred pounds of pork. Even so, I was not yet alarmed over Hamlet's potential, not even when January came and went and Hamlet didn't. There was still another month before I launched my bed and breakfast, and if I hadn't found a happy home for him by then he'd be old enough to shuffle off to the barn. Everything else was proceeding on schedule.

And then those "best laid plans of mice and men that oft gang agley," gang agleyed in the middle of my bathroom. That was before they went awry all over the place. One week prior to my first reservation, Hamlet broke his ankle. Somehow he got tangled up in the wrought-iron chair to my dressing table, turned it over, and ended up with a plaster cast encasing his right front leg from his toes to his shoulder.

Unwilling to subject him to the additional trauma of a move, I called on Kozby once again in hopes his soothing influence would at least keep the little porker quiet. Kozby quickly squelched that notion. He'd quiet Ham down, all right, but dispatching the little pig into the past tense was his strategy of choice. It was an unsatisfactory solution from Hamlet's point of view.

Obviously I could do nothing about the oinks and squeals emanating from the 27-pound pig, although I don't suppose it made much difference whether he weighed 27 or 127 pounds. There's just something about a pig, any size pig, living in the bathroom that destroyed any semblance of the "quiet elegance" the brochures proclaimed. The only antidote I could think of was turning up the stereo and overloading Hamlet with his Tail Curler Rockets to sedate him.

I didn't mention this setback to Priscilla Long, who was responsible for my first booking. Priscilla had arranged for her boss, sales manager for a computer software company based in Chicago, to be the guinea pig, and she was naturally anxious that the visit go well. Instead of burdening her with the news, I regaled her with a glowing account of wondrous deeds. Not only had I dusted and vacuumed and polished the silver and the crystal until not one water spot remained, I noticed a couple of stains on the living-room carpet and took action.

Henson Brothers Cleaners promised to work me into their schedule and so they did. They arrived the morning before the first guest was due. As the Messrs. Henson set to work, I went down to clean the tigers' pens, one of the social events of the day for the big cats. They rubbed against the sides of the fencing that separates our two worlds while I ran my fingers through their fur and scratched their ears, then they licked the hand I offered for their rough tongue kisses.

The socializing over, I lowered a guillotine door to confine the tigers in one section while I cleaned the other, and I'd just released the bolts and padlocks prior to entering when the senior Mr. Henson called me to the telephone. Securing all the safety devices I'd just released, a self-imposed rule, I headed for the house, took the call, and returned to the cages to repeat the ritual. This time I got all the way inside before Mr. Henson again summoned me to put ear to receiver.

Four times he beckoned and four times I responded. The telethon used up an hour during which time I'd gotten only one pen cleaned, and by then my mind was no longer on the original mission. How to put a halt to the constant interruptions occupied my thoughts. But it was a bit late for remedial action that might hurt Mr. Henson's feelings, I decided, so I did nothing.

The fourth call was from one of those wretched outfits that "happen to be in your area this week" and bend one's ear ten minutes with their resistible offer. Pondering on that particularly aggravating delay, I went back to the cats to take up where I'd left off, for the fourth time. Ivan and Deutchka were lolling around in the cleaned pen, separated from me by the lowered guillotine door, so I thought, the one I'd forgotten I'd opened.

Squatting down with the tools of my trade, I'd begun to scoop up the tiger uglies when I felt a tap, tap on my derriere that was so light I wondered absentmindedly which of the dogs it was. I didn't stop to look around. Concentrating on making up for the lost time, I went on about my business until a second tap, tap penetrated my consciousness, and I realized the patted area was at least ten times the size of any dog's paw I'd ever seen. It wasn't a tiger. I knew that; they couldn't open the door. Before I could look around to see who it was, a set of bristly whiskers grazed my face, followed by the rest of Deutchka as she rubbed against me, almost knocking me over in the process.

"Hello, Deutchka," I said in as normal a voice as I could muster with my heart crowding my throat.

The danger of the situation was twofold. Should Deutchka want to play, a friendly cuff could have the same end result as an intentionally lethal blow. If she was startled or somehow provoked, she might attack reflexively. Robert had given me a crash course in handling a tiger confrontation, and I was now facing the final exam, maybe "final" in the literal sense of the word. Ever so slowly I stood up and began to back away, extending the long-handled shovel between Deutchka and myself. Tigers won't strike unless they have a clear, unobstructed shot at the target. Supposedly.

"Don't stumble, for heaven's sake, don't stumble," I said out loud—to me—as I edged my way backward.

I'd only managed a couple of cautious steps when Ivan ambled over to check out the shovel that held Deutchka intrigued. Then both the big cats began batting at the new toy, neither the slightest bit interested in me or what I was doing.

When I got to the middle of the cage, about twenty feet from the first of the two doors I had to negotiate, Mr. Henson stepped out on the patio and I knew I was done for. I thought he'd appraised the situation accurately and, although I didn't expect him to rush down to save me, I figured he'd scream or dash wildly for his truck or somehow agitate the tigers. But I had underestimated Mr. Henson's dedication to duty as he saw it.

"Telephone," he called out cheerily.

"I'll be there in a minute," I answered, the humor of the farce escaping me until later—much, much later.

Ivan and Deutchka, as docile as two house cats, followed along, slapping at the shovel as I continued my slow-motion backtracking. When I reached the low opening to Ivan's boudoir, I had to get down on my knees to back through, with only one hand for support while the other brandished the shovel. Once through the door, I could resume a standing position, which I did hastily. Fifteen more feet. Ten more. Five. The tigers were with me every step. When I reached the last opening, I dropped all pretense of calm, leaped out backward, slammed the door, and began to tremble. Vibrate would be more accurate. All of me shook. I'm 99 percent certain they would never deliberately harm me, but wild animals can never be tamed, only trained. The 1 percent risk can be 100 percent fatal.

It was a memorable morning. So was the afternoon.

Since the tigers' annual shots and the camels' regular worming required extensive manpower, Don scheduled both procedures for the same outing to take advantage of the assembled brawn. There are never any volunteers. All of the recruits are badgered and coerced, and everyone is unhappy about the duty, Don in particular.

That afternoon's roster, averaging six foot two and two hundred pounds, included Kevin Francke, Gordie Haag, Todd Kogan, and Kevin Jowitt. They gathered inside the barn for the first event while I remained in the adjacent storeroom out of the combat zone but well within earshot of the free-for-all. Scuffling sounds and an occasional thud reverberated through the walls, along with a mixture of camel profanity plus the steady verbal bombardment directed at the opposition by the biped forces.

The camels, always strenuously opposed to the tubes forced down their throats, were excessively obstreperous, and the ordeal took even longer than usual that day. It was still in progress when I heard a car door slam and stepped outside to see a man I didn't know walking toward me, hand extended. He was probably in his early forties, wearing a business suit, and he smiled as he approached.

"I'm Dave Evans. Are you Moselle?" he asked.

Shock and horror must have registered on my face. I know my mouth flopped open. How could I have made such a mistake?

"Priscilla told me you'd just started your B&B, so I took a chance on your having room for me a day early," he continued.

Before I could answer, Don marched out of the barn. Tired and disheveled, with an eloquent scowl on his face, he ignored the stranger and got right to the point. "I want to tell you something, Moselle. ------- around with these camels is sure putting a strain on our friendship," he barked.

That was not the gracious welcome I'd envisioned for Camel Lot's first customer, and I knew of no antidote for Don's editorial comment. I didn't try to gauge my guest's reaction. To the contrary, I avoided any eye contact and restricted my gaze to his necktie. For lack of anything better to do, I proceeded with introductions as the rest of the bedraggled team appeared.

"Well, let's get the tigers' shots over with," Don said, once the formalities were concluded.

"Can I help?" Dave Evans asked.

"Sure," Don answered before I could decline the offer. "But not in those clothes."

"If you'll show me where to change, Moselle, I'll only be a minute," he replied.

Riding down to the house with Dave, I attempted a feeble apology for the uproar he'd walked into.

"Things are not always this chaotic," I said, neglecting to add that oftentimes they're worse.

"Does it take all these people to give the tigers shots?" he wanted to know.

"You bet. And you might want to forgo this happening," I

suggested. Although he measured up in size to the other men, his stamina quotient was an unknown quantity.

"Oh, no," he was adamant, obviously here to stay.

I showed him to his suite before hurrying down to the tigers. My role in that undertaking was critical. Ivan had to be lured into the "squeeze cage" first, the small connecting cage between the two large pens, and the guillotine doors at either end lowered almost simultaneously to trap the tiger inside. It required split-second maneuvering. If I fumbled with the pulleys or otherwise goofed up, Ivan was out of there and the project had to be scrubbed for the day. There was no second chance with Ivan, the cat was much too wary.

I was lucky. In a matter of seconds Ivan was incarcerated and Don and team charged out of the house like the first wave of Marines assaulting an enemy position. Far from being eager heroes, however, the motivation of these reluctant warriors stemmed from a strong desire to complete the mission and withdraw to a more secure position, namely anywhere with no view of any fierce, ferocious Siberian tigers. To them, the big cats' pens appeared as flimsy as mosquito netting and the irate animals ten feet tall.

The five musclemen took up their positions on the back side of the squeeze cage. Their job was to shove the wooden frame on the inside of it against Ivan, thereby "squeezing" him into relative immobility. It was no small feat considering the seven-hundred-pound tiger didn't want to be squeezed and made his sentiments unmistakably clear.

Don and I were stationed on the opposite side, my ineffective presence intended as a soothing influence while Don—the fastest shot in the West—administered the injections zap, zap, zap. The entire engagement, requiring less than ten minutes in terms of time, took a heavy toll on the nervous systems of the participants.

But Ivan was a pussycat compared to Deutchka. She became hysterical. Eyes blazing and roars erupting like explosions, she was a frenzy of teeth and claws, an awesome display of sound and fury signifying a whole lot—one enraged Siberian tiger bent on terminating her tormentors. As Don and I crouched down on our side of the cage, the stalwart citizens on the other side pushed the wedge forward, and although I didn't think Deutchka could become more violent, she did. Taking one steel reenforcing band after another into her powerful jaws, she snapped them in rapid succession. One bite was all it took.

It was then I learned there are degrees of terror. Up until that point, all the participants had been scared but still able to function. Then Don shouted over the uproar, "Is that side holding?" and all of a sudden there was no one around. Gone. Disappeared. Five robust men had vanished quicker than a puff of smoke in a fifty-knot gale.

"Release her," Don said to me, and I pulled the cables so the poor frantic animal could escape the close confines.

Everyone survived the melee, including the newcomer—grown years older in the course of an hour. It must have been a harrowing experience for one who'd never been closer to a tiger than the pages of Rudyard Kipling's *Jungle Book*. Dave left hurriedly for a real or imaginary dinner engagement, and I wondered if he hadn't seized the opportunity to put a couple of states between him and the "quiet elegance" of Camel Lot. No suitcase left with him, but he might have considered leaving his luggage a small sacrifice under the circumstances.

I wondered the same thing the next morning when there were

no sounds of anybody stirring, not even Hamlet, who was still flaked out, O.D.-ed on Tail Curler Rockets. I peeped out the front door and saw Dave's car, so I started breakfast. A few minutes before our agreed-upon time of 7:00 A.M. and still no sign of him, I was debating about whether to go ahead with the eggs when the question was resolved. The front door opened and one whiff of Dave told me he'd want a shower first. He'd sustained a direct hit from Charlie Lama and the ample evidence was running down his face and onto his warm-up suit.

"I didn't do a thing to that animal," he said with a laugh.

"You don't have to to get him riled up," I explained.

"I was jogging back down the driveway when he came running over to the fence, so I stopped and said good morning to him, that's all."

"I'm sorry, I should have warned you, but I didn't realize you'd be up and out so early."

"Hey, no problem," he brushed off my apology. "It won't happen to me again."

I'm sure it won't, I thought. Oh, well, there were still a few more careers I hadn't yet explored. Peddling apples on the steps of the Capitol might work out, and there are a lot of fringe benefits to the Apple Annie business, flexible hours, for one.

When Dave sat down to breakfast, he was dapper in suit and tie, every inch the successful executive. I joined him for a cup of coffee and we chatted easily. We had a lot to talk about.

"This has been one of the most incredible experiences I've ev—" The sentence trailed off as he pointed at a window, with a face in it. "Is that a deer?"

"Yes, that's Jane Doe."

"She's friendly? I can pet her?" he asked suspiciously.

"Oh, sure, she loves attention."

Dave opened the door, but before he could step out onto the patio, Jane Doe brushed him aside and made straight for the breakfast table. While he watched in wide-eyed astonishment, she stuck her nose in his orange juice and drained it, then rearranged everything on his plate, trying to corner an elusive wedge of coffee cake. The sunny-side eggs slid around easily without rupturing, and other than the missing coffee cake, everything else was undisturbed. Janie didn't care for bacon and had not yet gotten around to the toast. There was a tad of deer drool and a few crumbs, but what were a few crumbs among the gleaming china and crystal and silver—and the painstakingly ironed linens.

"Let's start over," I said, taking Dave's plate. "It won't take long."

"No, I'm just going to finish my coffee—Jane Doe doesn't drink coffee, I take it—and I need to be off," he protested.

Janie submitted to Dave's petting for a few minutes before indicating she was ready to leave. Just as I opened the patio door for her, a muffled "oink" caught Dave's attention, and he cocked his head to listen.

"I didn't realize deer made sounds like a pig," he said.

It was a statement of fact I saw no need to contradict. Not that it mattered at that point whether one pig or an entire tribe of aborigines was headquartered in my bathroom.

"I'm not sure when I'll get back," he said, on his way out. "I'll have my secretary call you."

Around the turn of the century, no doubt, I reflected glumly. I was not prepared psychologically for this business to bomb. I'd had unrealistic hopes for it, actual expectations that a visit to Camel Lot would be a treat guests would enjoy and remember. At least I was half right. My one and only customer would remember it.

When Dave's secretary did call two days later, I was surprised; what she had to say astounded me.

"I hope you're not already booked for next weekend; my husband and I would like to come down," she said.

"YOU WOULD?"

"Yes, Dave says people are going to be lining up to get in before long, and he wants to make a standing reservation for every other Tuesday," she said nonchalantly.

"HE DOES?"

"He's really looking forward to getting back. He says he can't imagine what will happen next."

Neither could I. More than likely he'd learn why some deer sound like pigs—among other things.